PRAISE FOR
Peeling the Onion

A *Christian Science Monitor* Best Book of the Year
A *San Francisco Chronicle* Best Book of the Year

"At heart, Grass is a robust maximalist, a metaphor-spinner to whom little that is human is alien. He does not linger long with handkerchief pressed to his face—he has a rich, ruminative, and ribald tale to tell . . . We see not only the peeled back essence of the inner and outer, but also feel, throughout, the potency of the shaping imagination . . . Grass comes through on every page as a man to whom it has been given to make powerful and controversial art."

—Sven Birkerts, *The News & Observer* (Raleigh, NC)

"*Peeling the Onion* is wakeful, twitchy, suspicious, shambling, and yet also—if we are still permitted to use this word as a compliment—sincere . . . [It] is wonderfully and dreadfully evocative."

—*Harper's Magazine*

"This is a wonderful book, a return to classic Grass territory and style . . . and a perfect pendant to his great 'Danzig trilogy' . . . *Peeling the Onion* repeatedly surprises, delights, and moves with passages of great descriptive power."

—*The New York Review of Books*

"Verbally dazzling . . . Mr. Grass's brief but searing wartime experiences, and his detainment in an American prisoner-of-war camp, account for the book's richest material, equaled only by the early chapters evoking his childhood in Danzig. Here and in the late, more diffuse chapters on his wandering years as a miner, mason, poet and sculptor, Mr. Grass offers tantalizing glimpses of a novelistic sensibility in the making."

—*The New York Times*

"A fascinating account of a powerful artist struggling with his inglorious past."   —*Entertainment Weekly*

"*Peeling the Onion* is immediately engaging in its recollections of childhood, and in its frank acknowledgments of the ways in which memory can warp, falsify, even efface some parts of past experience while leaving others unimpeachably clear . . . Grass's gift of rendering how things looked (and sounded, smelled, tasted, felt) makes for a rich and humanizing read."

—*The San Diego Union-Tribune*

"A fascinating book . . . Mr. Grass emerges from its pages as an endlessly appetitive *monstre sacre*, in the tradition of Wagner or Picasso."   —*The New York Sun*

"Grass is devastatingly severe in his treatment of his youthful self . . . The dialectic between his current and former selves gives this book its special resonance."   —*The Atlantic Monthly*

PEELING THE ONION

Günter Grass

PEELING THE ONION

Translated from German by
Michael Henry Heim

A HARVEST BOOK
HARCOURT, INC.
Orlando Austin New York San Diego London

www.HarcourtBooks.com

This is a translation of *Beim Häuten der Zwiebel*

The Library of Congress has cataloged the hardcover edition as follows:
Grass, Günter, 1927–
[Beim Häuten der Zwiebel. English]
Peeling the onion/Günter Grass;
translated from German by Michael Henry Heim.—1st U.S. ed.
p. cm.
1. Grass, Günter, 1927– 2. Authors, German—20th century—Biography.
I. Heim, Michael Henry. II. Title.
PT2613.R338Z4613 2007
838'.91409—dc22 [B] 2007009882
ISBN 978-0-15-101477-4
ISBN 978-0-15-603534-7 (pbk.)

Text set in Adobe Garamond
Designed by Cathy Riggs

Printed in the United States of America
First Harvest edition 2008
A C E G I K J H F D B

Dedicated to everyone from whom I have learned

CONTENTS

PEELING THE ONION

Skins Beneath the Skin

Today, as in years past, the temptation to camouflage oneself in the third person remains great: He was going on twelve, though he still loved sitting in his mother's lap, when such and such began and ended. But can something that had a beginning and an end be pinpointed with such precision? In my case it can.

My childhood came to an end when, in the city where I grew up, the war broke out in several places at once. It began with an unmistakeable bang—the broadsiding of a ship and the approach of dive-bombers over the Neufahrwasser dock area, which lay opposite the Polish military base at Westerplatte, and, farther off, the carefully aimed shots of two armored reconnaissance cars during the battle for the Polish Post Office in the Old Town of Danzig—and was heralded closer to home by our radio—a *Volksempfänger,* "people's receiver"—which stood on the sideboard in the living room. Thus the end of my childhood was proclaimed with words of iron in a ground-floor flat of a three-story building on Labesweg, in Langfuhr.

Even the time of day sticks in my mind. From then on, the airport of the Free State near the Baltic Chocolate factory handled more than just civilian planes. From the skylight in the roof of our building we could see smoke mounting duskily over the Free Port each time there was a new attack and a light wind from the northwest.

But the moment I try to remember that distant artillery fire from the *Schleswig-Holstein,* which had been retired from active duty after the Battle of Jutland and could no longer be used as anything but a training ship for cadets, and the layered sounds of the Stukas or *Sturzkampfflugzeug,* "dive-bombers"—so called because high above the combat zone they would tip to one side, then lunge down on their target, releasing their bombs at the last moment—I am faced with a question: Why go back to my childhood and its clear and immutable end date, when everything that happened to me between milk teeth and permanent ones—my first day at school, scraped knees, marbles, the earliest secrets of the confessional and later agonies of faith—all merged in the jumble of jottings that has since been associated with a person who, no sooner had he been put down on paper, refused to grow and shattered all manner of glass with his song, kept two wooden sticks at the ready, and thanks to a tin drum made a name for himself that thereafter existed in quotable form between book covers and claims immortality in heaven knows how many languages?

Because this as well as that deserves to be part of the record. Because something flagrantly significant could be missing. Because certain things at certain times fell into the well before the lid went on: the holes I left uncovered until later, growth I could not halt, the linguistic give-and-take I had with lost objects. And let this, too, be said: because I want to have the last word.

———

MEMORY likes to play hide-and-seek, to crawl away. It tends to hold forth, to dress up, often needlessly. Memory contradicts itself; pedant that it is, it will have its way.

When pestered with questions, memory is like an onion that wishes to be peeled so we can read what is laid bare letter by letter. It is seldom unambiguous and often in mirror-writing or otherwise disguised.

Beneath its dry and crackly outer skin we find another, more moist layer, that once detached, reveals a third, beneath which a fourth and fifth wait whispering. And each skin sweats words too long muffled, and curlicue signs, as if a mystery-monger from an early age, while the onion was still germinating, had decided to encode himself.

Then ambition raises its head: this scrawl must be deciphered, that code cracked. What currently insists on truth is disproved, because Lie or her younger sister, Deception, often hands over only the most acceptable part of a memory, the part that sounds plausible on paper, and vaunts details to be as precise as a photograph: The tarpaper roof of the shed behind our building shimmered in the July heat and in the still air smelled of malt lozenges . . .

The washable collar of my primary school teacher, Fräulein Spollenhauer, was made of celluloid and was so tight it put creases in her neck . . .

The propeller-shaped bows in the hair of the girls on the Zoppot Promenade when the police band played its snappy melodies . . .

My first *Boletus edulis* . . .

When we were excused from school because of the heat . . .

When my tonsils flared up again . . .

When I swallowed my questions . . .

The onion has many skins. A multitude of skins. Peeled, it renews itself; chopped, it brings tears; only during peeling does it speak the truth. What happened before and after the end of my childhood knocks at the door with facts and went worse than wished for and demands to be told now this way, now that, and leads to tall tales.

WHEN war broke out to a spell of glorious late-summer weather in Danzig and environs, and the Westerplatte's Polish defenders capitulated after seven days of resistance, I, that is, the boy I apparently was, gathered up a handful of bomb- and shell-splinters near the Neufahrwasser dock, which was easily accessible by tram via Saspe and Brösen, and traded them, at a time when the war seemed to exist only in radio bulletins, for stamps, colored picture cards from cigarette packets, books both dog-eared and hot off the press—including Sven Hedin's *Voyage Through the Gobi Desert*—and heaven knows what else.

An imprecise memory sometimes comes a matchstick's length closer to the truth, albeit along crooked paths.

It is mostly objects that my memory rubs against, my knees bump into, or that leave a repellent aftertaste: the tile stove . . . the frame used for beating carpets behind the house . . . the toilet on the half-landing . . . the suitcase in the attic . . . a piece of amber the size of a dove's egg . . .

If you can still feel your mother's barrettes or your father's handkerchief knotted at four corners in the summer heat or recall the exchange value of various jagged grenade- and bomb

splinters, you will know stories—if only as entertainment—
that are closer to reality than life itself.

THE picture cards I so eagerly collected in my boyhood and
youth were obtained with coupons that came in the packs out
of which my mother tapped her cigarettes after closing the shop.
"Ciggies," she called the accessories to her modest vice, and celebrated the nightly ritual with a glass of Cointreau. If the mood
was upon her, she could make smoke rings hover.

The pictures I lusted after were color reproductions of European masterpieces. From them I learned early on to mispronounce
the names of Giorgione, Mantegna, Botticelli, Ghirlandaio,
and Caravaggio. The naked back of a reclining woman gazing
into a mirror held up by a winged boy has been inextricably
coupled in my mind since childhood with the name of Veláz-
quez. What left the deepest imprint on me in Jan van Eyck's
Singing Angels was the profile of the hindmost angel: what I
would have given to have curly hair like him or like Albrecht
Dürer. Of the Dürer self-portrait hanging in the Prado in
Madrid one might ask: Why did the master paint himself wearing gloves? Why are the strange cap and right lower sleeve so
conspicuously striped? What makes him so self-assured? And
why did he write his age—he was all of twenty-six—under the
window ledge?

Today I know that a cigarette-picture service in Hamburg-
Bahrenfeld supplied these magnificent reproductions for the
coupons as well as square albums, which had to be ordered separately. Now that I have reclaimed all three albums, thanks to
my Lübeck gallery that maintains a second-hand bookshop on

Königstrasse, I can confirm that the number of copies of the Renaissance volume, published in 1938, ran to at least 450,000.

Turning page after page, I see myself at the living-room table, pasting in the pictures. This time it is the late Gothic as represented by the *Temptation of Saint Anthony* by Hieronymus Bosch: the saint in a group of very human-looking beasts. It is almost a ritual, the glue squirting out of the yellow Uhu tube . . .

Many collectors, hopelessly gone on art, probably took to smoking immoderately. I, however, took advantage of all the smokers who had no use for their coupons. I accumulated, traded, and pasted in more and more pictures, relating to them initially as a child would, but later with increasing sensitivity: Parmigianino's lanky Madonna, whose head budding on a long neck towers above the pillars that soared heavenward in the background, aroused the twelve-year-old to rub himself ardently, angel-like, against her right knee.

I lived through pictures, and because the son was so set on a complete collection, the mother in addition to the takings from her moderate consumption—she was a devoted smoker of flat, gold-tipped Egyptian cigarettes—slipped him a number of coupons contributed by one or another customer who couldn't care less about art. Sometimes the grocer father would bring the much-coveted coupons home from his business trips. My cabinetmaker grandfather's apprentices, diligent smokers all, also subscribed to my cause. The albums, full of blank spaces surrounded by explanatory texts, must have been Christmas or birthday presents.

I guarded all three as a single treasure: the blue album, which contained Gothic and early Renaissance art; the red album, which regaled me with the high Renaissance; and the golden yellow one, in which I was still trying to piece together the Baroque. I was distressed by the blanks calling for Rubens and van Dyck. I lacked reinforcements. Once the war began, the coupon boom died down. Civilian smokers turned into soldiers who puffed on their Junos and R6s far from home. One of my most reliable suppliers, a coachman at the local brewery, was killed during the battle for Modlin Fortress.

Then other series started competing: animals, flowers, glossies of German history, and the powdered faces of popular movie stars.

Besides, early in the war every household began to receive ration cards, and these included special slips for the consumption of tobacco products. However, as I had managed to secure a basic education in art history with the help of the Reemtsma cigarette company in prewar times, the officially ordained shortage did not affect me inordinately. I could fill in the gaps by and by. I was, for example, able to trade Raphael's Dresden Madonna, of which I had a duplicate, for Caravaggio's *Cupid,* a deal that did not pay off fully until later.

EVEN as a ten-year-old I was able to tell Hans Baldung, called Grien, from Matthias Grünewald; Frans Hals from Rembrandt; and Filippo Lippi from Cimabue—all at first glance.

Who painted the Madonna in the rose bower? Or the Madonna with the blue mantle and apple and Child? Quizzed by the mother, who covered the title and painter's name with two fingers, the son answered without missing a beat.

In these domestic guessing games and in school too I was an A student—at least in art. From my first year at the gymnasium I was utterly hopeless when it came to mathematics, chemistry, and physics. I was perfectly good at doing sums in my head but had trouble making equations with two unknowns come out right on paper. Until my second year I could compensate with As and Bs in German, English, history, and geography, and even my much-praised sketches and watercolors, whether done from nature or my imagination, seemed to help, but third-year Latin tipped the balance, and I had to repeat the whole year along with my fellow dunces. That upset me less than it did my parents: from early on I had prepared escape routes leading into the blue yonder.

Nowadays, a grandfather's confession that at school he was partly lazy, partly unambitious, but in the end an out-and-out dunce is not much comfort to grandchildren suffering from low marks or inept teachers. They groan as if they have pedagogical boulders hung around their necks, as if school were a penal colony, as if the demands of the classroom sour their sweetest dreams. Well, playground anxiety never troubled *my* sleep.

WHEN I was a child—before I donned the red school cap, before I started collecting cigarette cards—I would go down to one of the beaches along Danzig Bay as soon as summer with its endless promise came, and mold the wet sand into the high towers and walls of a citadel which I peopled with fantastical characters. Over and over the sea buried the structure, its towering turrets collapsing noiselessly. And yet again wet sand ran through my fingers.

"Kleckerburg" is the title of a long poem I wrote in the midsixties, in other words, when the forty-year-old father of three sons and a daughter seemed to have settled into a bourgeois existence. Like the hero of his first novel, its author had made a name for himself by trapping his dual self between the covers of a book and taking it thus tamed to market.

The poem is about my background and the sounds of the Baltic. "Born in Kleckerburg, west of," it begins, then poses questions: "Born when? And where? Why?" In a verbal torrent it evokes loss and memory, lost and found in sentence fragments: "The gulls are not gulls but."

At the end of the poem, which stakes out my territory between the Holy Ghost and Hitler's photograph, conjuring the beginning of the war with shell-splinters and muzzle-flashes, childhood peters out. Only the Baltic keeps going, in German, in Polish: "Blubb, pifff, pshsh . . ."

THE war was in its infancy when a cousin of my mother, Uncle Franz, a postman who took part in the defense of the Polish Post Office on the Heveliusplatz, was summarily executed by the Germans—along with nearly all the survivors of that brief battle. The military judge who pronounced, justified, and signed the death sentence went on pronouncing and signing sentences in Schleswig-Holstein long after the war, unscathed. A common story during Chancellor Adenauer's interminable term of office.

Later I adapted the skirmish over the Polish Post Office to my narrative prose style, changing the personnel and inserting a chatty description of the fall of a house of cards. My family was much less chatty. Our suddenly absent uncle, much beloved above and beyond or despite his politics and a frequent guest, along with his children, Irmgard, Grego, Magda, and little Kasimir for Sunday coffee and cake or an afternoon round of skat with my parents, was no longer mentioned. His name was passed over in silence, as if he had never existed, as if everything connected with him and his family were unspeakable.

This Kashubian side of the family—my mother's side—with its cozy kitchen babble, seemed to have been swallowed up. By whom?

Nor did I, even though my childhood had ended with the onset of the war, ask any insistent questions.

Or was it because I was no longer a child that I dared not ask?

Is it only children who, as in fairy tales, ask the right questions?

Can it have been the fear of an answer that would turn my world upside down that made me hold my tongue?

A demeaning disgrace it is to find such a blot on the sixth or seventh skin of that garden-variety, readily available, memory-boosting onion. So I write about the disgrace, and the shame limping in its wake. Rarely used words wielded in the service of belated compensation as my now lenient, now stringent eyes remain focused on a boy still in shorts, snooping into hidden affairs, yet failing to ask "Why?"

And as I clumsily interrogate and thereby clearly overtax the twelve-year-old, I weigh each step I take in this fast-fading present, hear myself breathing, hear myself coughing, and live my way, as cheerfully as possible, toward death.

FRANZ KRAUSE, my executed uncle, left a wife and four children, who ranged in age from somewhat older to three years younger than me. I was no longer allowed to play with them. They had to vacate their Old Town apartment on the Brabank—it had come with the job—and move to the country between Zuckau and Ramkau, where the widow had a cottage and piece of land. And there, in hilly Kashubia, the postman's children live to this day, plagued by the usual ailments of age. They have different memories: they missed their father, while mine was too present.

This employee of the Polish Post Office was an anxious, timid family man, not made for a hero's death, whose name appears on a bronze memorial plaque as Franciszek Krauze, and as such has entered eternity.

WHEN after much effort I was issued a visa for Poland in March of '58 and traveled from Paris via Warsaw to Gdańsk, a city still emerging from rubble, to seek out the former Danzig, I poked behind the façades of the ruins and along Brösen Beach, moved on to the reading room of the Municipal Library, the grounds of the still-standing Pestalozzi School, and the living rooms-cum-kitchens of two surviving Polish Post Office clerks, and then, having gathered a modicum of raw material for the novel, I went to see the surviving relatives in the countryside. I was greeted at the door of their cottage by the executed postman's mother, with the irrefutable: "Ginterchen! My, how you've grown!"

We had become so foreign, so alien to each other, that at first I had to assuage her doubts by producing my passport, but then she took me to see her potato field, which today lies underneath the cement runway of Gdańsk Airport.

BY THE summer of the following year, the war had grown into a world war, and during our holidays at the Baltic beaches we gymnasium students would not only rehash local events but carry on about happenings beyond our borders. We were entirely taken up with the Wehrmacht's occupation of Norway, though well into June the news bulletins were trumpeting the

French campaign as a blitzkrieg and celebrating the surrender of our hereditary enemy. Rotterdam, Antwerp, Dunkirk, Paris, the Atlantic coast . . . each new conquest was a geography lesson: blow after blow, victory after victory.

And yet all our pre- and post-swim admiration went to "the heroes of Narvik." We may have been lazing in the family bathing area, but the fjords under siege "up in Norway" were where we longed to be. Here we were smeared with Nivea cream; there, we could have been covered with glory.

Thanks to the setbacks dealt the English, our never-ending hero worship was directed at the navy, and several of us, myself included, dreamed of enlisting, if only the war lasted another three or four years, preferably in the submarine corps. Sitting there in our bathing suits, we would hold contests to see who could name the greatest number of military feats, beginning with Weddigen's U9 submarine triumphs in World War I, then First Lieutenant Prien sinking the *Royal Oak,* and always coming back to the "hard-fought victory" at Narvik.

One day, one of our gang—his name was Wolfgang Heinrichs, an acknowledged ballad singer who would even venture an opera aria upon request, but who had a maimed left hand that made him unfit for the navy and therefore an object of our sympathy—said plainly, "You must be crazy, all of you!"

Then he counted off on the fingers of his unmaimed hand how many of our destroyers had been sunk or badly damaged at Narvik. The five fingers on that hand did not suffice.

He went into almost professional detail, pointing out that one of the 1,800-ton ships—he called it by name—had had to be grounded. He knew all the particulars of the battle, even the weaponry on England's *Warspite* and its speed in knots. True, we too, seaport children that we were, could rattle off the specifications of our own and foreign vessels: the tonnage, the size of the crew, the number of torpedo tubes, the year of launching, but we were surprised at how well informed he was about Narvik, because his knowledge went far beyond what had come through to us from the Wehrmacht's daily radio bulletins.

"You haven't a clue about what really went on up there in the north. There were heavy losses! Damned heavy!"

Surprised or not, we simply accepted what he said. Nobody asked Wolfgang Heinrichs where he had got his amazing information. I certainly didn't.

FIFTY years later, when traces of what at the time was called "German unity," for want of a better term, began to appear, my wife, Ute, and I visited her native island, Hiddensee. Just off the East German coast, it lies between the Baltic and a shallow bay and is less endangered by stormy tides than by the tourist trade.

There are no cars on Hiddensee, so we took a long hike over the heath to the town of Neuendorf, where we visited a childhood friend of my wife's, Martin Gruhn, who, years after a daring rowboat escape to Sweden from the German Democratic Republic, had decided to return to the Workers' and Peasants' State and retire there. He did not look the part of an adventurer: he was too domestic, too settled.

Over coffee and cake we chatted about this and that: his career as a manager in the West, the many trips to India, Australia, and elsewhere he made on behalf of Krupp. He told us about his failed attempt to enter the world of joint East-West business ventures and about the only joy remaining to him, trap-fishing in local waters.

Then the obviously satisfied returnee changed the subject abruptly: he had a friend who lived in Vitte, another of the three villages on the island, who absolutely insisted that he had shared a school bench with me in Danzig. Heinrichs was his name, Wolfgang Heinrichs.

Pursuing the matter, I learned that yes, his left hand was maimed and yes, he had a good voice, "though he seldom puts it to use anymore."

For a while Ute and he switched exclusively to island matters, spinning yarns in which the living and the dead went on in their Low German dialect. Martin Gruhn, who had realized his boyhood dream and seen the world, proudly showed us the masks, colorful rugs, and carved fetishes on the walls. We had one last schnapps.

ON OUR way across the heath Ute and I searched for the house behind the dunes where Heinrichs lived with his wife. The door was opened by a giant of a man, breathing heavily. The only thing about him I recognized was his maimed hand. After a short hesitation, the school friends embraced and were somewhat moved.

We sat on the veranda, determined to be cheerful, and later all four of us went to a restaurant, for fish: crisply fried flounder. No, he had no desire anymore to sing "Erlkönig," but it was not long before we got to his beach talk of the summer of '40, still a mystery to me after all the intervening years.

"How did you know more than we did?" I wanted to hear. "How did you know what we, as you put it, hadn't a clue about? Where did you get the precise number of sunken and badly damaged destroyers at Narvik? And everything else you knew? For instance, that after a few bull's-eyes and with two torpedoes—all fired from shore—an outdated Norwegian coastal artillery unit sank the heavy cruiser *Blücher* in the Oslo Fjord?"

Heinrichs's otherwise impassive face showed the hint of a smile as he spoke. He had been roundly beaten by his father when he went home and mocked our ignorance. After all, his braggadocio could have had consequences. There were plenty of informers, not the least among schoolchildren. His father had listened regularly to British radio, and he had passed his knowledge on to his son under a strict vow of silence.

"Right," Heinrichs said, his father had been a true anti-Fascist, not one of your after-the-fact, self-proclaimed variety. He said this as though he, the son, felt the need to run himself down as after the fact and self-proclaimed.

And then I heard a tale of woe that, like a muffled wail, had completely passed me by—me, his school friend—because I did not ask, because here, too, I had failed to ask questions. Not even after Wolfgang Heinrichs suddenly disappeared from school, our venerable Conradinum.

Shortly after the summer holidays, maybe even while the last grains of beach sand were trickling out of our hair, our friend was either missing or was not, and nobody was willing to query the meaning of that casually tossed "vanished without trace," and I again failed to utter, swallowed the word *why.*

Only now, after all those years, did I learn what had happened. During the Free State period Heinrichs's father had been a member of the German Social Democratic Party and later a Social Democrat member of Parliament, and had opposed the Nazi Party bigwigs Rauschning and Greiser and the you-scratch-my-back-I'll-scratch-yours camaraderie that led to the alliance between the German Nationals and the Nazis in the municipal senate. He was kept under observation until early autumn of 1940, when the Gestapo arrested him. He was sent to the concentration camp that was set up near the Frisches Haff just after Danzig was annexed to the Reich. It was named after a neighboring fishing village, Sutthof, and could be reached by taking the narrow-gauge railway from the Werder Station in town, then the ferry that crossed the Vistula at Schiewenhorst. It was a two-hour trip.

Not long after Wolfgang's father was arrested, his mother committed suicide, and Wolfgang and his sister were sent to their grandmother in the country, far enough away to have been forgotten by their schoolmates. Their father was eventually released from the camp to serve in a penal battalion whose job it was to clear the mines at the Russian front. The Ascension Commando was what this squad was ironically nicknamed, but despite its high mortality rate it gave him the chance to go over to the Russians.

When the Second Soviet Army marched into the smoldering heap of rubble that was Danzig in March 1945, my schoolmate's father marched in with the victors. He searched for and found his children, and when the war was over he took them out of Poland in a protected transport reserved for German anti-Fascists and chose the port of Stralsund, in the Soviet-occupied zone, as the future home for what remained of his family.

There he was made head of the Landtag, the local parliamentary body, and as his political convictions had not been affected by the brainwashing to which he had been subjected in the concentration camp, he immediately founded a local Social Democratic association. But despite its popularity it fell on hard times after the German Communist Party and the Social Democratic Party were forcibly amalgamated into the United Socialist Party. Heinrichs's father refused to be brought into line from above and was harassed and threatened with arrest. An allusion was even made to the recently repopulated Buchenwald as a possible destination.

He died several years later, embittered at having been shunted aside by his comrades. His son, however, was able to complete his studies in Rostock, together with his school friend Martin Gruhn, and soon made a name for himself in the field of economics. After his rowboat escape Gruhn pursued his study of economics first in Lund and then with Karl Schiller in Hamburg, while Heinrichs made a career for himself in the all-powerful Party, serving through every regime shift, including the one from Ulbricht to Honecker. He had been rewarded in his old age with the post of director of the Economics Institute of the Academy of Sciences, a position so prominent that no sooner had the Wall come down and the dictatorship of the Workers and Peasants ceased to exist than the West German victors, the new masters of history, had had him "evaluated"—that is, reduced to a cipher.

Such had been the fate of many who were accused of falsifying their biographies and who always knew what in their actual biographies needed to be false.

By the time we visited Heinrichs in Vitte he was seriously ill. His wife gave us to understand that there was reason for concern: he complained of a tightness in his chest and had trouble breathing. Yet he still found occasional employment as a tax consultant in Stralsund and was, she assured us, getting good at finding loopholes in the system.

Wolfgang Heinrichs, a man laid low by German circumstances, died of a pulmonary embolism several months after our

visit. He was a school friend, I had shared my youth with him—
he sang "Die Uhr" by Carl Loewe at a graduation ceremony and
knew more about the navy than the rest of us put together—
and he remained in my mind because I had been content to
know nothing or to believe false information, because I had
used my status as a child to play dumb and accepted his disappearance without a murmur, and once more dodged the word
why, so that now, as I peel the onion, my silence pounds in my
ears.

GRANTED, the pain could be worse. But laments such as *If only
I'd had a strong father like Wolfgang Heinrichs and not one who,
when only thirty-six and when the pressure to do so in the Free
State of Danzig was not yet particularly great, joined the Nazi
Party* are cheap and likely to trigger the kind of laughter the
cynic in me laughs whenever I hear things like *If only we had . . .
If only we were . . .*

But I hadn't, I wasn't. My uncle was gone for good; my
school friend had vanished. Yet the boy whose life I feel the need
to trace was all too plainly present when atrocious deeds were
being done. Nearly a year before the war began. Violence in
broad daylight.

When shortly after my eleventh birthday synagogues in
Danzig and elsewhere were set aflame and Jewish merchants'
shop windows shattered, I took no part, yet I was very much a
curious spectator; I watched as the small Langfuhr synagogue on
Michaelisweg, not far from my school, the venerable Conradinum, was plundered, pillaged, and set on fire by a horde of SA
men. And the witness of this extremely clamorous operation,
which the municipal police—perhaps because the fire was so

long in kindling—simply stood by and observed, was, at most, surprised.

Nothing more. No matter how zealously I rummage through the foliage of my memory, I can find nothing in my favor. My childhood years seem to have been completely untroubled by doubt. No, I was a pushover, always game for everything that the times, which called themselves—exhilaratedly and exhilaratingly—modern, had to offer.

There was a great deal, and it was tempting. On the radio and the screen the boxer Max Schmeling was triumphant. Representatives of the Winter Charity Fund circulated with tin boxes in front of Sternfeld's department store shouting, "No one shall starve! No one shall freeze!" German racing drivers like Bernd Rosemeyer in his Mercedes Silver Arrow were the fastest. People gaped at the *Graf Zeppelin* and *Hindenburg* shimmering over the city or on picture postcards. The newsreels showed our Condor Legion helping to free Spain from the Red menace with the most up-to-date weapons. We reenacted Alcázar on the playground. Only a few months earlier we had thrilled to the Olympic Games, medal by medal, and later we had a marvel of a runner in Rudolf Harbig. The Third Reich glittered in the newsreel spotlight.

During the final years of the Free State—I was ten at the time—the boy bearing my name voluntarily joined the Jungvolk, an organization that fed into the Hitler Youth. We were called *Pimpfe,* "tykes," or—a term borrowed from the scouting movement—*Wölflinge,* "cubs." At the top of my Christmas wish list for the year was the Jungvolk's official uniform: cap, scarf, belt, and shoulder strap. True, I don't recall being particularly thrilled at the idea of carrying a flag at rallies or aspiring to the braiding that went with the rank of group leader, but I did my part unquestioningly, even when the endless singing and drumming bored me to tears.

The uniform wasn't the only thing that made the group attractive. The wishful thought of its slogan, Youth Must Be Led by Youth! was backed up by promises of overnight hikes and other outdoor activities in the woods along the beach, of campfires among the erratic blocks dragged together to form a Germanic tribal meeting ground, a *Thingstätte,* in the hilly countryside south of the city, of midsummer night celebrations under starry skies and hymns to the dawn in clearings facing east. We sang as if our songs could make the Reich bigger and bigger.

My unit leader, a working-class boy from Neuschottland, was barely two years older than I was, and a great guy who could tell a joke and walk on his hands. I admired him, laughed when he laughed, and trotted after him obediently.

I was lured away from the stifling petit-bourgeois atmosphere of familial obligations, away from my father, from the over-the-counter gossip of the customers, the confines of the two-room flat where the only space I could call my own was the low niche under the sill of the right-hand living-room window. Its shelves were piled high with books and my cigarette picture-card albums. It was also where I kept the modeling clay that I turned into my first figurines, my Pelikan drawing pad, a set of twelve watercolors, a rather lackadaisical stamp collection, a pile of miscellaneous junk, and my secret notebooks.

Few things do I see so clearly in retrospect as that niche under the windowsill, my refuge for years. (My sister, Waltraut, who was three years younger, was allotted the niche under the left-hand window.)

Which leads me to something that can be said in my favor, namely, that I was not only a *Pimpf* in uniform who did his best to march in step while singing, "Our Fluttering Flag Drives Us On," I was also a house mouse who guarded his niche treasures jealously. Even in formation I was a loner, though I took care not to stand out; I was a schemer whose mind was forever elsewhere.

Besides, the move from primary to secondary school had made me a Conradiner. I was allowed to wear the traditional red student cap decorated with a golden C and felt entitled to be snooty: I was a student at an elite institution, even if my parents had to pay for the privilege in installments with money they had put away with great difficulty. How much was involved I don't know: it was a monthly burden almost never alluded to in the son's presence.

THE grocery shop, which adjoined a narrow hallway leading to the door to our apartment and which my mother, Helene Grass, managed single-handedly and with a keen business sense—my father, Wilhelm (Willy to everybody), dressed the shop window, dealt with the wholesalers, and penned the price tags—had a success rate of middling to poor. During the Free State period, when the currency was the gulden rather than the mark, customs restrictions made trade unpredictable. There was competition on every street corner. For permission to sell milk, cream, butter, and cheese in addition to groceries, we had to sacrifice the half of the kitchen that faced the street, which left only a windowless cubbyhole for the stove and icebox. The grocery chain Kaisers Kaffee siphoned off more and more business. The sales representatives would not deliver goods to our store unless all our bills were paid up, and too many of our customers bought on credit. The wives of customs officers, civil servants, and policemen were especially prone to adding new purchases to an old bill. They griped, they pinched pennies, they demanded discounts. Every Saturday after closing the shop, my parents would look at each other and say, "Once more we've barely broken even."

It should therefore have been clear that my mother could not afford to give me a weekly allowance. But after endless laments on my part—everyone else in my class jangled a more or less ample supply of pocket money—she pushed over to me a well-worn ledger containing rows and rows of the debts of customers who paid on credit—"on tick," as she put it. I open it up.

I see a neatly penned list of names, addresses, and amounts of money owed, occasionally going down but more often going up, accurate to the last penny. It is the record of a business-woman with every reason to worry about her business, as well as a mirror of the general economic situation at a time of growing unemployment.

"The sales reps will be coming on Monday morning and they'll want to see cash," she always told me. All the same she never made either me, or later, my sister feel that the school fees she had to fork out every month put us under any special obligation to her. She never said, Look at the sacrifice I'm making for you. Show your appreciation.

She, who had little patience with cautious child-raising methods that took long-term consequences into account—when an argument between my sister and me got a bit too loud, she would say, "Just a second" to her customer, run out of the shop to wherever we were, and instead of asking "Who started it?" would simply slap both of us without a word, return immediately to the shop, and serve the customer as cordially as you please—she, who was so gentle and warmhearted, so easily moved to tears, who called everything she thought beautiful "genuinely romantic," she, the most concerned of all mothers, pushed the ledger over to me and offered to give me in cash—in guldens and pfennigs—five percent of the debts I collected if I was willing to make time—in the afternoon or whenever I was free from the (in her eyes) idiotic Jungvolk meetings—to visit the defaulting debtors, and armed with nothing but a saucy tongue (which I was not lacking!) and a notebook full of neat figures urge them most compellingly if not to settle their debts outright at least to pay them off in installments. She gave me just one specific piece of advice: "Friday is payday. Friday evening is the best time to collect."

And so at the age of ten or eleven I became a resourceful and, when all was said and done, successful debt collector. I was not to be bought off by an apple or cheap sweets. I came up with words capable of melting hardened debtors' hearts. Even the most pious, the most unctuous excuses sailed past my ears. I was not deterred by threats. I would stick my foot in the door when I felt it was about to be slammed. I was particularly aggressive on Fridays, making reference to pay packets, but not even Sundays were sacred for me. And on holidays, great and small, I was at it all day long.

I soon recovered such significant amounts that my mother felt impelled, now for ethical reasons, to reduce her son's extravagant percentage from five to three. I accepted the cut begrudgingly. Her response: "You were getting too big for your britches."

In the end I was better off financially than many of my classmates, even those who lived in high-roofed Uphagenweg or

Steffensweg private houses with colonnaded doorways and balconies and terraces and servants' entrances and whose fathers
were doctors and lawyers and grain merchants and even factory
and ship owners. My earnings piled up in an empty tobacco tin
hidden in my window niche. I spent it on a supply of sketching
pads and on books, including several volumes of Brehm's *Lives
of Animals*. The film addict in me could now afford to visit the
most out-of-the-way Old Town film palaces, even the Roxi in
the Oliva Castle Gardens, round-trip tram ticket included. He
missed not one offering there.

During those Free State days a Fox Movietone newsreel ran
before every documentary and feature film. I enjoyed watching
Charlie Chaplin eat his shoe, laces and all, in *The Gold Rush;* I
laughed at Laurel and Hardy; I was fascinated by Harry Piel. As
for Shirley Temple, I found her silly and only moderately cute.
Fortunately I also had the funds to see Buster Keaton, whose
funny scenes made me sad and sad scenes made me laugh.

Was it in February, for her birthday, or was it for Mother's
Day? In any case, I wanted to give my mother something special, something from abroad, sometime before the beginning of
the Second World War. I remember standing in front of the
shop windows, contemplating the possibilities, luxuriating in
the agony of choice, vacillating between an oval crystal bowl in
Sternfeld's department store and an electric iron.

In the end I decided on the beautifully designed Siemens ap-
pliance, whose exorbitant price the mother sternly extracted
from her son, though she avoided revealing it to the rest of the
family as if it were one of the seven deadly sins. No, not even the
father, who knew he had reason to be proud of his competent

son, was told the source of my sudden fortune. After each use, the iron disappeared into the sideboard.

I REAPED another reward from my career as a debt collector, though I did not cash in on it till decades later and then it came in the form of prose.

I would go up and down stairs in apartment buildings where smells varied from floor to floor: on one the smell of simmering cabbage would be overwhelmed by the stink of laundry soaking; on the next a cat smell or a diaper smell would force its way through. Behind each door lurked a special rankness: a sour must or the reek of burning hair, because the mistress of the house had just been styling her locks with the curling iron. There was the odor of elderly ladies—mothballs and Uralt Lavender cologne— and the schnapps breath of the retired widower.

I learned by smelling, hearing, seeing, and by experiencing: the poverty and anxieties of large working-class families, the arrogance and fury of civil servants who cursed in stilted High German and refused to pay their bills as a matter of principle, the need of lonely women for a kitchen-table chat, the ominous silence and fierce quarrels among neighbors.

I collected it all in my internal savings account: fathers sober and fathers drunk, beating their children, mothers screaming at the top of their lungs, close-mouthed or stuttering children, whooping cough, permanent cough, sighs, curses, tears of all sizes, dog-and-canary love, people hatred, the prodigal son who has not yet returned, tales of the proletariat and tales of the petite bourgeoisie, the former in Low German larded with Polish expletives, the latter in clipped bureaucratese and shortened to arm's length, some generated by infidelity, and others—about the strength of the spirit and the frailty of the flesh—that I did not recognize as stories until later.

That and much more—not only the blows I was dealt as I made my rounds—got stowed away in me, a stockpile for times when the professional storyteller was short of material, at a loss for words. All I had to do then was let time run backward, sniff the smells, sort the stenches, trudge up and down the stairs, ring the doorbells or knock on the doors, mostly on Friday evenings.

It may even be that this early contact with Free State currency, pfennigs as well as guldens, and then, starting in 1939, with the Reichsmark and its much-coveted silver five-mark coins—that is, my early initiation into the financial world—made it easy for me to trade unscrupulously in black-market commodities like flints and razor blades after the war, and then later on as an author negotiate doggedly with hard-of-hearing publishers. So I have ample reason to be grateful to my mother for my early lessons in the businesslike handling of money even if they were based on debt collecting. And when my sons Franz and Raoul coerced me into drawing them a verbal self-portrait in the early seventies while I was working on *From the Diary of a Snail,* I came up with the lapidary "I was very well badly brought up." Among other things, I was referring to my career as a debt collector.

I have forgotten to mention the bouts of tonsillitis that even after my childhood ended not only kept me out of school for days but also interfered with my money-mad professional life. The convalescent boy was fed egg yolk mixed with sugar by his mother at his bedside.

Encapsulations

One word evokes the other: *Schulden, Schuld,* debts, guilt. Two words so close and so deeply rooted in the soil of the German language. But while debts can be mitigated by installment payments, long-term as they may be (witness my mother's clientele), guilt—whether proven, presumed, or concealed—remains, ticking on and on, and holds its place, even on journeys to nowhere. It says its piece, fears no repetition, is mercifully forgotten for a time, hibernates in dreams. It remains as sediment—not a stain to be removed or a spill to be wiped away. Penitent, it learns early to seek refuge in the shell of an ear, to think of itself as beyond the statute of limitations, as long since forgiven, as smaller than small, next to nothing, yet there it is, as the onion sheds skin after skin, permanently inscribed on the youngest skins, now in capital letters, now in a subordinate clause or footnote, now clear and legible, now in barely decipherable hieroglyphics. The brief inscription meant for me reads: I kept silent.

But because so many kept silent, the temptation is great to discount one's own silence, or to compensate for it by invoking the general guilt, or to speak about oneself all but abstractly, in the third person: he was, saw, had, said, he kept silent . . . and what's more, silent within, where there is plenty of room for hide and seek.

As SOON as I summon up the boy I was at the age of thirteen, subject him to the third degree, and feel tempted to judge him as I would a stranger to whose needs I am indifferent, to condemn him, I see a kid of average height in shorts and kneesocks constantly grimacing, running to his mother, and crying, "I was just a child, just a kid . . ."

I try to calm him down and ask him to help me peel the onion, but he rejects all entreaties and refuses to let himself be exploited as my early self-portrait. He denies me the right to—as he puts it—do him in and "from your high horse" to boot.

Now he is narrowing his eyes to observation slits, pressing his lips together, screwing his mouth into an uneasy grimace while hunching over his books; then he's gone, nowhere to be found.

I observe him reading. It's the only thing he can do for any length of time. He habitually stops up his ears with his index fingers to shut out his sister's gleeful noise. Here she comes, warbling away. He'd better watch out, because she likes to close his book on him. Or she may want him to play with her. That's all she thinks about, play; she never stops. The only time he likes her is when she keeps her distance.

Books have always been his gap in the fence, his entry into other worlds. But he also makes faces when he's not reading, when he's just standing in the living room, looking so absent that his mother calls over to him, "Where are you, anyway? What's going on up there in your head?"

Where was I when I was only pretending to be there? What far-off spaces was the grimacing youngster inhabiting without leaving the living room or classroom? In what direction was he spooling his thread? As a rule, I was moving backward in time, ravenously hungry for the bloody entrails of history and mad about the Pitch-Dark Ages or the Baroque interim of a war lasting thirty years.

And so the boy who answers to my name liked to see the passing days as a series of appearances in ever changing costumes. I always wanted to be someone else and somewhere else, the Soonother whom I met a few years later, immersed in a cheap edition of *Simplicissimus,* a strange, yet attractive figure, who at the end of the eponymous hero's adventures, helps him to slip out of a musketeer's baggy breeches into a hermit's shaggy habit.

Even though the present, with the Führer's speeches, the blitzkriegs, submarine heroes, ace pilots, and suchlike military details, was a subject I knew backward and forward, and my knowledge of geography was expanding to include the mountains of Montenegro, the Greek archipelagos, and—starting in the summer of '41, as the front shifted eastward—Smolensk, Kiev, and Lake Ladoga, I was simultaneously on the march with the Crusaders as they entered Jerusalem, I was a squire to the Emperor Barbarossa, fought fiercely as a knight of the order against the Prussians, was excommunicated by the Pope, joined Conradin's retinue, and went down, intrepid, with the last of the Hohenstaufens.

Blind to the injustices that were becoming daily occurrences in the city's environs—between the Vistula and the Haff, only two villages away from the Nickelswald country house used by the Conradinum for school excursions, the Stutthof concentration camp was growing and growing—I was incensed by the crimes of sanctimonious clerics, the tortures of the Inquisition. On the one hand I thrilled to the description of pincers, red-hot pokers, and thumbscrews, on the other hand I saw myself avenging the deaths of witches and heretics. I reserved my ire for Gregory IX & Co. Polish peasants and their families were being turned out of their farms in the West Prussian hinterland; meanwhile I was a vassal of Frederick II, who settled his loyal Saracens in Apulia and spoke Arabic to his falcons.

In retrospect I see that the grimacing gymnasium student had managed to transfer his book-learned sense of justice entirely to the Middle Ages. Perhaps that is why in my first attempt at writing a sustained piece I used a setting far from the sieges of the summer of forty-one and the deportation of the remaining Danzig Jews from the Mausegasse ghetto to Theresienstadt. I could scarcely have chosen a more remote backdrop for my plot than the mid-thirteenth century.

It all began with *Hilf mit!* (Lend a Hand), a children's newspaper, which had sponsored a contest with prizes for narrative prose submitted by youthful readers. Thus did the grimacing youth, or my I, by now well-established though forever ducking behind fiction's bushes, maculate a till-then-immaculate notebook with no, not a meager short story, but a full-fledged novel right off the bat. And off my own bat: the novel bore the title *The Kashubians*—that I remember clearly. They were, after all, my relatives.

During my childhood we often crossed the Free State border in the direction of Kokoschken and Zuckau to visit Great-Aunt Anna, who lived with her large family in cramped quarters under a low roof. Cheesecake, brawn, gherkins pickled with mustard seeds, mushrooms, honey, prunes, and giblets (stomach, heart, liver), morsels sweet and morsels sour, and schnapps, potato schnapps—she would lay it all out on the table at once, and we would all laugh and cry at once.

In the winter, Uncle Joseph, Great-Aunt Anna's eldest son, would come for us with his horse and sleigh. What fun it was. We would cross the border at Goldkrug. Even though Uncle Joseph greeted the customs officers in German and Polish, he would get an earful from each uniform. That was less fun. Just before the war broke out, the story goes, he took a Polish flag and a flag with a swastika out of the wardrobe and said, "When war starts in, I climb tree and look who comes first. Then I raise flag—this one or that . . ."

Even later, when times had changed, we would go on seeing the mother and sisters and brothers of the late Uncle Franz, though only in secret, after the shop was closed. Trade in kind was useful in that war economy: they gave us soup chickens and farm eggs; we gave them raisins, baking powder, yarn, and kerosene. Next to the herring barrel there was a kerosene tank the size of a man. Its smell has survived its time. As has the picture of Great-Aunt Anna pulling a plucked goose she had brought to trade out from under her skirts and tossing it onto our counter with, "One of them ten-pounders . . ."

I was familiar with Kashubian speakers' linguistic peculiarities in German: whenever she abandoned grumblings in her ancient Slav tongue for expressions of woe in Low German, she would also abandon all articles, definite and indefinite, and say *nein* twice instead of once just to be certain. Her slow-motion speech was like clotted milk mixed with sugar and topped with grated pumpernickel crumbs.

The Kashubians, what remained of them, had lived from time immemorial in the hilly hinterland of the city of Danzig and depending on who was in power were considered either not Polish or not German enough. When the Germans took over government of the Free State, many Kashubians were classified by decree as Ethnic Group Three. This was done under pressure from the authorities, that the Kashubians might prove themselves worthy of being made fully fledged Germans, *Reichsdeutsche,* the young women eligible for the Labor Service, the young men, like Uncle Jan, who was now called Hannes, for the military.

Here were issues that cried out for airing. That is why I placed the action of my entry into literature, a tale of mayhem and manslaughter, during the interregnum of the thirteenth century—"a terrible time with no emperor." I had the urge to flee reality for as rough-and-tumble a historical period as possible. Nor did the life and customs of an ancient Slav culture have a chance. No, my literary debut was more about the medieval German vehmic court and its injustices after the downfall of the Hohenstaufens, which made for amply violent narrative material.

Not a word of that novel remains: I haven't the slightest memory of its episodes, other than that they dripped with blood because they dealt with bloodlust; not one character's name—knight or peasant or beggar—has stayed with me; nothing, no cleric's pronouncement of guilt, no witch's cry has stuck. Yet streams of gore must have flowed, a dozen or more stakes been erected and victims set afire with torches, because by the end of the first chapter all the heroes were dead: beheaded, garroted, impaled, burnt to a cinder, or drawn and quartered. Not only that: there was nobody left to avenge them.

Thus my trial by fire in narrative prose found a premature end on a corpse-strewn battlefield. Had this notebook survived, it would have been of interest only to fragment fetishists.

To bring back the strangled and the beheaded, the quartered and the burnt, the corpses dangling from the oaks as crow fodder—to bring them back in later chapters as ghosts, and scare the hell out of the remaining rank and file population could not have been further from my mind: I was never partial to ghost stories. But it may be that this early case of writer's block, brought on by my uneconomical treatment of fictional personnel, led me later, as a carefully calculating author, to be more sparing of the heroes of my novels.

Oskar Matzerath survived as a media mogul. And with him, his grandmother, his *babka,* for whose hundred-and-seventh birthday celebration, in the crisscrossed time frame of the novel *The Rat,* he even took upon himself the strain of a trip to Kashubia—and that despite the agony of serious prostate problems.

And because Tulla Pokriefke's early demise could be only presumed—in fact she was rescued at the age of seventeen, and very pregnant, from the sinking refugee ship *Wilhelm Gustloff*—she was ready for recall as a seventeen-year-old survivor when the novella *Crabwalk* was ready for paper. She is now the grandmother of a young rightist radical who glorifies his "martyrs" on the Internet.

The same holds for my favorite Jenny Brunies who, though badly damaged and forever down with a cold, managed to outlive *Dog Years,* much as I too have been spared, the better to re-discover myself over and over in new pastures.

In the end, the immoderate youth, a sketch of my still-to-be revealed self, was unable to enter the competition of the children's newspaper *Hilf mit!* Or, to put it in a more favorable light, I was spared participation, possibly prizeworthy, in a National Socialist competition for the literary youth of the Greater German Reich. Because had a successful first story been crowned with a second or third prize—to say nothing of first—the premature debut of my literary career would have been Nazi-tarnished; it would have been tantamount to handing the evidence—complete with chapter and verse—to the always ravenous journalists on a silver platter. I could have been labeled a Young Nazi, and, thus hand-icapped, declared a collaborator, indelibly branded. There would have been no shortage of judges.

But I can take care of the labeling and branding myself. As a member of the Hitler Youth I was, in fact, a Young Nazi. A be-liever till the end. Not what one would call fanatical, not lead-ing the pack, but with my eye, as if by reflex, fixed on the flag that was to mean "more than death" to us, I kept pace in the rank and file. No doubts clouded my faith; nothing subversive like the clandestine distribution of leaflets can let me off the hook; no Göring joke made me suspicious. No, I saw my father-land threatened, surrounded by enemies.

I HAD been properly appalled by the "Bromberg Bloody Sun-day" horror stories that were plastered all over the local Nazi daily, *Danziger Vorposten,* which made all Poles out to be treach-erous murderers, and I perceived every German deed as justifiable retribution. If I had any criticism, it was against the local party bigwigs—known as golden pheasants because of their gold braiding—who had wormed their way out of active duty at the front and who would bore us, after we had marched past the requisite rostra, with their tedious speeches, speeches that took in vain the holy name of the Führer we so believed in—no, I so believed in, believed in with untroubled, unquestioning fervor, until everything fell, as our song foresaw—"So onward we'll march, ever onward, till everything falls to pieces"—to pieces.

THAT is how I see myself in my rearview mirror. The image cannot be wiped out: it is not chalk on a blackboard; it is permanent. And though with time a few erasures have appeared in them, the songs are still there too: "Onward, onward! Trumpets are blaring their fanfare! Onward, onward! Youth knows nothing of danger!" Claiming "They seduced us!" does not excuse the youths who sang them and hence does not excuse me. No, we let ourselves, I let myself, be seduced.

But, the onion might say timidly, pointing to a few unblemished spots on the eighth skin, you've got a clean record. You were just a foolish boy, you did nothing bad: you didn't denounce anyone, the neighbor, for example, who dared tell that cynical joke about Göring, the fat Reichsmarschall; you didn't turn in the soldier on leave from the front who bragged of steering clear of assignments that might get him the Knight's Cross; nor were you the one to denounce the history teacher who had dared, if only in subordinate clauses, to question the "final victory" and call the German people "a herd of sheep," and who, to top it all, was hated by the entire school.

That was true: ratting on students to our janitor, turning them in to the Nazi block or ward leader—that was not my style. But when our Latin teacher, who because he was a priest as well had himself addressed as "Monsignor," was suddenly no longer there to test us on our vocabulary, when he suddenly disappeared, I again asked no questions even though the moment he was gone the word "Stutthof" was on everyone's lips by way of warning.

I was fourteen when our People's Receiver started to broadcast bulletins preceded by brass-and-drum fanfares announcing victorious sieges on the Russian steppes. Day after day Liszt's *Preludes* was misappropriated, and while my knowledge of geography was soaring, my Latin hovered at unsatisfactory.

After yet another change of school I found myself at Saint John's, an Old Town gymnasium on Fleischergasse near the Municipal Museum and the Church of the Trinity, an institution that turned out to rest upon a Gothic cellar and whose low-ceilinged corridors found their way into *Dog Years.* That is why I later had no trouble enrolling two of my characters—Eddie Amsel and Walter Matern, simultaneous friends and foes—in the school and having them make their way from the locker room to the Franciscan corridors.

When after a few months my Latin teacher, Monsignor Stachnik, returned to Saint John's and started teaching again, I again failed to pose any urgent questions, although I had the reputation of being obstreperous in general and a big-mouth in particular.

Oh, well, he wouldn't have answered them anyway. That's the way it always was when people were let out of the camps. He didn't look any different, and questions would have only added to his problems.

Still, I must have been sufficiently disturbed by my own silence to have felt the need to erect an unmistakable monument to the man—he was not only my Latin teacher but also the former head of the Free State Centrist Party and a tireless spokesman for the blessed Dorothea von Montau—in my deliberately retrogressive novel *The Flounder*. Monsignor Stachnik and his Gothic hermitess. His efforts to have her canonized. He would go into raptures whenever we prompted him to talk about her slimming cure. We had no trouble luring him away from the formal garden of Latin syntax: all we had to do was to bring up the woman who was, to him, Saint Dorothea.

What had spoiled her marriage with the armorer?

What miracles were ascribed to her?

Why had she had herself immured in the cathedral at Marienwerder?

Did she still have a beautiful figure after losing all that weight?

All these things, and his invariably closed collar, I called forth from my memory to pay him tribute.

BUT this belated hymn of praise was not completely to Monsignor Stachnik's liking. We assessed the penitent Dorothea's life and her death by starvation from quite different perspectives. When my wife and I were traveling through the countryside around Münster in the mid-seventies, researching the remnants of Baroque local color for *The Meeting at Telgte*, we paid him a visit. He had taken up residence in a nunnery in his old age and had a spacious and comfortably furnished cell conducive to conversation. I carefully avoided provoking any conflict on this very Catholic soil. Ute, a Protestant by birth, was a bit surprised at the elderly gentleman's serene existence in the midst of a community of nuns, who appeared before us, in their all-concealing habits, only to let us in.

In a coquettish tone that I had never heard from him in his teaching days, he called himself the cock of the walk. The figure before me was also rounder than my memory had preserved it: refectory cooking clearly agreed with him.

We did not spend much time on Dorothea, who had finally been beatified. In matters political he was still very much the centrist, a position he felt was poorly upheld by the Christian Democrats at the time. He praised Father Wiehnke, my confessor at the Sacred Heart Church, because he had looked after the Catholic workers in his congregation "with great valor." He reminisced about this or that teacher at Saint John's and about the principal, whose two sons, as he put it, had "found their death" with the battleship *Bismarck*.

Yet he looked back with reluctance: "Those were hard times, they were . . ." "No, no. Nobody denounced me . . ."

That I was bad at Latin had mercifully slipped through the cracks.

We spoke about Danzig when it was a picture postcard of towers and gables. He was glad to hear I had made repeated trips to Gdańsk—"I hear Holy Trinity has been restored to its former beauty"—and when I brought up the topic of my silence during those years in school Monsignor Stachnik dismissed it with a smile and a wave of the hand. I thought I heard an *"Ego te absolvo."*

THOUGH seldom admonished by my moderately pious mother to go to church, I was early marked by Catholicism, and always crossed myself when I passed between the confessional and the main altar and altar of Our Lady. *Monstrance* and *tabernacle* were words I loved uttering, if only for their melodious sound. But what did I believe in before I believed only in the Führer?

The Holy Ghost struck me as more fathomable than God the Father or God the Son. My faith, nurtured by the altar figures, the age-darkened paintings, and the incense-impregnated ghost-like atmosphere of the Sacred Heart Church, was more heathen than Christian. I felt physically close to the Virgin Mary: as Soonother, I was the archangel who recognized her.

In addition, I was nurtured by the truths in books, truths that led lives of their own, lives rich in meaning, and it was in their hothouse beds that my own preposterous stories germinated. What, then, did the fourteen-year-old read?

No religious tracts, that's for sure, and no alliterative *Blut und Boden* propaganda: blood and soil were not for me. Nor was I attracted to Tom Mix or the endless volumes of our very own spinner of westerns, Karl May, which my classmates couldn't put down. Above all, I read everything—what luck!—that my mother's bookcase had to offer.

On the occasion of receiving a prize in Budapest about a year ago—a mantelpiece clock I found monstrous because it was set in a lead-gray casing that implied I had only leaden moments ahead of me—I asked my Hungarian editor, Imre Barna, if he knew who had written a novel that had bewildered me in my youth, a novel entitled *Temptation in Budapest.* Before long, a thick tome was delivered to me by a dealer in secondhand books. Its author, long since forgotten, was Franz Körmendi. His book, published by Propyläen Verlag in Berlin in 1933, is a five-hundred-page tale of men sitting around in coffeehouses after

World War I, bored and longing for happiness and stability. There is an undercurrent of proletarian revolution and counter-revolution and anarchist bombings. The hero is a rootless member of the coffee house group, poor but ambitious, who leaves the city on the Danube, goes out into the world, and returns with a rich wife, only to fall prey to a perplexing and in the end spurious love.

It is as fresh a novel today as it was when it was published and I found it in my mother's collection—a motley combination of books that the son made short work of and whose titles must remain unlisted for the time being because, hungry for more reading material, I now picture myself at a table in the Municipal Library near Saint Peter's.

Saint Peter's was my intermediate stop. I was transferred there by decree of the school board after being expelled from the Langfuhr Conradinum for having been, as the son's disappointed parents were informed, "unruly and shamelessly insolent" to a physical education teacher who was known for torturing his pupils on the horizontal and parallel bars.

But what does it mean to say, "I now picture myself in the Municipal Library"? With the help of the few snapshots my mother managed to save from the war I can put together another self-portrait of the adolescent I was then. The pimples I later vainly laid siege to with Pitralon lotion and almond bran have not yet made their appearance, but my protuberant lower lip and congenitally jutting jaw make me look less like a child. I am serious, almost somber, the kind of prematurely pubescent pupil who can be expected to rise up against his teachers: rub him the wrong way and he's likely to lay hands on you.

Then there was the time a fat music teacher sang us "Hei-deröschen" in his falsetto voice, and when we provided a jazz accompaniment of sounds and gestures I was the only one he scolded and dared to shake, which led me to grab his tie with my left hand and throttle him with it until it tore just under the knot (because of the war it was made out of paper). That incident provided the grounds for yet another transfer—as a pedagogical precaution, according to the euphemistic report—this time from Saint Peter's to Saint John's. No wonder I was cutting myself off from everybody, even from my mother.

And I picture myself wearing the same brooding look on my way to the Municipal Library for whose existence we had the Hanseatic sense of civic duty to thank and which one could reasonably have assumed to have burned down when the entire city was in flames just before the end of the war. But when I visited the by then Polish city of Gdańsk in the spring of 1958 to search for traces of Danzig, that is, to take notes on loss, I found the Municipal Library intact, down to its old wood-paneled interior, so that I had no trouble seeing myself as an adolescent in knee-length trousers seated at one of its tables enjoying the use of its collection. Right: no pimples yet, but a lock of hair falling over the forehead; the bridge of the nose already arched; chin and lower lip thrust forward; the mouth twisted into a grimace. He still grimaces, and not only when he reads.

TIME lays layer upon layer. What it covers is at best recovered through chinks. And it is through one such gap in time, which I do my best to enlarge, that I view him and myself simultaneously: he shamelessly young, I getting on in years; he reading the future in books, the past catching up with me. My cares are not his: what he fails to see as disgraceful, that is, what makes him feel no shame, I, who am more than related to him, must somehow grapple with. Sheet upon sheet of time consumed lies between us.

While the thirty-year-old father of newborn twin sons, who has recently tried to balance out his protruding lower lip by growing a mustache, is poking around for local morsels to feed an always ravenous manuscript, his rejuvenated self will not let anything, not even him, the man in the corduroy suit, distract him.

But my eyes can't stay still. As I leaf through the 1939 issues of the *Danziger Vorposten* that have been brought to me from the stacks, I am only superficially involved in what the paper reports about everyday life at the beginning of the war. Granted, my thirty-year-old self is scribbling things in his notebook: the films being shown during the first week in September in Langfuhr and in the Old Town cinemas—*Water for Canitoga* with Hans Albers, for instance, at the Odeon near the Dominikswall—but at the same time his roaming eye catches sight of the fourteen-year-old boy sitting three tables away, engrossed in a richly illustrated volume of the Knackfuss World Artist Monographs.

There is a pile of other volumes in the series beside him: he is clearly hoping to expand the knowledge he has gained from his cigarette cards. Without so much as raising his head, he sets aside the volume devoted to Max Klinger and opens another.

While the grown-up morsel-collector copies out random market prices and stock quotations (Bemberg silk steady, grain commodities on the rise) and before he can be mortified by yet another multicolumn horror story—here is one that goes on for pages, squeezing the last gory drop out of the "massacre perpetrated by Polish monsters" on September 3, "Bromberg Bloody

Sunday"—he sees himself, no, sees the boy, who, thanks to Knackfuss has just admired the versatility of Klinger, painter, sculptor, draftsman, and is now, after being fascinated by Caravaggio's tumultuous biography, wishing he could have been an apprentice in Anselm Feuerbach's studio. His current favorites are the Deutschrömer, the "German Romans" of the mid-nineteenth century. He wants to become an artist, and famous, no doubt about it.

The mature time-traveler from Paris, who may already be an artist but is not yet famous, realizes that his youthful counterpart is totally absorbed: even if he called out to him, he would get no response.

THIS meeting with myself is transferable: when I cut myself off from the world, I often see my younger self in different places, in the Jäschkental Forest or on the steps of the cast-iron Gutenberg monument. Or on the deserted shore before the beach season began, when I would take a pile of borrowed books down to the Baltic and huddle up in one of the empty wicker chairs to read, though my favorite reading place was the attic of our apartment building, where I could read under the skylight. I can also picture myself in our cramped apartment standing before my mother's bookcase. It is more memorable than any other piece of furniture in the living room. It reaches only to my forehead. Its glass front and blue curtains are meant to protect the books' spines from too much light. The wood is walnut with egg-and-dart edging. It is said to be the piece that an apprentice working at my paternal grandfather's joining bench happened to finish just before my parents' wedding and submitted to his master, my grandfather, as his bid to become a journeyman.

Ever since, it had stood to the right of the living-room window, just beside my niche. Beneath the sill of the left-hand living-room window, which provided side lighting for the piano and the music open on its stand, my sister kept her poetry album and dolls and stuffed animals, my sister, who never cracked a grimace or a book, yet was Papa's pet, because she was always cheerful and practically never made a fuss.

After closing the shop, my mother not only played languorous pieces on the piano, she also subscribed to a book club, though which one I cannot recall. She must have let her membership lapse, because shortly after the war began the books stopped coming.

Still, the case contained Dostoevsky's *Possessed*, Wilhelm Raabe's *Sparrow Street Chronicle*, Schiller's *Collected Poems*, and Selma Lagerlöf's *Gösta Berling*. Something by Sudermann stood side by side with Hamsun's *Hunger*, Keller's *Green Henry* next to his *Holiday from Myself*. Fallada's *Little Man, What Now* was between Raabe's *Hunger Pastor* and Storm's *The White Horseman*. Dahn's *Battle for Rome* was most likely the support for the illustrated volume with the title *Rasputin and Women*, which I later gave to a certain character to read as an antidote to Goethe's *Elective Affinities*, though he was book-mad for a completely different reason, using the explosive mixture to teach himself his ABC's, in upper and lower case.

All these and more were grist to my mill. Did *Uncle Tom's Cabin* and *The Picture of Dorian Gray* have a place in the treasure trove behind the blue curtains? What did it include of Dickens, of Mark Twain?

I am certain that neither my mother—who had less and less time to read as her business gave her more and more trouble—

nor her son realized that one of the books in her bookcase was on the blacklist: Vicki Baum's *Helene Willfüer, Chemistry Student.* Baum's novel, which had unleashed a scandal even before the Nazis took power in 1933, is about a young woman who is as diligent as she is without means, about love and longing for death in the idyllic atmosphere of a university town, and, because the heroine becomes pregnant, about quacks and abortionists—the latter subject illicit by definition. I assume my mother never actually read the account of the brave chemistry student's sufferings, because when she saw her fourteen-year-old son sitting at the living-room table totally absorbed in the heroine's misfortunes—and in the joy Helene later finds in motherhood—she made no objection whatever.

Over the years I've gone back to Vicki Baum. I read *People in a Hotel,* the novel the famous Garbo film, *Grand Hotel,* was based on. And in the early eighties when I was working on a travelogue that appeared under the title *Headbirths, or The Germans Are Dying Out,* and predicted the self-serving lives of the childless and the continuation of their me-generation ego-cult to the present day—as well as the graying of the German population, the long-term crisis in the pension system, the dreariness of forced togetherness—Baum's exotic story "Love and Death on Bali" helped me to fill in the melodramatic background. But never again have I given myself up to her books, considered to be mere entertainments, with such abandon as I did in my youth.

As SOON as it was time to set the table for supper, Father would say, "Books won't fill your stomach."

Mother, however, liked to see me with my nose in a book.

Beloved by customers and sales representatives alike, she was, though inclined to bouts of dreamy melancholy, of a basically cheerful and at times even bantering nature; nor was she averse to harmless practical jokes, which she called "pranks," and she enjoyed demonstrating to her visitors—a friend she had apprenticed with at Kaisers Kaffee, for instance—how lost her son became in the printed page by replacing the slice of bread and jam I bit into now and again as I read with a slab of Palmolive soap.

Her arms crossed, her face smiling, sure of success, she would wait for the result of the exchange. She was especially jubilant when her son bit into the soap and noticed only after another three quarters of a page what he had demonstrated to the amused visitor. Since then, my palate instantly recognizes the taste of Palmolive.

The boy with the protuberant lip must have bitten into Palmolive quite often, because in my memory, which tends to get caught up in variations, the food the soap replaced is now a sausage or cheese sandwich, now a slice of raisin cake. As for the lower lip, its brashness came in handy whenever I needed to blow my hair from my eyes. And I needed to all the time when I was reading. Every once in a while Mother would remove a barrette from her carefully permed hair and pin back the offending shock of soft hair. I put up with it.

Her one and only. Despite the worry I caused her—by having to repeat the third year at the gymnasium, by being expelled from two schools for obstreperous behavior—she maintained an unwavering pride in her son, forever reading, forever sketching, but easily lured back from his dreamworld to become, as they both desired, her darling little boy.

The litany of my boasts, which would open with "When I'm rich and famous, you'll . . . ," never failed to beguile her. Nothing seemed to please her more than to be showered with extravagant promises: "And then we'll travel to Rome together and to Naples . . ." She, who dearly loved beauty and all things melancholy, who would don her Sunday best and go off to the Municipal Theater on her own or with my father as an appendage, had a name for me whenever I took it into my head to promise her the moon: she would call me her little Peer Gynt. This blind devotion granted her braggart of a mama's boy presumably had its roots in the passing of her youth.

My FATHER's family could not have lived closer—just around the corner on Elsenstrasse, where the circular saw in Grandfather's workshop set the tone from morning till night—and I had great trouble keeping out of their constant feuding, which let up for only brief periods of reconciliation. They were always at it—"Not another word to them" and "They'll never darken our door again, they won't." My maternal grandparents and my mother's three brothers and only sister, on the other hand, were known to me only through stories and a few mementos. Apart from the sister, who was named Elisabeth but called Betty, and who had married "into the Reich," my mother was on her own.

True, there was the Kashubian side of her family, but they lived in the country; besides, they weren't really German and didn't count anymore, now that there were reasons to keep them under wraps. Mother's parents, who had adapted to middle-class city ways, had died young. Her father fell in battle at Tannenberg early in World War I. Then, after two older sons were killed in

France and the youngest, likewise a soldier, was carried off by influenza, her mother died as well: she had lost the will to live.

Arthur had made it to twenty-three, Paul to twenty-one; the influenza took Alfons at the very end of the war, when he was nineteen. My mother, née Helene Knoff, spoke of her brothers as if they were still alive.

One dateless day—was I fourteen by then or still twelve?—in the attic of the Labesweg apartment building, where we occupied one of nineteen units, I was on the way to my favorite reading place, the threadbare armchair under the hinged skylight, when in one of the storage areas allotted to each of the units and partitioned off by slats I found a suitcase bound by string. I—or the boy in whom stories started accumulating at an early age—had made a momentous discovery. Under piles of junk, between abandoned pieces of furniture, this suitcase had been waiting for me. At least that was how I interpreted the find.

Was it under a tattered mattress?

Was a pigeon that had flown through the skylight dancing on the leather, cooing?

Had my presence scared it into leaving a dropping?

Did I rush to undo the knots?

Did I grab for my pocket knife?

Did I hold back out of fear?

Or did I drag the suitcase down the stairs like a good boy and hand it over to Mother?

There are other, mutually interchangeable possibilities: according to air-raid regulations promulgated in mid-1942, all attics had to be cleared; the suitcase had turned up during the process and was opened by her, me, or a third party.

In any case, it contained the few possessions of both brothers who died in the First World War and the brother taken by
the epidemic that impartially dispatched friend and foe.

Everything my mother had so often told me, the ineradi-
cable pain of this loss, which she would evoke with tears, was
confirmed by the contents of that suitcase: three young men
prevented from living the lives for which their inclinations and
talents had prepared them.

Each of the three piles she had bound with a silk ribbon
had its own distinct tale to tell. The middle brother, Paul, had
wanted to be a painter and had tried his hand at theatrical
scenery. I found color drawings of stage settings and costumes
for the operas *Der Freischütz* and *Der fliegende Holländer,* or
maybe it was *Lohengrin,* because what I now see in my mind's
eye are sketches for a stageworthy swan that want me to think
of them as belonging to the colored-pencil stack left behind by
Uncle Paul, who died near the Somme. There were no medals
among the sheets of paper.

The youngest brother, Alfons, who died of the Spanish influenza, had been trained as a professional cook and dreamed of
rising to the rank of chef in a grand hotel in some European capital—Brussels, Vienna, or Berlin—in recognition of the exquisite menus he had concocted. He poured it all out in letters
written on the Baltic Sea island of Sylt, where he had his first
and last job, as a cook at a resort, just before he was conscripted
and sent to basic training.

The letters he wrote to his sister Helene were long and
packed with breezy boasts. After hinting at adventures with the
noblewomen taking the cure at the resort, he would detail the
dishes he had learned to make: cod stewed in mustard sauce,

filet of loach on a bed of fennel, eel soup spiced with dill, and other fish dishes that I later attempted myself, with Uncle Alfons in mind.

The eldest brother, Arthur, whom Mother spoke of as her favorite, saw himself—until a shot in the belly finished him off—as a poet crowned in glory. During his apprenticeship in a branch of the Imperial Bank near the High Gate, a building that survived the last war and currently supplies a Polish bank with all the pomp of the Bismarck-era boom, a local Danzig paper occasionally published verses of multiple stanzas under his name, a dozen or so spring and autumn poems, an All Saints' Day poem here, a Christmas poem there, and these clippings I found collected in the suitcase—in my momentous discovery, as Mother was later to call it.

Her son too was tempted to see it as momentous and, in the mid-sixties, when, having suffered enough under the burden of lengthy novel manuscripts, he found himself producing short stories, he decided to sign them with the name of his mother's favorite brother and published them in a series of pamphlets put out by the Literarisches Colloquium Berlin, a pleasure I indulged in partly to shield them from the malice of capricious critics, partly to illuminate the brief life of Arthur Knoff with a bit of posthumous glory.

Knoff's debut—apart from poetic juvenilia, which owed much of its coloring to Eichendorff—was quite well received. Despite his recognizable similarity to a well-known author of the day, critics believed he was gifted and had a future. An Italian publisher felt it was too early to think of translating the stories, but she hoped they could expect something more monumental from him soon, something along the lines of a family

chronicle. It was clear, people said, his talent was more conducive to the novel.

The stories of Arthur Knoff were in print for more than
two decades, holding their own under the pseudonym until
Klaus Roehler, who when sober was a rather fussy editor with
Luchterhand-Verlag, unmasked my literary uncle one day when
he was plastered.

THE attic with its slatted storage areas full of odds and ends and
spider webs, where later Oskar Matzerath, like me, would find
refuge, that is, until the neighborhood children followed him up
there and tortured him. Oskar could practice his powerful song
there; I had my suitcase.

I can still see the sun dappling its smooth leather surface.
No, no cooing pigeon gave me advice. I was the only one privileged to open it, up there in my secret reading place. Impatient.
With my three-blade penknife. I was hit by a smell, as if a tomb
had been opened. A cloud of dust danced in the light. I took
what I found as a sign: it sent me on a lifelong journey. Only
now is the traveler beginning to tire: looking back is all that
keeps him awake.

I was drawn again and again to my hiding place. The hinged
skylight gave me an unobstructed view of the back courtyards, the
chestnut trees, the tarred roof of the candy factory, the postage-
stamp gardens, the half-covered sheds, the carpet-beating frames,
the rabbit warrens, all the way to the houses on Luisenstrasse,
Herthastrasse, and Marienstrasse, which bordered the spacious
square. But I saw farther than that. From the place of my meeting with the painter, the poet, and the chef—Paul, usually gloomy,
Arthur, often dreamy, Alfons, always blithe—I followed a flight

pattern into the somewhere, just as now on my flight back, I am trying to land in a place where no relics, no worn-out armchair, nothing I can touch or lay my hands on awaits me.

Oh, if only there were a suitcase, or at least a cardboard box, full of my earliest scribblings. But not a fragment from my first poems, not a page from the Kashubian novel remains; not one of the muddled fantasies or fastidiously detailed moss-covered bricks I drew or painted has survived. Neither the rhymed verse in Sütterlin script nor the black-and-white hatched drawings found a place in the luggage my parents packed for our escape. Nor is there an exercise book of school compositions that earned "good" or "very good" despite my execrable spelling. There is no record whatsoever of my beginnings.

Or should I tell myself, "How good not a scrap has remained!"?

For how embarrassing it would be if the preadolescent's gushings included a poem, dated April 20, influenced by the panegyric style of such Hitler Youth bards as Menzel, Baumann, or von Schirach and celebrating the Führer in hymn-like terms reflecting the young poet's unbending faith. Rhymes like *Ehre gebäre* ("may honor give birth to"), *Blut und Glut* ("blood and ardor"), *Fanfaren und Gefahren* ("fanfares and dangers") would have been awful to face later on. Or if some racist claptrap had found its way into a passage in my first novel at the expense of the poor Kashubians: *A long-faced knight beheads round-faced Slavs by the dozen.* And suchlike products of the delusions that come of brainwashing.

At best, I can be certain that should a stack of drawings be found, if not in the attic then in the basement, not one of them would depict a highly decorated war hero like Lieutenant Captain

Prien or Galland the fighter pilot, though I thought of them both as idols.

What if? The speculations induced by the contents of lost suitcases are as futile as they are inevitable.

What treacherous whispers might go on in a detergent box that the mother used to pack her son's belongings when the family was forced to flee and that she overlooked in the rush to depart?

What else would it take to expose a man needy of a fig leaf?

Having grown up in a family that was expelled from house and home, in contrast to writers of my generation who grew up in one place—on Lake Constance, in Nuremberg, in the North German lowlands—and are therefore in full possession of their school records and juvenilia, and having ipso facto no concrete evidence of my early years, I can call only the most questionable of witnesses to the stand: Lady Memory, a capricious creature prone to migraines and reputed to smile at the highest bidder.

So WHAT we need here are other means, helpful in other ways. Objects round or angular waiting on the shelf above the stand-up desk. Found objects, which, when invoked with sufficient intensity, will begin to reveal their mysteries.

No, not coins or clay shards. They are honey-colored and translucent, their hues are autumn's red and gold. Fragments the size of cherries, and this one, large as a duck's egg.

The gold from my Baltic pond: amber. Found on Baltic beaches or bought a year ago now in a Lithuanian town once called Memel from a dealer hawking his wares on the street. The standard tourist fare, polished and buffed—amber chains and bracelets, amber paperweights and boxes—but some of it uncut or only partially smoothed pieces.

Ute and I had gone there with Jürgen and Maria Manthey by ferry from the Kurische Nehrung. Actually we only intended to visit the monument to Anke von Tharau and pay tribute to the poet Simon Dach. A windy day with fast-moving clouds. I made my selection, hesitated, then took the plunge.

Objects were preserved in all the pieces I found or bought: in the petrified bead there are pine needles, in that found object mossy lichen, in this one a mosquito, its tiny legs countable, its wings poised for flight. Holding the duck's-egg piece up to the light, I see a fossilized, ice floe-like mass wedged in tight and surrounded by minute insects. A matter of encapsulation. Is this a worm? Is that a centipede halted in mid step? Only under prolonged scrutiny does amber yield the secrets it once presumed secure.

Whenever my primary means, the imaginary onion, has nothing to say to me or delivers its message in all but indecipherable codes, I reach for the shelf above the stand-up desk in my Behlendorf studio and rummage among the bought and found fragments there.

This honey-colored piece is transparent all the way to its crusty rim, where it turns milky. If I hold it up to the light long enough and switch off the tick-tock in my head and refuse to allow current events—or anything current—to sidetrack me, that is, if I am completely and utterly focused, what I see instead of the object, which until then claimed to be a tick, is the full-length outline of my own person, fourteen and naked. My penis, which at rest was still boyish, like Cupid's, as painted by a brilliant yet potentially homicidal artist on one of my cigarette cards, claimed grown-up status the moment it stiffened, willfully or after a brief fumble, and freed its glans.

Cupid's willie, as created by Caravaggio, has a sweet, innocuous look to it—a nice little nib—though the winged rascal is smirking as he climbs out of a bed where he has initiated or promoted the proceedings, but my willie, harmless as it was when asleep, once awake, would rise to the occasion of sin with grim determination: relentlessly manly, it tried to penetrate whatever bore penetration, be it only the knotholes in the Brösen Baths changing cabins.

The amber will reveal even more if you persist in questioning it. The member attached to me—or as willie, to my self-portrait, embedded in resin—lacks reason and intends to remain without reason to the bitter end. It may be appeased daily and for brief intervals by the traditional biblical method, yet the hand alone is insufficient. Its head, also yclept *glans,* will have its way and swift deliverance. Its proven idiocy notwithstanding, it grows inventive when in need. It claims athletic prowess, nor is it free of ambition. Recidivist that it is, it shrinks from no penalty.

As long as I was a believing Catholic—the transition to nonbelief was smooth—my penis paid off as a ready perennial subject for confession. I ascribed the most outrageous sins to it: illicit relations with angels. With a virgin sheep. Even Father Wiehnke, my highly experienced confessor, to whose ear nothing human was meant to sound alien, found its deeds and misdeeds astonishing. But confession helped me to release what was assigned to, ascribed to the pigheaded appendage as pleasure. It was my weekly relief.

Later, however, when the fourteen-year-old had reached the

stage of absolute godlessness, his correspondingly more mature member was of more concern to him than the military situation on the eastern front, where the till then unstoppable progress of our Panzer divisions ground to a halt: first in the mud, then in the snow and ice. Father Frost rescued Russia.

And what helped me in my need?

The goal of all my desires had gradually acquired a name: I experienced the pain of first love. No later fit of love's madness had so powerful an effect. Toothache is nothing in comparison, though the love torture too was accompanied by swellings and achings that came and went.

Since I cannot with any precision date the onset of my first love, and since it did not lead to a course of action that can be described as steps in the direction of physical contact to say nothing of more intrusive possession, I am left with mere words, the stutter that leads to perfervid outpourings and has circulated in letters and bed whispers since Goethe's *Werther*. I shall be brief.

THE GIRL on whom I trained my desire like a hound would pass me on the way to school. For a time the Conradinum building was used not only by its own male students but also by female students of the Gudrun School (the former Helene Lange School), which had been requisitioned. We attended classes in morning and afternoon shifts. She was the oncoming traffic on Uphagenweg: she came, I went. That is, I was on my way home from five hours of lessons; she had the same number of hours yet to sit through. She was always with a bunch of girls, while I, the notorious loner, was on my own. I would walk straight through the bevy of gigglers, risking no more than a glance at her.

She was neither pretty nor ugly, just a black-haired girl with rather long braids. The dark frame made her face look small: two dots the eyes, a comma the nose, a dash the mouth. Her lips were thin, her mouth pinched. Her eyebrows grew together over her nose.

I knew prettier girls. I had even groped a cousin of mine in my grandfather's woodshed. And there was another girl named Dorchen, who came from Bartenstein in East Prussia, spoke the local dialect, and stayed all summer long.

No, I will not identify my black-plaited love by name. She may be alive somewhere, and having, like me, survived, not wish to be molested in her old age by an old man, his mind full of vague memories, who struck her as awkward during their school days, and in the end grievously offended her.

So my first love shall remain nameless, unless when I reach for the amber I find her in an encapsulated mosquito or spider whom I wish to summon, invoke, curse . . .

I was tenacious. It is a trait that has become part of me and continues to grant me staying power in my various endeavors. Since we schoolboys were more or less aware of where each Gudrun girl sat in our classroom, I planted notes for her—the unfillable receptacle of my desires—at her seat, secret missives stuck under the lid of her desk, silly trifles that sometimes spawned silly replies. No, there was no verse in my classroom correspondence. I cannot even say for sure whether her notes or mine were signed.

This went on until I was forced to change schools and take the tram, Line Five, from the suburb of Landform to Danzig and my new school, and then from the Old Town back home. The narrow streets, the towering brick edifices, the medieval spirit behind the lopsided walls and gabled façades—history's petrified offerings—I found, if not soothing, then at least distracting, especially during the winter of 1942–1943, before and after the battle of Stalingrad, when a young woman by the name of Lilli, who was fulfilling her compulsory civilian war service as an art teacher at Saint Peter's, came to be more important to me.

Not until I had changed schools twice and the students in my year had been called up as Luftwaffe auxiliaries and given spiffy uniforms to wear did I receive a letter from my first love. I received it in the field, where I had been trained as an artilleryman sixth class with the Kaiserhafen battery.

I don't remember what she wrote in her best handwriting, but the newly baked artilleryman was arrogant enough to correct her spelling, give the letter a mark in red ink as if he were her teacher, and send it back to her together with a note of his own, possibly of a poetic nature.

That was the last I heard of my first love. Prone to spelling errors at fifteen—and even now less than confident in matters orthographical—I had destroyed something I was only vaguely beginning to understand, something that had promised more than enough for my ever ready Caravaggio-sized member.

A vacuum. Gratification pursued in isolation. Desire now dozing, now wide-awake and lasting well after my days as a Luftwaffe auxiliary, which found expression in the description of barracks life in the desolate port area, far from home, in the novel *Dog Years:* with completely different stories told in the school slang of completely different boys, but who were, like me at the time, relieved that both their Hitler Youth service, which was growing increasingly idiotic, and school were over.

Although love plays an incidental role in the plot, I hasten to point out that the spindly Tulla Pokriefke, who plagues the boys of the Kaiserhafen battery during weekend visiting hours, has nothing in common with my first love.

AMBER may tell us more than we wish to remember: it preserves what should have been digested and secreted long ago. It retains everything it receives in its soft, still liquid state. It refutes excuses. And it is amber, which forgets nothing and takes the deepest-buried secrets to market, which steadfastly maintains that the boy bearing my name, twelve years old and still religious—that is, he still believed in Mary if not in God—teased the girl with the braids during catechism. A curate was preparing my coevals and me for our First Communion in the rectory of the Sacred Heart Church. The list of sins we would be expected to confess—and which were venial, which grave, and which mortal—flowed from our lips. I was even supposed to serve as an altar boy by the side of one of her brothers, bell and censer in hand, eye on the tabernacle and the monstrance.

And yes, to this day I can recite the *introit.* Like Mulligan at the beginning of *Ulysses,* I whisper *"Introibo ad altare Dei . . ."* while shaving.

If at thirteen—that is, beyond the miracles of the Catholic bag of tricks—I still went to church, it was only to ambush the girl on Saturday afternoon, to get as close to the confessional as possible, one pew behind her braids.

That honey-colored piece of petrified resin even reveals the secrets of the confessional: it reports that the details of my youthful masturbation procedure rolled from my tongue so unimpeded into the priest's ear that the name of their object, the harbor of my desire, would spring from my lips, whereupon His Reverence, seasoned as he was, could be heard to clear his throat behind the grill.

It goes on to state that later, while the girl with the braids was sitting next to the confessional sorting out her sins, I would jump out of the pew and go up to the Altar of Our Lady and with either mischief or malice aforethought . . .

No, I say, placing the piece with the mosquito next to the pieces containing the fly, the spider, the tiny beetle. That wasn't me. That is in the book and is true only in the book. There is no evidence for the crime. Recently, early in the summer of 2005, when my editor, Helmut Frielinghaus, and I met in Gdańsk with ten translators from all over the world having another crack at my first effort, we visited one scene of the crime after another in the novel's energetically shifting plot, including the Church of the Sacred Heart, which had survived the war and in which a copy of the Madonna of Vilnius with her tin-gilt wreath sends forth radiance and draws in pious Poles. Just next door, in a niche behind the candles, we saw photographs of the Polish Pope's public death and of his recently elected German successor.

And there, at this neo-Gothic scene of a youthful crime, a young priest with a cryptic smile, a man with more than a passing resemblance to Father Wiehnke, asked me to sign a copy of the Polish edition of the book in question, and the author, to the astonishment of his translators and editor, did not hesitate to write his name under the title. Because it was not I who tore the censer from the Christ Child's hand that day at the Altar of Our Lady; it was someone with a completely different will: someone who had never renounced evil, someone who had refused to grow . . .

I grew and grew. By the time I was sixteen and eligible for Labor Service, I was considered full-grown. Or did I not measure one meter and seventy-two centimeters—five feet, six and a half inches—until I became a soldier, who survived the war's end only by luck or chance?

That is an issue neither onion nor amber cares about. They want accurate information about other things, about what else has been encapsulated, about what has been swallowed in shame, about secrets in varying disguise, about nits nesting in sackhair. Eloquently avoided words. Slivers of thought. Things that hurt. Even now . . .

His Name Was Wedontdothat

I'D CATCH myself leafing back, watch myself skipping pages, and when gaping blanks came up I doodled flourishes and stick figures. Facile, beside-the-point stories flowed from my pen—a diversionary tactic—only to be crossed out at once. Off with you!

What is lacking are the links in a process no one stopped, an irreversible process whose traces no eraser can rub out. But no onion need be peeled, no amber consulted in the case of the fatal step of the fifteen-year-old schoolboy in uniform. It is clear: I volunteered for active duty. When? Why?

Since I do not know the date and cannot recall the by then unstable climate of the war or list its hot spots from the Arctic to the Caucasus and on other fronts, all I can do for now is string together the circumstances that probably triggered and nourished my decision finally to enlist. No mitigating epithets allowed. What I did cannot be put down to youthful folly. No pressure from above. Nor did I feel the need to assuage a sense of guilt at, say, doubting the Führer's infallibility, by my zeal to volunteer.

It happened while I was serving as a Luftwaffe auxiliary—which was not voluntary, though we experienced it as a liberation from our school routine and accepted its not very taxing drills.

The way we boys saw it, our uniforms attracted all eyes. Rabidly pubescent, we considered ourselves the mainstays of the home front. The Kaiserhafen battery became our second home. To the east the flats leading down to the Vistula; to the west the loading cranes, the grain silos, and the far-off towers of the city. At first there were attempts to keep school going, but as classes were too often interrupted by field exercises, the mostly frail, elderly teachers refused to travel the wearisome dirt road to our battery.

Finally we were taken seriously. Six artillery weapons had to be aimed at their target. We had had the appropriate training and could, should it come to that, help to protect the city and port from the enemy's attacks. In test drills we reached our command posts within seconds.

We got to use our eight-point-eight guns only two or three times, when a few enemy bombers were sighted in our air space in the beam of the searchlights. It all looked very festive. But massive raids—the kind known as firestorms that Cologne, Hamburg, Berlin, and the Ruhr Basin cities suffered, and that we knew of only through rumors—we did not experience. No damage worthy of the name: two houses hit on the Fuchswall near the Schichau Shipyard, few casualties. We were proud to have shot down a four-engined Lancaster bomber, even if the hit was attributed to the Zigankenberg battery on the southern border of the city rather than to ours. The "rather charred" crew members were said to have been Canadians.

As a rule, however, service in the Luftwaffe auxiliary was dreary, though dreary in a different way from school. We were especially turned off by nightly guard duty and ballistic classes, which dragged on forever in the musty classroom barracks.

When bored, we fell back into childlike behavior, or regaled one another with made-up sexual exploits. So the days passed.

We had every other weekend off. We could, as they put it, "go home to Mama." And each time my joy at the thought of the visit was tempered by my pain at the thought of our cramped quarters.

Not even the vanilla pudding with almond slivers that Father, who loved to cook for the family, made from ingredients he skimmed off his meager deliveries and hoarded for special occasions was of any help. Having loosened the pudding from the mold, he would douse my portion with chocolate sauce and serve it to me as a welcome at the table set specially for his son.

No, no sweet could offset the cramped feeling. I kept bumping into things and into the lack of things: a bathroom and toilet, for instance. All we had at the Kaiserhafen battery was a common shower room and, beyond it, a common latrine. There we would squat next to one another shitting into a pit, and that didn't bother me at all.

But at home, the toilet on the landing, shared by four flats, had grown more and more distasteful to me: it was always filthy from the neighbors' children or occupied when you needed it. It stank, and its walls were smeared with fingerprints.

I was ashamed of that shared toilet and hid its existence from my schoolmates, who took bathtubs and private toilets for granted. I would never ask them over. Only Egon Heinert, who also had an outside toilet that stank, would come and lend me books.

The two-room hole. The family trap. Everything there conspired to constrain the weekend visitor. Not even the mother's hand could smooth away the son's distress. True, he was no longer expected to sleep in his parents' bedroom, like his sister, but even on the couch made up for him in the living room he remained a witness to the married life that continued unbroken from Saturday to Sunday, that is, I could hear—or thought I could hear—sounds I had heard, muffled as they were, from childhood on, sounds that had lodged in my mind in the form of a monstrous ritual: the anticipatory whispers, the lip-smacking, the creaking bedsprings, the sighing horsehair mattress, the moaning, the groaning, the entire aural repertory of lovemaking, so potent, especially in the dark.

As a child I had been curious about the nearby noises, but accepted them innocently. What the Luftwaffe auxiliary who wore a uniform by day heard in his pajamas, when his father fell upon his mother during his weekends on leave, was unbearable. Yet it is far from certain that the two of them went at it when the son lay awake on the couch within hearing range; in fact, it is more likely they took his presence into account and left each other alone. But the mere expectation of those noises in their more or less unchanging sequence was enough to keep me awake.

In the dark I had a clear picture of all the variations on marital coupling, and in my cinematic version of the act the mother was always the victim: she yielded, she gave the go-ahead, she held out to the point of exhaustion.

The hatred of a mother's boy for his father, the subliminal battleground that determined the course of Greek tragedies and has been so eloquently and sensitively updated by Dr. Freud and his disciples, was thus, if not the primary cause, then at least one of the factors in my push to leave home.

I racked my brain for flight routes. They all ran in one direction: the front, one of the many fronts, as quickly as possible.

I tried to pick a quarrel with my father. It wasn't easy. It would have taken massive recriminations, and, peace-loving family man that he was, he was quick to give in. Anything to maintain harmony. The progenitor had a constant wish for the offspring on his lips: "I want your life to be better. . . . You will have a better life than ours . . ."

Try as I might to turn him into a bugbear, he was not made for the role. Seen through his bright blue eyes, I was an alien being; I might as well have been illegitimate. That my little sister was devoted to him may have made amends for her brother's coldness.

And our mother? She would sit at the piano without playing, worn down from having to deal in an ever diminishing supply of goods or depressed, like the father and sister, by the son-and-brother's brief visits and the burdens he seemed to be shouldering.

YET THE suddenly unbearable two-room flat and four-family toilet on the half-landing could not have been the sole cause for my urge to enlist. My schoolmates had grown up in five-room flats that had their own bathrooms, toilets supplied with rolls of toilet paper instead of the newsprint we tore into squares. Some of them even lived in fancy private houses on Uphagenweg and the Hindenburgallee and had rooms of their own, yet they, too, yearned to get away, go to the front. Like me they wanted to face danger without fear, sink ship after ship, knock out tank after tank, or fly through the skies in the latest-model Messerschmitts, picking off enemy bombers.

After Stalingrad, however, the front situation went downhill. Anyone who, like my Uncle Friedel, was tracking it with colored thumbtacks on specially enlarged, cardboard-backed maps had trouble keeping up with developments in the East and in North Africa. At best, they could register the successes of our ally Japan at sea and in Burma, though our submarines occasionally padded the bulletins with the number and register tonnage of ships they had sunk. In the Atlantic and up near the Arctic they would attack convoys in packs.

Not one newsreel failed to show submarines returning home victorious, and since the Luftwaffe auxiliary home on leave would lie awake for hours on the living-room couch after seeing them on the screen, I had plenty of opportunity to picture myself as a ship's mate during a stormy tower watch, swathed in oilskins, covered with spray, spyglass trained on the dancing horizon . . .

With anticipatory zeal, the future volunteer saw himself returning from victorious campaigns to one of the submarine bunkers on France's Atlantic coast, safe at last from the enemy's merciless depth charges. He would stand in formation with the crew next to the bearded lieutenant-commander, under pennants representing all the ships they had sunk. They had been presumed lost and would be given just the kind of welcome, brass band and all, that the moviegoer had seen over and over when his heroes returned home triumphant. No scenes of the boats that had gone down with every last man.

No, it wasn't the papers that fed my hero worship. My parents didn't subscribe to the *Vorposten;* they subscribed to the more objective, somewhat fuddy-duddy *Danziger Neueste Nachrichten.* It was the newsreels: I was a pushover for the prettified black-and-white "truth" they served up.

They would come before the feature film. In the Langfuhr Cinema or the Old Town's Elisabethkirchengasse Ufa Palace I would see Germany surrounded by enemies, valiantly fighting what had been defensive battles abroad—on Russia's endless steppes, in the burning sands of the Libyan desert, along the protective Atlantic Wall, at the bottom of the sea—and on the home front I would see women turning out grenades, men assembling tanks: a bulwark against the Red Tide. The German folk in a life-and-death struggle. Fortress Europe standing up to Anglo-American imperialism at great cost. Every day the *Neueste Nachrichten* published more and more announcements rimmed in black and decorated with the thick black crosses indicating soldiers' deaths for Führer, Folk, and Fatherland.

Could this have stood behind my desire to enlist? Was one of the ingredients of my muddled daydreams a pinch of death-wish? Did I yearn to see my name immortalized inside the black rim? I don't believe so. I may have been an egotistical loner, but I was no stereotypical world-weary adolescent. Maybe just dumb?

There are no data available about what goes on in the head of a fifteen-year-old who longs to enter a fray in which—he might well presume, as he knew from his books—death takes its toll. But there are any number of speculations: Is it the pressure of emotions with no outlet, the desire to be totally independent, the will to grow up overnight, to be a man among men?

It must have been possible for a Luftwaffe auxiliary to trade a weekend leave for a Wednesday or Thursday off. In any case, one thing is clear: after one long day's march I took the tram from Heubude to the Central Station and from there the train via Langfuhr and Zoppot to Gotenhafen, a city that in my childhood was called Gdingen in German and Gdynia in Polish. It had grown up too quickly and had no history to speak of.

Modern flat-roofed construction ran all the way down to the harbor, where quays and moles faced the open sea. It was there that navy recruits were trained to handle submarines. There were other places as well—Pillau, for instance—but Gotenhafen was the closest.

It took all of an hour to reach the goal of my dreams of heroism. Was it in March or during April showers? Yes, it was probably raining, the harbor misted over. The former Strength-Through-Joy ship *Wilhelm Gustloff* was moored and at anchor at the Oxhöft Quay: I'd heard it was being used as a floating barracks by a submarine training division, though I didn't know for sure, the harbor and shipyard being off-limits to us.

Sixty years later, a human lifetime away, I was finally able to write a novella, *Crabwalk,* about that ship, about its much-heralded launching, its much-loved peacetime cruises, and its wartime conversion into a quayside barracks, about its one last voyage, with a human cargo of a thousand recruits and several thousand refugees, and about its sinking on January 30, 1945, off the Stolpebank. I knew the catastrophe's every detail: the temperature that day (twenty degrees below zero), the number of torpedoes (three) . . .

Since I was reporting a swatch of time-compressed action, yet simultaneously writing fiction, I imagined myself into one of the submarine recruits on board the sinking *Gustloff.* I thus imagined what those seventeen-year-olds doomed to an early death in the icy Baltic must have had in their sailor-capped heads: first, girls promising instant bliss, then, heroic deeds to come. Like me, they believed in a miracle: the final victory.

I found the recruitment office in a low, Polish-period building where behind a row of doors with signs bureaucratic rigamarole was processed, passed on, filed. After signing in, I was told to wait for my name to be called. There were two or three older boys ahead of me. I did not have much to say to them.

The sergeant and seaman first class I spoke to rejected me out of hand: I was too young; my age group hadn't come up yet; it would soon enough; no reason for excessive haste.

They were smoking and drinking coffee with milk out of big, bulbous cups. One of the—from my perspective—elderly gentlemen (the sergeant?) was sharpening a supply of pencils while I spoke. Or did I pick up this dramatic detail from some movie or other?

Was the Luftwaffe auxiliary in uniform or in mufti? Short trousers and kneesocks, perhaps? Did he stand at attention, the requisite distance from the desk, and deliver a timid but much rehearsed "I hereby volunteer for service in the submarine corps"?

Was he asked to take a seat?

Did he see himself as courageous, already displaying signs of heroism?

A blurred image is the only answer.

I must have stood my ground even as I was told there was no need for submarine volunteers at present: they had stopped accepting applications. And then they said, as we all know, the war was not being fought entirely under water, and they would make a note of my name and pass it on to other branches of the military. Provisions were being made for new Panzer divisions. There would be possibilities galore once your age group came up. "Patience, young man, patience. We'll come and get you soon enough . . ."

Did the volunteer prove flexible? "If submarines are out, well, why not tanks . . . ?"

Did he ask about the latest models? "Would I get to drive one of the new Tigers?"

Again, it was the newsreels that had been the moviegoer's first training camp: he had seen Rommel's tanks in the desert sand.

I may also have shown off the knowledge I had cribbed from *Weyer* and *Köhler's Fleet Calendar*. I was even familiar with the particulars of Japanese battleships, aircraft carriers, and cruisers and their victories in the Pacific: the taking of Singapore, the battle for the Philippines. To this day I can spout the weaponry and speed in knots of the heavy cruisers *Kurutaka* and *Kako*. The memory likes to hoard scrap metal, objects promising to stand up to time even in their eroded state.

At a certain point, though, the avuncular sarge and rather brusque seaman must have heard enough as they broke off our discussion and assured me my application would be looked upon with favor. But first came Labor Service, after all. Not even enlisted men could get out of Labor Service. "That's where you do your rifle drills. And learn what real army discipline means . . ."

As I summon forth the boy I was then, making him stand at attention in laced-up, spit-shined shoes and striped kneesocks topped by naked knees, and taking care to avoid secondhand images from the screen or from the page, I seem to hear the two middle-aged—or old, in my young eyes—gentlemen in uniform laughing sardonically, thinking perhaps of what the boy still in shorts had in store: the sergeant's left sleeve was empty.

TIME passed. We boys grew accustomed to barracks life, to bunk beds, to a summer without Baltic beaches and bathing. The Heideggerian turns of phrase of a corporal who claimed to have studied philosophy threaded their way through our school slang.

"You forgetful-of-being dogs, you!" he would scream at us. "We'll knock the essentiality out of you yet!" The sight of us put him in mind of "the facticity of a pile of shit." But otherwise he was harmless. No slave driver he. Just someone who liked to hear himself talk. The boy later put him to use in the *Dog Years'* Materniads.

When the wind blew from the north, it wafted an evil stench our way from a mass of indefinable whitish substance near the factory grounds over by the port. The things I saw and smelled. Things that left their mark. Other things, too. And we ate God knows what.

Toward the end of August a group of Ukrainian "volunteer laborers" moved into a barracks erected especially for them. They were not much older than we were, and their job was to free the gunners from such nonessential activities as kitchen duty and building earthworks. In the evening they would sit quietly in front of the tool shed.

But between rifle drills and ballistics lectures we would hunt long-tailed rats with them, in the washroom, behind the barracks kitchen, in the dugouts under the eight-point-eight artillery. One of us—or was it one of them?—would catch them with his bare hands. For every ten tails presented we received a reward: the Luftwaffe auxiliaries got fruit drops, the veteran ack-ack soldiers got cigarettes, and the Hiwis (which is what we called the Ukrainians—it was short for *Hilfwillige,* "volunteer laborer"), got a kind of tobacco they liked, called *makhorka.*

No matter how successful we were at collecting loot, we no more than stemmed the tide. The Kaiserhafen battery could not even begin to celebrate a victory over the creatures. Perhaps this is why decades later I gave the floor for the length of a novel to an indestructible rodent. I would dream of rats separately and in clans. The rats made fun of me because I kept hoping. They knew better; they dug in before it was too late. Only they had the wherewithal to survive mankind and its squabbles . . .

SHORTLY after my sixteenth birthday I was transferred with part of the Kaiserhafen team to the Brösen-Glettkau beach battery, which was equipped with four-barreled anti-aircraft artillery to protect the nearby airport from strafing. There we had more rabbits than long-tailed quarry.

During my free time I would disappear into the dunes and, sheltered from the wind, scribble autumn poems into a notebook. Overripe rose hips, the daily tedium, mussels and Weltschmerz, wind-bent shore grass, and a rubber boot washed ashore provided the inspiration, and when fog rolled in, what I called my love pains would pay off. After storms there were fragments, or, if I was lucky, hazelnut-sized nuggets of amber to be gathered from among the tangles of seaweed. Once I even found a nugget big as a walnut, containing a centipede-like insect that had survived the Hittites, the Egyptians, the Greeks, the Roman Empire, and who knows what else. But I no longer molded wet-sand citadels.

Things at home ran their wartime course. I managed to keep the animosity I felt toward my father within bounds for the length of my weekend leaves. I presumably enjoyed disdaining him: first, because he existed; next, because he would stand or sit in the living room wearing a suit and tie and felt slippers; next, because he was forever mixing pastry dough in the same stoneware bowl while clothed in the same apron; next, because he was always the one who carefully tore up the newspapers into toilet paper; and finally, because having been declared "exempt from military service," he would never go to the front and therefore never get out of my hair. But my father did give me a Kinzle wristwatch for my birthday.

Mother had all but stopped playing the piano. Her take on the general situation boiled down to the following: "I have my doubts." Though I once heard her say, "Too bad Hess is gone. I liked him better than our Führer . . ." She was also known to come out with, "I can't understand why they've got it in for the Jews. We used to have a haberdashery sales rep by the name of Zuckermann. As nice as could be and always gave a discount."

After Sunday supper she would cover the table with the food ration stamps for all the goods she had been allocated. Then she'd paste them onto newsprint with a mixture of potato starch and water. She was required to hand them over to the officials, as the volume of groceries delivered had to correspond to the volume of stamps collected. The Max-Halbe-Platz branch of Kaisers Kaffee had closed its doors, and our clientele increased.

I often helped her with the pasting. The *Danziger Neueste Nachrichten* provided not only the day's events but also the backing for the stamps. Flour- and sugar-stamps may therefore have obscured the report by the Wehrmacht's high command that tried to tone down the retreat by dubbing it a front-straightening operation. Names of cities being evacuated were names I had learned when they were being taken. Stamps for shortening and cooking oil concealed pages of announcements of soldiers fallen in battle; stamps for peas and beans covered up cinema schedules, which still changed from week to week, or classified advertisements.

Father sometimes lent a hand as well. The stamp-pasting process brought us all closer. He called his wife Lenchen; he was Willy to her. They called me "son." Daddau, my sister, she never helped.

While the paste dried, the Sunday music-by-request program would broadcast all of Mother's old favorites: "Oh, Alas, Alack, I've Lost Her" . . . "Hark to the Dove's Sweet Song" . . . "Alone, Once More Alone" . . . Solveig's song, "Cold Winter May Leave Us" . . . "Bells of Our Homeland" . . .

All winter long the front moved closer to home. Bulletins virtually ceased, but more and more bombardment victims were seeking refuge in our city and its environs. They included my father's sister, Aunt Elli, with her invalid husband and twin girls, both of whom I liked—one in particular. They had come from Berlin with the few belongings they had managed to salvage to a city the war had left whole, a city so ensconced in its stolid brick obsolescence that it seemed as if no battles would ever come near it.

Since the picture palaces were generally open for business, the moviegoer took advantage of his leaves to escort one of his Berlin-accented cousins to *Quax, Crash Pilot* with Heinz Rühmann, and *Homeland* with Zarah Leander. We may have sat together through other films as well. My cousin was a year older than I and more dexterous in the dark.

Presumably the signature I had put to paper in a Gotenhafen office to enlist in this or that arm of the service had in the course of that winter been treated as a whim and vanished without consequences. The urge to break away, to flee to any front that would have me, had lost its force. My desire was moving in another direction: I read Eichendorff and Lenau at their most romantic, pored over Kleist's *Kohlhaas* and Hölderlin's *Hyperion,* and stood guard by the ack-ack guns lost in thought, my eyes wandering over the frozen sea. There, in the fog above the roadstead, freighters were riding at anchor, Swedish freighters, perhaps.

It was at about this time, in the dead of winter, that the military post delivered the letter that the black-plaited object of my exceedingly fervent first love had written in her best handwriting and whose spelling mistakes I had felt constrained to correct. What she wrote vanished into thin air. Before bliss came to pass, it shattered to pieces.

For years after the war I searched through the Red Cross missing-persons lists and the newspaper for Germans expelled from Danzig, the *Danziger Heimatblättchen der Vetriebenen,* which occasionally reported on reunions of students from the Gudrun School, for the name of a girl whose form kept changing, who at one moment seemed but an arm's-length away and at the next completely unreal, and who had first one name, then another, in my books.

Once, in the mid-sixties, I thought I saw her at the main entrance to Cologne Cathedral, much the worse for wear, begging. When I addressed her, a practically toothless woman, she babbled something back in the local dialect . . .

And when in the late nineties, back in Gdańsk to attend the debut of an adaptation of my *Call of the Toad* staged in the cramped quarters of a private apartment, Ute and I passed an old building on what had once been Brunshöferweg, I said, "This is where she lived" and felt a fool.

WHAT I had lost seemed impossible to get over at first, but I dealt with it in time. There was that cousin I liked, after all. Besides, work, boring as it was, was going okay. Our instructors, war-weary NCOs, weren't particularly hard on us and seemed grateful to be far from the fray, "putting the fear of God" into "you muttonheads."

The waves broke monotonously against the battery's beach position. Rifle practice consisted of shooting at rabbits or— though it was forbidden—seagulls with small-caliber weapons. I waged a futile battle against pimples. When it rained and we were off duty, we played card games or board games.

This leisurely pace could have gone on all spring, which had finally come, and into the summer, but shortly after I was called in for the physical given to all potential recruits, in the building of the local military command near the Wiebenwall, I received official notification that I had been inducted into the Reich's Labor Service.

I was not the only one who received that piece of certified mail. It all went like clockwork, according to age group. Length of service: three months. I was to report in late April or early May. A whole group of us were discharged from our Luftwaffe auxiliary unit, which was immediately replenished by an influx of Danzig schoolboys, and suddenly I was back in short trousers and kneesocks. Looking in the mirror or visiting friends with pretty sisters I felt I no longer had anything to offer. It had all happened quickly and close to home while at the same time and far away the dead were having tin dog tags removed from their necks and the living were having iron medals hung around theirs.

Throughout the winter and into spring my knowledge of geography had been expanding again with reports of front movements in the east (Kiev evacuated), of battles for islands in the Pacific between the Japanese and the Americans, of developments in southern Europe. After our Italian allies broke with us, a move we saw as base treason, and our parachutists liberated Il Duce from his hideout in the Abruzzi Apennines—Skorzeny was the latest hero's name—came the battle for the ruins of Monte Cassino Abbey. The British and Americans had landed on the coast just south of Rome and were extending a bridgehead that was still under fire when I had to give up my chic Luftwaffe auxiliary uniform for the less than flattering Labor Service garb. Shit-brown, it made us look shitty, we would say. The most ludicrous part of it was the headgear, a felt hat that looked like a big bump with a crease down the middle and seemed to have been made only to be torn off. We dubbed it "ass with a handle."

In my early novella *Cat and Mouse,* which was branded unsuitable for young readers when it first came out but eventually became required reading in schools and is therefore exposed to the interpretive whims of the syllabus-faithful, my tragicomic hero, Joachim Mahlke, dons this unattractive headgear for a while. Pilenz, the narrator, sees him wearing it at the Oliva Castle Park. Furthermore, the Tuchel Heath—the region where my Labor Service camp, a quadrangle of barracks plus mess hall, was located—matches the flat-to-rolling countryside in which an episode of Joachim Mahlke's evolution to war hero takes place: ". . . beautiful clouds floating over birches and butterflies not knowing where to go next. Shiny black, ring-shaped pools in a bog where you could fish out perch and moss-covered carp with hand grenades. Nature wherever you shat. And movies in Tuchel . . ." Also worthy of mention were the stretches of sandy soil, the woodland of trees both deciduous and coniferous, and the juniper bushes. The perfect setting for Polish partisan action.

But my time with the Labor Service is layered differently in my memory. My recollection differs from what Pilenz, in his compulsion to get it down on paper, tells us about the Great Mahlke, and not only in the details but also in the way it exposes me: I missed the opportunity to learn to doubt, an activity that—much too late, but then pursued all-out—enabled me to clear every altar and go beyond faith in making decisions.

It was not always easy, because the fires of hope were constantly being rekindled, trying to warm up the chilly atmosphere. For a time it was the desire for a lasting peace and justice for all, then the consumer bliss of the American way of life, and now the new Pope is supposed to work miracles . . .

FROM the outset, I had what was known in the Labor Service as a cushy job: I was good at drawing and had a way with colors and was therefore considered privileged. The walls of the canteen in the stone mess hall were to be adorned with pictures inspired by the juniper bushes, the water hole complete with reflected clouds, and the birches of the half flat, half hilly heath. Desired but not essential: a frolicking water nymph.

After the usual morning drill—rifle practice, first with a spade, then with a ninety-eight carbine—I was released to make sketches from nature: all afternoon I could absent myself from the camp with my watercolors, water bottle, and drawing pad. Beautiful clouds, shiny black ponds, birches in front of or behind gigantic erratic boulders made their way onto the paper in saturated colors. I soon had a pile of sketches to paint in distemper on the canteen's white walls. Having had a tree fixation since childhood, I may well have made a single, isolated oak my motif of preference. And because in my old age I still enjoy watercolor painting from nature, whether on the road or in my Behlendorf orchard, I have no trouble picturing myself seated at the edge of a bubbling bog hole or perched on a humpback rock left behind by the last ice age.

As I sat painting the flat land or hills fading into the horizon, I was not, if I am to be perfectly honest with myself, completely free of fear. Partisans with looted carbines could have been lying in ambush, crouching behind a thick juniper bush or hidden by boulders jutting out of the heath. A private who sighted a Labor Serviceman screwing up his face as he plied his brush would have had no trouble picking him off.

The wartime volunteer's career would have ended before it began. Besides, I was unarmed: at first the carbines were distributed only for regular and silhouette target practice. As dim and fuzzy as the picture of myself and my routine in my Labor Service days that has come down to me is, the picture of the distribution of arms is painfully sharp and very much alive, even now.

DAY after day we went through a ceremony conducted by the corporal in charge of weapons, a man who looked serious on principle. He handed them out, we grabbed them. One man after another experienced what it meant to be armed. It goes without saying: every member of the Labor Service was to feel honored by the touch of the wood and metal, the butt and barrel of the carbine in his hands.

And we boys did in fact inflate ourselves to men when we stood at attention with our guns by our sides or presented them or marched with them on our shoulders. You might say we took the expression "A soldier's gun is a soldier's bride" literally. We thought of ourselves as engaged, if not quite married, to the ninety-eight carbine.

Though I make a point of using "we" here, there was an exception to that rank-and-file, somewhat facile plural, an exception whose image I can conjure more clearly than that of the privileged muralist, his assiduous brush strokes, and all else that transpired under the partly sunny, partly cloudy skies of the Tuchel Heath.

This exception was a lanky boy who was so blond and blue-eyed and whose profile revealed a skull so elongated that the likes of him could be found only in propaganda promoting the Nordic race. Chin, mouth, nose, forehead—each was the epitome of "racial purity" at a stroke. He was a Siegfried, a Baldur, and like Baldur, the Teutonic god of light, he shone brighter than the day. He was untainted: no trace of a wart on neck or temple. He neither lisped nor stuttered when ordered to report. No one could beat him in long-distance running, no one could match his daring when leaping over musty ditches or his agility when clambering over a wall. He could do fifty knee bends without getting tired. He was born to break records. There was nothing, no flaw, to sully the picture. But what made him an exception was that he—whose name, first and last, eludes my memory—was an insubordinate.

He refused to take part in rifle drill; worse still, he refused to take butt or barrel in hand; and, worst of all, when our dead-earnest drill instructor pressed the carbine on him, he would drop it. Which made him or his fingers criminal.

Was there any greater crime than to let a gun, a weapon, the soldier's fiancée fall into the parade ground dust absent-mindedly, let alone intentionally?

With the spade, a basic utensil for everyone in the Labor Service, he did all that he was ordered to do. When he presented the blade, it gleamed before his Nordic profile like a shield. To gaze upon him was to worship him, make him your ideal. As long as the Reich had cinemas to show newsreels, the screen would have been graced by his celestial countenance.

He would also have received top marks in camaraderie. When a nut cake came from home, he would willingly share it. He was the friendly, good-natured type, always ready to help, to do anything asked of him, and he never complained. Upon request, he would give his comrades' boots such a regulation shine that they would be a feast for sore eyes, even the eyes of the strictest NCO during roll call. He had no trouble with brushes or dust cloths; it was only the firearm he refused to wield, the ninety-eight carbine we were being trained on to ease our entry into the military.

Every possible sort of punitive labor was imposed upon him—they were patient—but nothing helped. He would work conscientiously for hours without a peep, emptying the latrine with a worm-infested bucket on a long stick—a punishment known as "honey-slinging" in soldiers' slang—filling the bucket to the brim from the pit the men shat into and carting it off, only to appear, freshly showered, at rifle drill shortly thereafter and refuse to wield the weapon once again. I can see it falling to the dust as if in slow motion.

At first we merely asked him questions and tried to talk him out of it. We actually liked the fellow, this oddball, this knucklehead: "Take it! Just hold it!"

His response ran to a scant few words, which soon made the rounds in the form of a whispered quote.

But when they took to punishing us on his account and tormented us in the hot sun until we collapsed, we all began to hate him.

I, too, worked up my ire against him. We were expected to give him a hard time, and so we did. He had put us under pressure; we would return the favor.

He was beaten in his barracks by the very boys whose boots he had polished mirror bright. All against one. Through the boards dividing room from room I could hear his whimper, the snap of the leather belt, the loud counting. They are ingrained in my memory.

But neither the hazing nor the beatings nor anything else could force him to carry arms. When some of the boys pissed on his straw pallet so as to label him a bed wetter, he swallowed his humiliation and delivered his by then famous phrase at the next opportunity.

Nothing could be done about this unprecedented state of affairs. Morning after morning, when we gathered for roll call and the drill instructor with his immutable solemnity started passing out the weapons, the insubordinate would let the one meant for him fall to the ground like the proverbial hot potato and immediately return to his ramrod position, hands pressed to trouser seams, eyes fixed on a distant point.

I cannot count the number of times he repeated his mantra, which had now reached even those in command, but I remember the questions his superiors, all the way up to the commanding officer, asked him and we plagued him with: "Why are you doing this, Labor Serviceman?" "What makes you do it, you idiot?"

His unvarying reply became a catchword that has never left me: "We don't do that."

He stuck to the plural. In a voice neither loud nor soft, yet sonorous, a voice that carried well, he pronounced what he and his refused to do. It was as though he had if not an army then at least a goodly battalion of imaginary insubordinates lined up behind him ready to repeat the phrase after him. Four words fusing into one: Wedontdothat.

When asked what he meant, he repeated the indefinite "that" and refused to call the object he would not take in his hands by its name.

His behavior transformed us. From day to day what had seemed solid crumbled. Our hatred was mixed first with amazement, then with admiration expressed in questions like "How can that idiot keep it up?" "What makes him so hardnosed?" "How come he doesn't report sick? He's been pale as a ghost lately."

We let him be. No more beatings on the bare behind. The most obstreperous among us—some boys from Alsace or Lorraine who stuck together during time off, carrying on in their incomprehensible patois, and who whenever the opportunity presented itself, as after a pack march in the pouring rain, reported sick in their strange attempts at High German—would whisper in French, which was taboo, words that probably meant "one of a kind."

The insubordinate stood above us, as if on a pedestal. What is more, the insubordination of this individual seemed to our superiors to have affected general discipline. They imposed extra duties on us, as though everyone in his year shared his guilt.

In the end this morning ritual was cut off by his arrest. "Off to the cooler with him!" came the command. Yet out of our sight though he was, he remained palpable as an absence.

From then on, discipline and order reigned. My afternoon plein-air sessions soon came to an end—the brushes rinsed clean, the murals incomplete, the distemper dry. My cushy days gone forever, I was entitled to nothing more than instruction in hitting bull's-eyes, throwing hand grenades, lunging with fixed bayonet, and crawling through fields.

Every once in a while the "convict" came up in our conversations. Someone—was it the drill instructor or one of us?—would say, "He must be a Jehovah's Witness." Or "He's a Bible nut. No doubt about it." But the blond, blue-eyed boy with the racially pure profile had never referred to the Bible or Jehovah or any other almighty; he had said simply, "Wedon'tdothat."

ONE day his locker was cleared out: private things, including religious pamphlets. Then he was gone—transferred, it was called.

We did not ask where to. I did not ask. But we all knew. He had not been discharged as proven unfit for service; no, we whispered, "He has long been ripe for the concentration camp."

Some made jokes, without garnering much laughter: "It'll do him good, the crackpot, help him to concentrate." Others knew: "It's a sect that doesn't do that. That's why they're banned, the Jehovah's Witnesses."

That's what we said, though no one knew precisely why they were banned, what they witnessed, or what they did when they weren't witnessing. Everyone agreed, however, that such an intransigent insubordinate could end up in only one place: Stutthof. And since we knew of the camp only by hearsay, we thought Wedontdothat, which was what we called him in secret, was in good hands. "They'll bring old Wedontdothat down a peg or two."

Was it all as simple as that?

Did no one shed a tear?

Did everything go on the way it had before?

What could have passed through my head or otherwise disturbed me when on the one hand he was taken off to quarantine as if carrying a disease and was therefore out of sight, yet on the other was so palpably missed that in a visible hole off to the side he seemed to go on drilling, standing guard, crawling through fields, eating potato soup at our long table, squatting in the latrine, shining boots, sleeping, having wet dreams or giving himself a helping hand, and welcoming the incipient summer. Summer came; it was dry, hot, and windy. Sand dust settled everywhere, covering much, including thoughts that might have gnawed at me.

But setting aside all subplots and going straight to the point, I must say, I was if not glad, then at least relieved when the boy disappeared. The storm of doubts about everything I had had rock-solid faith in died down, and the resulting calm in my head prevented any further thought from taking wing: mindlessness had filled the space. I was pleased with myself and sated. A self-portrait from that period would have shown me well nourished.

But later, much later, when I was developing the hero of the novella *Cat and Mouse*, Joachim Mahlke, a marvelous, off-beat character—fatherless altar boy, student, master diver, Knight's

Cross recipient, and deserter—I used the insubordinate we called Wedontdothat as a model. Even though Mahlke had to do battle with an enlarged Adam's apple, he seemed unblemished when, time after time, he dropped his weapon, slowly, deliberately, the better to ingrain it in our memory.

WHEN the bulletin of the Wehrmacht high command, which was tacked up daily on the notice board, announced the landing of the British and American forces on the Atlantic coast, thus enriching yet again my knowledge of geography (only the Alsatians and Lorrainers among us could wrap their tongues around the names of the Norman and Breton towns and villages), the battle for the Atlantic Wall pushed everything that preceded it—including the model for the propagation of the Nordic race, and thorn in our side—into the background.

Increased vigilance was the order of the day. Twice the camp was roused by a partisan alert, but no shooting—or anything else—followed. Our quadrangle of barracks was constantly patrolled by one or two guards.

When I was on duty by myself, I would allay my fears by letting my thoughts wander. I got plenty of practice. History would immediately give way to legends: Old Prussian deities like Perkun, Pikoll, and Potrimp; the Pomeranian princess Mestwina; Prince Swantopolk; and, going back even further, Goths wandering from the mouth of the Vistula to the Black Sea. The legions peopling my daydreams—all of them armed in the fashion of their times—helped me hold my fear of partisans at bay.

One of our duties was to fortify the camp: we dug trenches, set up mined wire barriers. We also had to install a complex alarm system, though nothing alarming ever happened except that one Sunday we were ordered out onto the parade ground in full force, all two hundred and fifty of us, and not in the light gray of the troops but in our own shit-brown garb plus ass-with-handle headgear on our closely cropped hair.

In the middle of the square, right next to the flagpole, a Reich Labor Service leader, who had arrived out of nowhere with a tightly knit retinue, was reeling off clipped pronouncements about shame and craven betrayal, that is, about the base and insidious plot on the part of a coterie of well-born officers—unsuccessful, thank Heaven—to assassinate our dearly beloved Führer, and about merciless revenge, the "extermination of this vile clique." And on and on about the Führer, who—"It was truly a miracle!"—had survived.

With ever-longer sentences his rescue by fate was celebrated, and we were told to renew our vows on his behalf. In this hour of need, from now on, from this moment on, it was our duty, yes, here and throughout the German Reich, in this hour of need, the duty of—more than anyone—the youth representing the movement which bears his name to stand unswervingly by him until the final victory . . .

A shiver ran through us. Something akin to piety sent the sweat seeping out of our pores. The Führer saved! The Heavens were once more, or still, on our side.

We sang both our national anthems. We shouted *Sieg Heil!* three times. We were irate, we were incensed at the still nameless traitors.

Although I had never—not in school, let alone in my mother's grocery—met anyone who could be called well-born, I tried to work up the requisite hatred for the reputed blue bloods, but in fact I was torn. From the period of my mental excursions into the dark corners—and enlightened ones—of German history I had retained my admiration for the Hohenstaufen line of emperors: I would have been only too happy to serve as a squire to Frederick II in thirteenth-century Palermo. And when it came to the Peasant Wars a few centuries later, I was not only a fan of Thomas Müntzer's, I also sided with the upper-class ringleaders of the insurrection, men with noble names like Franz von Sickingen, Georg von Frundsberg, and Götz von Berlichingen. Ulrich von Hutten was my idol, the Pope and his clerics my enemies. When in time the names of the conspirators and the man who had pulled the trigger—names like von Witzleben and von Stauffenberg—became known, I had trouble reaffirming the hatred I had vowed against the "craven band of aristocrats" as weeds to be rooted out of our society.

THE chaos that raged under our closely cropped hair! The image that had been crystal clear in the sixteen-year-old Labor Serviceman's mind until then was turning fuzzy around the edges. Not that it had become alien, no. But my uniformed self seemed to be slipping away. It had even given up its shadow and wanted to belong among the less guilty.

There were plenty of people like that later on, people who "were only obeying orders." First they belted out "No Land More Fair in These Fair Times . . . ," then they listed the mitigating circumstances that had blinded and misled them, feigning their own ignorance and vouching for one another's. No matter how elaborate their excuses and protestations of newborn-babe innocence, these all-too-eloquent anecdotes and human-interest stories, densely inscribed on onion skins, are actually meant to divert attention from something intended to be forgotten, something that nevertheless refuses to go away.

I reach for the transparent amber on the shelf over my desk to examine the extent to which my faith in the Führer withstood the verifiable cracks in its surface, the increasing whispers, and the retreat, now from France as well.

But faith in the Führer was not hard to maintain—it was child's play, in fact: he had remained safe and sound and was what he claimed to be, his gaze steady, ready to meet every eye, his field-gray uniform free of flashy medals. He was everywhere portrayed with only his Iron Cross from the Great War, majestic in his simplicity. The voice seemed to come from on high. He was impervious to attack. Did he not have the protection of something beyond understanding, of Providence?

The only thing that rankled was the persistent memory of that blond, blue-eyed boy who never tired of saying "Wedon't-dothat." From the time he was gone, he was sorely missed. He did not, however, become a role model.

WE WERE dismissed soon after the assassination attempt. We handed in our drab uniforms and the spades we had presented mirror-bright at the final ceremonial roll call, after which we heard ourselves sing the Labor Service anthem: "Brown like the earth our uniform . . ."

Back in mufti, I was ashamed of my naked knees, my forever sagging kneesocks: I was beyond all that now, no longer a schoolboy. Back in summery Langfuhr the parents awaiting the homecomer were their same old selves but found their son, as they put it, "somewhat different."

The two-room flat I so detested weighed even more heavily on me, though things were much quieter within its wallpapered precincts, almost too quiet. Daddau was gone and with her the laughter and mayhem she provoked with her dinner-table antics and her hopping back and forth between living room and bedroom. There was no little sister who always wanted to play—only wanted to play—and kept closing my book. All that was left of her were her dolls and stuffed animals under the left-hand windowsill.

By official decree, all schoolchildren had been evacuated to the country to save them from the enemy bombers' attacks. Their teachers had gone with them, and the lessons continued in their refuge near the fishing village of Heisternest, on the Hela Peninsula. My sister wrote us postcards full of homesickness.

My parents indulged me—Father with sauerbraten, Mother with the way she smiled whenever I launched into my Goethe paraphrase: We shall go south to where the lemons grow. But the son was tired of being a mama's boy, even as the mother lived in dread of the postman. Her only hope she put into these words: "Maybe it will somehow be over before that."

It took less than two months for the induction letter to arrive, an interval of listless waiting of which I can retrieve only snippets of memories in no special order.

It was like a relapse: as I had feared, after the Labor Service, I slipped back into the schoolboy-on-vacation pattern, though minus the beach, minus the necking and fumbling in the dunes behind the rose-hip bushes.

Everywhere I went, I saw chests of drawers with photographs rimmed in black, heard people talking in subdued voices about men—sons, brothers—fallen in action. The Old Town looked shabby, as though anticipating gradual if not sudden decay. Blackout regulations made the night streets look eerie to their own inhabitants. Posters proclaimed THE WALLS HAVE EARS and COAL THIEVES ON THE PROWL wherever you turned. Shop windows displayed merchandise no one wanted. My mother offered a whipped-cream substitute called Sekosan over the counter but off ration.

In front of the Central Station, on Mottlau Bridge and Speicher Island, at the entrance to the Schichau Shipyard and along the Hindenburgallee, the military police and Hitler Youth patrols would stop and check the identification papers of civilians, soldiers on leave, and the increasing number of girls who let themselves be accosted by privates as well as officers. There was talk of deserters, of a band of young toughs who had broken into the Food Supply Office or set a fire in the harbor area, of conspirators gathering in a Catholic church . . . Eventually, when I finally had the words at my command, I devoted several chapters to the "riffraff" to whom all these unbelievable activities were attributed.

In *The Tin Drum,* one of the ringleaders is called Störtebeker. He survives the war and mutates logically in the postwar period into an anti-confrontational teacher by the name of Starusch, a supremely adjusted type who in another novel, *Local Anesthetic,* is morbidly fearful of pain and assesses everything with the formula "on the one hand . . . on the other . . ."

All I did was listen. When I visited schoolmates who, whether they had volunteered or not, were awaiting induction letters as a kind of redemption, I would hear rumors of other schoolmates who had suddenly disappeared, "gone underground," as they put it. One of these, whose father was a high-ranking police inspector in the Rhineland, told us about a band of youths known as the Edelweiss Pirates who were shaking people up in bombed-out Cologne.

Out of habit more than interest, I would go to the movies. Watching *Romance in a Minor Key* at the Langgasse Tobis Palace, I couldn't help comparing Marianne Hoppe to the beauties on the cigarette picture-cards of years past: the Renaissance women had something of her well-defined profile.

I also whiled away the time in the backstreets of the Old Town and in the Jäschkental Wood, unconsciously gathering details that eventually turned into an enduring source of material. I can still picture myself sitting in the pews of the Gothic churches, from Trinity to Saint John's, imprinting every ogive and brickwork buttress in my mind.

I also had my reading places. The attic was still my favorite, although without its threadbare armchair and the clutter in its slatted storage-area, which had been removed because they would act as tinder in case of firebombing, it was now merely a space under undamaged roof tiles, swept clean in anticipation of things to come. For the same reason, there was a row of water buckets standing next to a few fire-swatters and a barrel of sand.

But what did I read beneath the skylight? Probably *The Picture of Dorian Gray*, a dog-eared, leather-bound edition, one of my mother's treasures. Wilde's copious roster of sins outdoing one another provided me with a suitable mirror.

It was most likely at this time that I borrowed Merezhkovsky's *Leonardo da Vinci* from somebody and devoured it in the attic. I would sit on an upside-down fire bucket and read more than I could digest. I was especially drawn to heroes who took me out of myself and into other spheres: Jürg Jenatsch, August Weltumsegler, *Der grüne Heinrich,* David Copperfield, or the Three Musketeers—all three at once.

I can't say for sure when I plucked *All Quiet on the Western Front* from my uncle's bookshelf. Was it not until I was waiting to be called up or was it at the same time that I read Jünger's *Storm of Steel,* a war diary that my German teacher at Saint Peter's had prescribed as good preparation for the front?

The teacher, a stiff-legged veteran of World War I whose name was Littschwager, praised the "fantastically colorful" and "vivid" quality of my compositions and even their "exceptionally daring wordplay," though he bemoaned their "total lack of gravity"—gravity, in his opinion, being called for by the "fateful trials to which the Fatherland is being subjected."

Whether it was as a schoolboy or as a recently discharged Labor Serviceman, I found Erich Maria Remarque's *All Quiet on the Western Front* in the bookcase of my father's youngest brother. As the man in charge of transporting the barrack components—walls, windows, doors—turned out by the five apprentices who kept my grandfather's saw in operation nonstop, Uncle Friedel was exempt from military service. He spent a lot of time down at the port or shipyard, because more and more emergency barracks for Ostarbeiter, workers brought in from occupied territories in the East, needed to be assembled and wound around with barbed-wire fences.

I assume my uncle had no idea that Remarque's novel, the story of the pitiful death of a young enlisted man in the First World War, was on the index; I hadn't. To this day the delayed effect of that early reading experience is with me. The way one pair of boots keeps changing owners who one after the other give up the ghost . . .

Over and over, author and book remind me of how little I understood as a youth and how limited an effect literature may have. A sobering thought.

WHEN I was in Ticino with my first wife, Anna, and our four children in the mid-sixties—my daughter Laura and I on the lookout for mountain deer along the wooded slopes because they would lick salt from our hands—I took the opportunity to pay a visit to Remarque, arranged by my American publisher Helen Wolff, in his villa stuffed with antiques on the Lago Maggiore. I told him about the hot and cold baths of my readings: Jünger's celebration of war as an adventure and test of manhood had fascinated me; his contention that war makes a murderer of every soldier had made my blood run cold.

The elderly gentleman laughed softly to himself and in Prussian-inflected English passed on my youthful reading experience to his late-in-life love, the onetime film star Paulette Goddard, who had been Charlie Chaplin's third wife. Then he showed off a few of his antiques, among them Chinese vases and woodcuts of the Madonna. No, we did not have a grappa together.

But later, much later, when I was writing the stories for *My Century*, I was moved to bring the antipodes of Remarque and Jünger back into play. When I got to the First World War, I sat the two cavaliers at a table in the Zurich Storchen Hotel and set up a debate between them making a young Swiss historian— who, true to her kind, claimed neutrality—their foil. As wine-connoisseurs they were courteous to each other, but remained petulantly divided when it came to the meaning of deadly trench warfare: their war had never ended; they could not be reconciled; something had been left unsaid.

But I, too, gazing out on the silver platter of Lago Maggiore, had left unsaid the confession that the fifteen-year-old schoolboy had volunteered for the submarine corps or the Panzer division despite having read his book, which enumerates more than enough varieties of death perpetrated by war. Then again, the émigré, weary of his superannuated fame, had been less than forthcoming about the famous novel that overshadowed everything he had written since.

THERE it was on the dinner table, the induction letter, frightening Father and Mother. Had Mother run to the piano and played something from the *Rose Garden* folk-song collection? And only then burst into tears?

No, we have to rewind a bit. A few days before the paper with the official stamp struck my parents dumb, we had taken the train to Putzig via Zoppot and Gotenhafen to visit my evacuated sister. A bus then took all of us on to Heisternest. It was a benign August day.

That the children's home was near the sea is evidenced by a picture my mother preserved in a family photo album that survived the war and exile: brother and sister sitting side by side on the luminous sand that covered the length and breadth of the Hela Peninsula beach. Shortly before or after bathing in the Baltic I have put a brotherly right arm around her. Siblings who know next to nothing about each other. And would not be so close to each other again for a long time.

She looks pretty, my sister, whom I've called Daddau since

we were kids. She is laughing. Her brother, still somewhat boy-ish, though of manlike proportions, is doing his best to look se-riously into the box camera's lens.

The father has taken advantage of the fine late-summer weather, and the picture comes out well. It is the last picture taken before I left.

And what has long been repressed is now a fact. It lies in black-and-white on the table, signed, dated, and stamped: the induction letter. But what does it say, large print and small?

NOTHING helps: the letterhead is blurred; the rank of the man behind the signature is unclear, as if he had been demoted ex post facto. Memory, usually a chatterbox only too willing to tell its tales, draws a blank. Or am I at fault, unwilling to decode the message the onion skin contains?

Exculpations leap to mind. The induction letter and its con-sequences, that has all been chewed over, turned first into words and then into a book, to the tune of seven hundred pages. *Dog Years.* All about how this fellow named Harry Liebenau starts a diary the day he goes into the army and writes letters to his cousin Tulla from his training camp at Fallingbostel, letters riddled with quotations from the nationalist poet Löns, and how later, no matter where his travel orders take him—from the Lüneburg Heath all the way to the retreating eastern front—he tries, and fails, to find a rhyme for Tulla in the letters. "I haven't seen a Russian yet. Sometimes I stop thinking of Tulla. Our field kitchen is gone. I keep reading the same thing. The streets are clogged with refugees. They don't believe in anything now. Löns and Heidegger are wrong about lots of things. In Bunzlau I saw five soldiers and two officers hanging from seven trees. This morning we shelled a wooded area. I couldn't write for two days because we met up with the enemy. Many men died. After the war I'm going to write a book . . ."

As for me, perched in knee-length trousers on the wooden seat of a third-class train compartment in September 1944, I had no future novel, no action-packed pages in mind, though I did intend to fill a notebook with my collected experiences.

The train pulled out of Danzig Central Station, left Langfuhr behind, and headed for Berlin. I had hoisted my cardboard suitcase, bought especially for the occasion, into the net above my seat. My thoughts were a jumble, even more muddled than usual. I can't pick out one to quote, not even to mumble or stumble through. The only thing I hear is the crackle of the induction letter in the breast pocket of my tight jacket.

MOTHER had refused to accompany son to the station. She was smaller than I was, and when she hugged me in the living room she seemed to dissolve into tears between the piano and the grandfather clock. "All I ask is that you come back in one piece . . ."

When Harry Liebenau said good-bye to his cousin Tulla Pokriefke, she was wearing the dashing cap of an assistant tram conductor. "Watch out you don't get your nose shot off!"

Father accompanied me. We didn't say a word to each other on the tram. Then he had to buy a platform ticket. His velvet hat gave him a soigné, bourgeois look: a man in his middle forties who had managed to stay a civilian and stay alive.

He insisted on carrying my cardboard suitcase. The man I had pushed away the moment I started growing, the man I blamed for the cramped two-room flat and the four-family toilet, the man I had wanted to murder with my Hitler Youth dagger and had stabbed many times over in my thoughts, the man whom somebody later built into a character who turned feelings into soups, the man who, though he was my father, I had never got close to except when we quarreled, this vivacious, easygoing, easily tempted man with a mania for good posture and, as he put it, "nice, neat handwriting," who loved me after his fashion, the eternal husband, called Willy by his wife, this man stood next to me as the train pulled in through a cloud of steam.

I didn't cry; he did. He hugged me; I hugged him back. I insist. Or did we only do the manly handshake thing?

Were we provident, even stinting with our words: "Take care, my boy," "See you, Papa"? Did he take his hat off as the train rolled out of the station? Did he pat down his blond hair?

Did he wave good-bye with his hat? Or his handkerchief? The handkerchief he would wear on his head on hot summer days—ridiculous! I thought—after tying its four tips in knots. Did I wave back out of the open window and watch him grow smaller and smaller?

All I remember seeing clearly was the city with its towers against the evening sky in the distance. I also think I heard the bells of nearby Saint Catherine's: "Be ever true and forthright till to the grave thou comest . . ."

OF ALL the churches in the city that rose again out of the rubble stone by stone in the postwar years, it was Saint John's over near the Mottlau that attracted me most during my visits to the city as it came increasingly—and by design—to resemble the city where I was born. Though unharmed on the outside, the church, built entirely of brick, had been badly burned and plundered within. For decades it served the Polish restoration team as a warehouse for undamaged fragments waiting to be reincorporated.

When visiting in March 1958, I asked an old man, who was one of the few to identify himself, in the local dialect, as *"emmer noch deitsch,"* still German, what he could tell me about the church. I learned that when the city was subject first to bombing, then to heavy shelling, and Saint John's was surrounded by whole streets of burning houses—Häkergasse and Johannisgasse, Neunaugengasse and Petersiliengasse—a hundred and more men, women, and children took refuge in the church. Those who were not suffocated or burned to death were hit by falling masonry, vault fragments, and plaster and buried alive. "But nobody wants to hear about that kind of thing nowadays," the old man said.

Another story I heard, this one in Polish, took a different tack: because many women fled to Saint John's, the Russians had set it on fire. Whoever did it, only the charred walls survived.

Later people used the damaged but still standing church to store what they had picked up all over the city—stone gable ornamentation, bits and pieces of bas-reliefs, of balustrades from the Renaissance balconies along Brotbänkengasse, Heiligen Geistgasse, and Frauengasse, of Baroque door embrasures made of granite. Not only what was left of the tracery on the façade of the Artushof but anything yielded by the piles of rubble, anything of interest was carefully labeled, numbered, and stored for later use.

Whenever I slipped inside the hall of the Gothic church— they were careless about locking the portal—I would find human bones, large and small, among the dust and piles of stones, and I could only wonder whether they were of late medieval origin or whether they should remind me of the men, women, and children who were said to have died in the flames of Saint John's when the town and all its churches were burnt.

No one knew for sure. Graves under the cracked memorial slabs had probably supplied at least some of them. Bones, from whatever time, resemble one another at first sight. In Saint John's, where sailors and barrel makers had their own altars, well-to-do merchants and shipowners had been laid to rest beneath slabs of sandstone and granite until the eighteenth century.

No matter to whom the bones had belonged, they formed part of what had been preserved and thus bore witness. That was said to be one of the reasons why, starting in the fifties, the desolate church interior was used as a set for Polish films—that and the light falling through the partly boarded windows were effects that attracted directors and pleased cameramen.

On one of my last visits to Danzig, I found Saint John's different: no more stones, no more bones, large or small; the floor smooth, the windows glazed, the brick masonry renovated. I was giving a reading from *Crabwalk,* and the audience sat on chairs arranged in rows stretching all the way to the back of the hall.

And while I was trying out the church's acoustics and the ship full of human cargo sank line by line, the part of my mind that prefers moving backward sought out the boy who left the city at a time when all its towers and gables were still intact.

How I Learned Fear

Could it be that during the journey to Berlin it was the memory of my first trip in that direction that so reduced me to a child? Was it in '36, the year of the Olympic Games, or a year later?

While still in primary school I was taken on a train to the Rhineland, all the way to the Dutch border, by an organization called Children Visit the Countryside. Because we were visiting the countryside at the time of the Free State, we children experienced a contemporary variant of the Punch-and-Judy show, going through first Free State customs, then two sets of differently uniformed Polish customs, and finally, at the Schneidemühl border station, the German customs and their set of uniforms. The customs officers had different ways of saluting: the Germans with a flat hand, the Poles with two fingers at the peak of the cap.

These inspections took place at brief intervals. We children had our papers hanging from our necks in transparent cases, which made us very proud.

From a peasant who raised dairy cattle and pigs, and whose son Matthias was my age, I learned how to cut asparagus from its carefully smoothed, raised beds in such a way as to avoid damaging it. So it must have been May. The name of the village was Breyell. Breyell was more Catholic than the Church of the Sacred Heart in Langfuhr. The peasant's wife made Matthias and me go to confession every Saturday. I still believed in hell and knew plenty of sins.

The road from the farmyard to the village school left no trace in my memory. Nor did much else. Though I do see countless colorful flies on the white-tiled walls of the peasant kitchen. The fat ones could be caught and subjected to an operation I had learned from a schoolmate whose love of animals knew no bounds: gluing colored threads to their bodies. It was a grand sight to watch them fly off or circle the kitchen table trailing red, blue, or yellow tails.

Matthias and I would compete to see how many flies we could catch from the wall with one hand. "Catching flies is better than idle lives," said Matthias's grandmother, who would sit all day in her easy chair, fingering her rosary. Outside the land stretched flat. Three steeples away lay Holland . . .

ONLY a cynic could have viewed my second trip west as children visiting the countryside. When, after a night's journey broken by repeated stops, the train finally pulled in late to the Reich's capital, it was going so slowly as to invite the passengers to write everything down or at least fill in the potential memory gaps ahead of time.

Here is what I retained: there were houses, whole apartment houses, on fire on either side of the embankment; there were flames coming out of the windows of the upper stories, and glimpses of dark gorge-like streets and courtyards with trees. The only people I saw were isolated silhouettes. No crowds.

Fires were considered normal by then: Berlin was in the throes of dissolution, and the situation worsened by the day. The city had just been bombed and the all-clear signal sounded. That was why the train was moving so slowly, offering what seemed like a personal sightseeing tour.

Until then the moviegoer had seen only brief fade-ins and fade-outs of ruins, which served as illustrations for banners with slogans like We Are Not To Be Undone! or Our Walls May Crumble, Our Hearts Never! and the like.

Goebbels, the Reich's minister of propaganda, had recently appeared on the screen of the Tobis Palace, skillfully playing himself, bucking up men and women whose houses lay about them in ruins, shaking the hand of a soot-black air-raid warden and patting the heads of awkwardly grinning children.

A few days before the induction letter lay on our table, I had visited an uncle on my mother's side, a projectionist at the Tobis Palace who for years had been responsible for moviegoing experiences that, like *The Bath on the Threshing Floor*, were rated unsuitable for young audiences. Did I peek through the peephole next to the projector and watch *Kolberg*, with Heinrich George in the leading role, immediately after the newsreel showing Goebbels chatting with air-raid survivors?

Later there were rumors from who knows what quarter to the effect that a number of the fellows who in period costumes had fought bravely against Napoleon for the cameras found themselves back in Kolberg the following year as combatants in the Volkssturm, the German Home Front Army, when Kolberg was under siege by real-life Russians and Poles. This time there was no one on hand to film their heroic deaths.

People at the station seemed oblivious to the fires. It was business as usual: shoving crowds, curses, sudden salvoes of laughter; soldiers on leave hurrying back to the front, soldiers on leave hurrying home; representatives from the female arm of the Hitler Youth, the League of German Girls, passing out hot drinks and giggling when the soldiers pawed them.

What had the stronger smell: the smoke of the steam locomotives, compressed under the only slightly damaged roof of the station concourse, or the fires?

I stood before a confusing array of signs indicating assembly points, registration desks, and the like. Two troop leaders—identifiable as such by the metal nameplates hanging from their necks, from these came their appellation "chain-hounds"—told me where to go. In the hall with the ticket windows (in which of the Berlin stations was it?) I joined a group of recent recruits my own age and after a brief wait was handed marching orders naming Dresden as my destination.

I can picture my fellow recruits jabbering. We are curious, as if on an adventure. We're in a good mood. I hear myself laughing too loudly, what about I don't know. We get marching rations. They include cigarettes. A nonsmoker, I give mine away. What I get from one of the boys in exchange is something I associate exclusively with Christmas: marzipan potatoes rolled in cocoa powder. Crushed by the reality of it all, I think I'm dreaming.

Suddenly an air-raid siren chased us all into the station's voluminous basement, the nearest shelter. A motley crew was soon crammed together there, soldiers and civilians, and a lot of children. There were wounded soldiers lying on stretchers and leaning on crutches. There was also a troupe of music-hall performers that included midgets. They were all in costume: the siren had sent them directly from stage to cellar.

While outside the ack-ack gunfire hammered on and bombs dropped far and near, they carried on their show: a dwarf juggler who kept ninepins, balls, and colored hoops all in the air at one time had us mesmerized; a number of his colleagues performed acrobatic feats; a dainty little lady tied herself gracefully in knots while blowing kisses to the wildly applauding crowd. The troupe, whose job it was to entertain front-line soldiers, was led by a tiny old man who performed as a clown. He also coaxed a sweet, melancholy music out of a row of empty to full glasses by stroking their rims with his fingers, the smile never leaving his rouged lips. An image that stuck with me.

As soon as the all-clear sounded, I took a tram to another station. Again I saw flames leaping out of apartment windows, whole façades destroyed, long lines of streets reduced to rubble after nights of bombing. In the distance, a factory lit from within, as if for a ceremony. The train for Dresden waited for departure in the gray light of morning.

NOTHING about the journey there. Not a word about the content of the sandwiches in our marching rations and no anticipatory, no previously accrued thoughts to be deciphered. All that remains to be said and therefore to be questioned is that it was not until here, in a Dresden as yet untouched by the war, or, to be more precise, in the upper story of an upper-middle-class mansion in the Weisser Hirsch district near Dresden-Neustadt, that I learned what division I had been attached to. My new marching orders made it clear where the recruit with my name was to undergo basic training: on a drill ground of the Waffen SS, as a Panzer gunner, somewhere far off in the Bohemian Woods ...

The question is: Was I frightened by what was obvious then in the recruitment office as I am terrified now by the double S, even as I write this more than sixty years later?

There is nothing carved into the onion skin that can be read as a sign of shock, let alone horror. I more likely viewed the Waffen SS as an elite unit that was sent into action whenever a breach in the front line had to be stopped up, a pocket like Demyansk forced open, a stronghold like Kharkov regained. I did not find the double rune on the uniform collar repellent. The boy, who saw himself as a man, was probably more concerned with the branch of the service: if he was not destined for the submarines, which hardly came up in the radio bulletins any longer, then he would be a tank gunner in a division which, as everyone in the Weisser Hirsch regional headquarters knew, was to be freshly raised under the name "Jörg von Frundsberg."

Von Frundsberg was known to me as the leader of the Swabian League during the sixteenth-century Peasant Wars, and as "father of the Landsknechts"—crack infantry mercenaries. Someone who stood for freedom, liberation. Besides, the Waffen SS had a European aura to it: it included separate volunteer divisions of French and Walloon, Dutch and Flemish, and many Norwegian and Danish soldiers; there were even neutral Swedes on the eastern front in the defensive battle, as the rhetoric went, to save the West from the Bolshevik flood.

So there were plenty of excuses. Yet for decades I refused to admit to the word, and to the double letters. What I had accepted with the stupid pride of youth I wanted to conceal after the war out of a recurrent sense of shame. But the burden remained, and no one could alleviate it.

True, during the tank gunner training, which kept me numb throughout the autumn and winter, there was no mention of the war crimes that later came to light, but the ignorance I claim could not blind me to the fact that I had been incorporated into a system that had planned, organized, and carried out the extermination of millions of people. Even if I could not be accused of active complicity, there remains to this day a residue that is all too commonly called joint responsibility. I will have to live with it for the rest of my life.

BEHIND and between woods, in churned-up fields. Trees and barracks roofs weighed down with snow. The onion-domed helmet of a church in the distance. Not a word of Czech spoken on the drill ground, only German-commandese, which in the frosty air carried farther than usual.

We were trained on outdated equipment—Panzer III and Panzer IV, which were used during the first years of the war—and driven like slaves. At first I thought that was how it had to be, but my initial supply of enthusiasm soon dwindled. All of us—recruits my age and old-timers who had been transferred to the Waffen SS as part of what was ironically called the Hermann Göring Fund—were drilled hard from dawn to dusk and, as we had been warned from the outset, constantly raked over the coals.

I had read about it in books. I intentionally suppressed the names of the slave drivers, even the worst of them. All that I learned from the experience was mute compliance or clever tricks. I got out of drill once by feigning jaundice—I swallowed

some heated oil from sardine cans—and once because of an outbreak of boils that swept the camp, but the chronically packed
infirmary could offer only temporary refuge. Then back to the
torture.

Our instructors, who were young in years but had been
turned into hard-boiled cynics by their year or two at the front,
were eager now, as NCOs and proud bearers of close-combat
and frozen-flesh medals, to pass on the experience they had
gained at the Kuban bridgehead and in tank warfare at Kursk.
They would do so in bitter earnest or with merciless wit or however they felt like. Now loudly, now softly, they plied us with
military lingo and outdid one another in bullying us with newfangled or time-honored army tortures.

A lot of it escapes my memory, but one method they had of
humiliating us recruits sticks in my mind, though I am not certain whether the reaction on the part of the bullied party was
merely wishful thinking or whether my act of vengeance actually took place, and in the form of a tale I could tell. In any case,
it is a tale with a point.

It is early morning. I am making my faltering way through
a snowy patch of pitch-black woods with metal cans in both
hands. I ran out there in double time, but have to return slowly.
Hidden among the trees, but visible because of its lighted windows, is a castle-like farmhouse where important offices are located. Once I thought I heard music coming from there; today
I'm positive it was a string quartet rehearsing Haydn or Mozart.
But that has nothing to do with my story, which took place in
total silence.

For days I had been ordered by the troop leaders to see to

their breakfast, which meant hauling two cans of coffee especially for them. The coffee had to arrive hot and was repeatedly
warmed up throughout the day. It came from the canteen on the
other side of the woods. The malt or barley substitute that we
recruits got—and that was rumored to be mixed with bicarbon-
ate of soda to keep our urges down—also came from there.
What I delivered piping hot to the head troop leader and the
five or six troop leaders who had preferential treatment owed its
taste to genuine coffee beans. At least what emanated from the
cans had the smell of authenticity.

The way there and back not only cut my breakfast time in
half, it also cut into the few minutes that remained for me to
give my mud-encrusted uniform a few whacks and a brushing,
so I was often late to morning roll call and got punishment drill:
running up and down a hill wearing a gas mask and heavy pack,
picking up sticky clay on my boot soles as I went. It was a torture that inspired lifelong hatreds in the gas-masked recruit.

Not surprisingly, I plotted my revenge to the last detail while
howling behind the misted-up mask.

On the way back from the canteen I make a stop behind
one of the snow-laden pines. I can see the farmhouse gleaming
in the distance, but it can't see me. The woods are so quiet I can
hear myself breathe. I pour two fingers of coffee into the snow,
put the cans down, and piss first in one can, then the other, till
they are full. The remainder between trees to color the snow
yellow.

Then snow falls and covers my traces.

Suddenly I go hot in the cold. I am overwhelmed with something akin to happiness.

Inner whisper: Good. They'll chug the stuff down—true, sweetened with sugar cubes, which they manage to hoard God-only-knows-how. Now, right now, for breakfast, and at noon, and then warmed up again at night: they always grab for the coffee pot when they've shouted their throats hoarse. I can just picture them, the troop leaders, the head troop leader. I keep count, swallow after swallow.

And pot after pot of what I delivered, more or less hot, they did in fact down. Why doubt it? We may assume that my repeated revenge, my regular morning gesture of futility, helped me to endure the drills, and even the worst tortures, with an inner grin. Just before one of those punishment drills, a recruit in the company next to ours hanged himself with the strap of his gas mask.

Otherwise I did everything I was ordered without a second thought. Crawling under the sump of our practice tank to the command "Measure ground clearance!" Brief training on heavy equipment. Shooting at moving targets. Night marches with combat pack. Knee bends with rifle held at arm's length. It was all supposed to make a man of me.

Every once in a while we were rewarded with a delousing session in a hygiene barracks specially set up for the purpose, after which we could take a group shower naked and laugh over Hans Moser and Heinz Rühmann at the camp cinema.

Letters came with less and less regularity. Afternoons we were force-fed theory. We learned about the tanks' Maybach engine. I can't recall one technical detail. To this day I cannot and will not drive. They drummed the Morse alphabet into us; not one letter remains.

And once a week we yawned our way through a class in *Lebensraum und Weltanschauung*, in *Blut und Boden*... The verbal refuse left behind by that rhetoric has not decomposed: you can call it up on the Internet even now.

CLEARER in my mind, because it can be told as a story, is an incident that took place outside the hazing routine. Several recruits, myself among them, were summoned one after another to the farmhouse I had found so intriguing during my morning excursions. Everywhere—behind the piano in the vestibule, along the winding staircase, and on the walls of my destination, a room the size of a banquet hall—there were deer antlers and sumptuously framed paintings of hunting scenes, dark with age. The room was devoid of furniture, except for a desk with bulbous legs. Seated at the desk was a storm trooper who could have been a venerable teacher.

Doing his best to look friendly, he told me to stand at ease, then asked me about my career plans after the final victory. He spoke like an affable uncle inquiring after the future of his favorite nephew.

I made no mention of my determination to become an artist, limiting myself to something vague, like studying art history, whereupon he held out the possibility of support if I were willing and qualified to attend a Junker school for future leaders.

Such schools were even now training young men with the proper national and racial consciousness to assume positions of responsibility that would need to be filled after the final victory to handle *Lebensraum* issues, resettle the non-German population, rebuild the cities, manage the economy. There would be posts in the financial sector, perhaps even in the arts you have your heart set on . . . Then he asked me what I could tell him about art.

This kindly, avuncular figure, who wore rimless glasses and whose rank grows more questionable the more I think about it—could he really have been a storm trooper?—appeared genuinely interested in what he dignified by calling it my career, so I unraveled before him what I had skeined together on the basis of my cigarette cards and Knackfuss volumes. I talked nonstop, and like as not ostentatiously, about Dürer's self-portraits, the *Isenheim Altarpiece,* and Tintoretto's *Miracle of Saint Mark,* praising the apostle's nosedive as an example of the artist's bold use of perspective.

Having crisscrossed his way through his three-volume, bird's-eye view of art history and thus exhausted his accumulated knowledge, the future Junker school graduate added a few brash assertions about Caravaggio's "gory genius" and an overly enthusiastic tribute to Anselm Feuerbach and the Deutschrömer and, finally, Lovis Corinth, whom Lilli Kröhnert, his art teacher at Saint Peter's, had called brilliant. As a result, he placed Corinth's work far above anything you could see in the exhibition of contemporary painting at the House of German Art.

With a shake of the head, my kindly old uncle waved me to the door. I had clearly disqualified myself for a position of responsibility after the final victory: no Junker school whisked me away from drill.

THOUGH belatedly, a present for my seventeenth birthday arrived in the mail: a package containing woolen socks, a cake that was mostly crumbs, and a double-sided letter full of clueless worries in my father's fine penmanship. From then until Christmas, only letters; after Christmas, nothing.

The notice board led us to believe that the Ardennes offensive—the Battle of the Bulge—was going swimmingly and would turn things around at last, but soon came the bulletin admitting that the Russians had entered East Prussia. Reports of the rape and murder of German women in the Gumbinnen region occupied my thoughts during the theory lectures.

All day we saw enemy squadrons sending bundles of vapor trails through the frost-bright sky, wending their unimpeded way—where? It looked quite beautiful, actually, but where were our fighter pilots?

There was still a lot of talk about the V1 and V2 rockets, to say nothing of the miracle weapon that was expected to materialize at any minute. Toward the end of February, when rumors of the Dresden firestorm started making the rounds, we took the oath. The moon was full, the night freezing cold. A chorus sang "If Others Prove Untrue, Yet We Shall Steadfast Be," the song of the Waffen SS.

SOON thereafter I witnessed an event that should have made the downfall of the German Reich evident—the organized chaos of defeat moving slowly, then with dispatch, and finally at breakneck speed. Was I able to recognize what things were coming to? Did I realize what was going on with us, with me? Did the never-ending activity, the all-consuming need for a ladle of soup and crust of army bread, along with fears of various magnitudes, leave any room for insight into the general situation? Was the seventeen-year-old at all conscious of the beginning of the end, of the gradually increasing dimensions of what was later called the collapse?

When my first attempt at sorting out and putting down on shiny white paper the confusion reigning in the head of a young soldier, whose oversize steel helmet keeps slipping, ended up as the novel *Dog Years* in the early sixties, the war as constant retreat gets mixed up in the pages of the diary kept by tank driver Harry Liebenau with the urgent entreaties of Harry's cousin Tulla, who, rumors lead him to believe, has gone down into the Baltic's icy deep on the refugee ship *Wilhelm Gustloff.*

I, too, kept a diary of sorts. I kept it in a notebook that I lost along with my winter coat and other items in my pack either at Weisswasser or near Cottbus. It is not an easy loss to write off: it has often made me feel lost to myself.

What did I scribble on those sheets of lined paper during breaks brief or extended?

What flights of fancy freed me from the matters at hand or the boredom that loomed whenever we had to wait for the eternal straggler or the field kitchen or the orders that would send us off in this or that direction?

Did intimations of spring move me to rhymed couplets?

Did I wallow in apocalyptic thoughts?

And even if it yielded no abstruse idea to decipher, no vernal verse to transcribe, no desired doubts to glean, the lost notebook could have thrown some light on the question: What did the battle-ready recruit do?

Did he sit in a tank as a gunner or as a gun loader?

Did he switch from cardboard to moving targets?

Where and when was I assigned to what unit?

I can't seem to turn the other members of the Jörg von Frundsberg division, which now feels quite unreal, into flesh and blood. From the training camp in the Bohemian Woods we were transferred group by group to a number of outlying garrisons: one lot set off in the direction of Vienna, another was sent to defend Stettin. Mine was taken one night on a freight train via Tetschen-Bodenbach to Dresden, then farther east into Lower Silesia, where the front was reputed to be.

All that remains in my mind of Dresden is the smell of burning and the sight—through the slightly open sliding door of the freight car—of charred bundles piled one on top of the other between tracks and in front of scorched façades. Some claimed to have seen shriveled corpses, others heaven knows what. We covered up our horror then by quarreling over what had happened, much as today what happened in Dresden lies buried under verbiage.

We seemed to have arrived at a reality only to abandon it or exchange it for something that claimed to be another reality. After being shifted from one direction to the next, we finally found the company we had been assigned to and joined its as yet incomplete squad in an evacuated school. The school benches piled up outside were being sawed into firewood by the kitchen crew. The accommodation awaiting us in the courtyard made it clear that the barracks existence I had led since my days as a Luftwaffe auxiliary was not over yet.

There we sat, waiting for our famous Tiger tanks to arrive. The wait proved long but, given the regular meals and loose discipline, tolerable. We even got to see movies. Did I have a second crack at *We Make Music,* which featured a gaily whistling

Ilse Werner and had served as a jazz substitute in my school days? Or was it there I first saw *Kolberg*?

How long did this motley troop composed of Wehrmacht regulars and ground personnel garnered from surrendered air bases wait for those tanks—and for the army postal service, which never came?

I cannot put a date to it. I picture that period as a film pieced together out of random episodes—now in fast, now in slow motion, jumping forward, jumping back, breaking off, then starting up again with a completely different script and plot.

The only person I remember clearly is an NCO sitting with us at the long wooden table we take our mess tins to, your typical "front swine." Forced to heed an urgent call of nature, he plucks a glass eye out of his right socket with a practiced pinch and plunks it, bright blue, onto the middle of the palm-sized slab of meat which—along with boiled potatoes, cabbage, and brown gravy—each of us is allocated for lunch. He shouts, "I'm keeping a glass eye on it," and we sit there agape till he returns from the shithouse.

What does memory cling to? A still life with a practical goal and no pretensions to art. There were plenty of soldiers marked by their wounds who returned to active duty straight from the field hospital: it didn't take much by the end to be declared fit for combat.

Eventually we received three or four Jagdpanthers, Hunting Panthers, instead of the promised Königstigers, King Tigers. There they stood under their camouflage netting: guns with no revolving turret. And although we lacked the training to operate them, we had to clear out of the barracks and mount them in our capacity as escorts, equipped with rifles and other assault weapons.

The front was supposedly the Silesian town of Sagan, which had been recaptured but was still under fire. From Sagan there was to be an offensive, or so we were told, to liberate Breslau, which the Russians had besieged and which was therefore being called the fortress city, but we got no farther than Weisswasser, where we fell apart as a company and I lost the pack containing my diary and the winter coat buckled onto it . . .

AT THAT point the film rips, and when I splice it together and switch the projector back on, all I get is a jumble of images: somewhere I throw away my threadbare footcloths and put on the woolen socks we have found in an evacuated military storehouse, which also contained piles of undershirts and tarpaulins. We have stopped in an alluvial plain and I am stroking the first pussy willows.

Did I hear an early cuckoo? Did I count its calls?

And then I see my first bodies. Soldiers young and old, in Wehrmacht uniforms. Hanging from trees still bare along the road, from linden trees in the marketplaces. With cardboard signs on their chests branding them as cowards and subversive elements. A boy my age—his hair, like mine, parted on the left—dangling next to a middle-aged officer of indeterminate rank or, rather, stripped of his rank by a court-martial. A procession of corpses we ride past with our deafening tank-track rattle. No thoughts, only images.

Off to the side I see peasants working their fields, furrow after furrow, as if nothing were wrong. One has a cow hitched to his plow. Crows following the plow.

Then I see more refugees, filling the streets in long processions: horse carts and overladen handcarts pushed and pulled by old women and adolescents; I see children clutching dolls, perched on suitcases and rope-bound bundles. An old man is pulling a cart containing two lambs hoping to survive the war. The image collector sees more than he can take in.

At a stop during the retreat I set my sights on a girl whose name is—this time I'm sure—Susanne. She is fleeing Breslau with her grandmother. Now she is stroking my hair. She lets me hold her hand, though nothing more. This exciting event takes place in the undamaged stable of a farmhouse that has been riddled with bullets. A calf looks on. If only the story had a message that would have justified sacrificing that bore named Truth.

But all I probably noted in my diary was: "Susanne wears a necklace made of cherry-red wooden beads. . . ." Or was it a completely different girl who wore the necklace, not the flaxen-haired one but the girl with the long black braids, whose name I refuse to tell?

Anything that occurred outside my field of vision does not make it into my cobbled-together film. Since rumors are rife, I will have heard that the Russians have taken my native city; what I don't know, however, is that the Old Town has long since been turned into one big heap of smoking rubble and that the ruins of the burnt-out brick church are waiting for photographers whose mission it will be to document each and every steeple stump, each and every fragment of the façade before reconstruction gets under way, so that schoolchildren will later recognize . . .

In my thoughts, though, the image of the city was still unblemished: the steeples could be counted from left to right; every gable ornament was in place, the paths to and from school intact. I also forced myself to see my mother behind the counter, my father in the kitchen. Could I have been tormented by the fear that my parents, together with my sister and their scant luggage, had in the end found room on the *Gustloff*?

AT THIS point the reel of my first contact with the enemy must be singled out from the arbitrary concatenation of images produced and directed by Chance, though with no indication of place or time or even of my having laid eyes on that enemy.

One can only assume that the encounter took place sometime in mid-April, when, after lengthy artillery bombardment, the Soviet armies had broken through the German lines along the Oder and Neisse between Forst and Muskau to take revenge for their ravished land and millions of dead, to conquer, to triumph.

I see our Jagdpanthers, a few armored personnel carriers, several trucks, the field kitchen, and a thrown-together troop of infantrymen and tank gunners taking up position in a grove of young trees, either to launch a counteroffensive or form a line of defense.

Buds on the trees—birches among others. The sun giving warmth. The birds chirping. We wait, half drowsing. Someone no older than I am is playing a harmonica. A private lathers up, starts shaving. And then, out of the blue—or was the birds' sudden silence a loud enough warning?—a Stalin organ overhead.

There is no time to wonder where the expression comes from. Is it the way it howls, hisses, and whines? Two or three rocket launchers blanket the grove. They are ruthlessly thorough, mowing down whatever cover the young trees might promise. There is no place to hide, or is there? For a simple gunner, at least.

I see myself doing as I was taught: crawling under one of the Jagdpanthers, where I find someone else—the driver, the gunner, the commander?—measuring the space between sump and soil. Our boots touch. We are protected by the tracks on either side. The organ goes on playing for what is most likely a three-minute eternity—scared to death, I piss my pants—and then silence.

Beside me chattering teeth.

No, the chattering had begun even before the organ had played its piece to the end, nor did it stop when the screams of the wounded overpowered all other noise.

Brief as the interval was, it was sufficient: my very first lesson taught me how to fear. Fear took possession of me. When I crawled out from under the Jagdpanther, I was no longer crawling the crawl I had practiced. I see myself crawling through a churned-up forest floor of decomposed leaves, into which I pressed my face for as long as the Stalin organ set the tone; the smell of them clung to me long after.

Still wobbly on my feet, I was assaulted by images. The birches looked as if they had been broken over somebody's knee: the falling treetops had set off some of our explosives. There were bodies everywhere, one next to the other and one on top of the other, dead, still alive, writhing, impaled by branches, peppered with shell splinters. Many were in acrobatic contortions. Body parts were strewn around.

Isn't that the boy who'd been tootling away on the harmonica? And there's that private, his lather not yet dry . . .

The survivors were either crawling here and there or, like me, rooted to the spot. Some wailed, though not wounded. I made not a sound; I just stood there in my piss-soaked pants, staring at the innards of a boy I had been shooting the breeze with. Death seemed to have shrunk his round face.

But I had already read everything I write here. I had read it in Remarque or Céline, who—like Grimmelshausen before them in his description of the Battle of Wittstock, when the Swedes hacked the Kaiser's troops to pieces—were merely quoting the scenes of horror handed down to them . . .

Then, suddenly, the teeth-chatterer was at my side, pulling himself up to his full height and exhibiting the rather elevated Waffen SS rank on his collar, his Knight's Cross medal only slightly awry under his chin, the very picture of a newsreel hero such as we schoolboys had been fed from the screen for years.

"Get a move on, soldier," he barked at me, the witness to his fear. "Assemble all able men. On the double. Get them back into formation, chop-chop. Prepare for the counterattack."

I watch him stepping over shattered bodies, both dead and alive. He looks ridiculous striding along, waving his arms, the picture-book hero no more. I later recalled him with gratitude, because his demeanor in the midst of the mutilated unit—only two Jagdpanthers and a few personnel carriers would still be of use in the field—completely undermined the image of the hero I had cherished during my schooldays. Something had gone wrong. The foundation of my faith, which had first developed a crack because of the blond-haired, blue-eyed Wedontdothat, was weakening again, though it would eventually stabilize . . .

FROM then on, the units I belonged to had no names. Battalions, companies kept dissolving. The Frundsberg was no more—if it ever had been. The Soviet armies had moved on beyond the Oder and Neisse and formed a broad front. Our main battle lines, steamrollered and broken through, existed only on paper, but what did I know of battle lines and what they were or meant?

In the chaos of retreat I sought to join up with scattered soldiers who were likewise trying to find their units. Even though I had had no direct contact with the enemy, I was scared to death. The soldiers hanging from the trees along the road were constant warning of the risk run by every one of us who could not prove that he belonged to a company or was on his way to this or that unit with signed and sealed travel orders.

The central section of the eastern front, now pushing inexorably west, was under the command of the infamous General Schörner. According to "Schörner's orders," military police—bloodhounds, the lot of them—were to go after soldiers without marching papers and haul them, no matter what their rank, before mobile courts-martial as malingerers, cowards, and deserters. They would then be summarily and conspicuously hanged. The phrase "hero-catcher on the prowl" served as warning. Schörner and his orders were more to be feared than the enemy.

I had Schörner on my back for a long time after the breakthrough between Forst and Muskau. In the mid-sixties I drafted a play, *Lost Battles,* meant to deal with the much-feared chief bloodhound. In the end, nothing came of this sandbox project: once more, fiction took the upper hand. But so relentlessly did that beast of a casual hangman hold me in his thrall that in the novel that replaced the play, *Local Anesthetic*—which is about the jutting jaw of a teacher by the name of Starusch, its orthodontic treatment, and the side-effects thereof, and about a student who wishes to burn his dachshund Max in protest against the Vietnam War—General Field Marshal Ferdinand Schörner is in evidence under the name of Kring.

Fear became a pack I could not throw off. Having, like the boy in the tale, gone forth to learn fear, I received daily lessons: ducking, dodging, cowering—such were the lapidary techniques of survival to be applied without drill. Woe betide the man unwilling to learn. Sometimes the only thing that helped was Luck, the child of Cunning and Chance.

Later I would call to mind several situations from which escape had been possible only with the aid of luck and chance. I summoned them so often that they turned into stories, which, as the years went by, grew more and more pertinent the more insistent they became on being believable down to the last detail. Yet everything that has been preserved as danger survived in the war must be doubted, even if it boasts of concrete detail in stories claiming to be true and as tangible as the mosquito in my amber.

It is a fact that twice in mid-April I ended up behind Russian lines as part of an improvised unit. It happened in the haste of retreat; both times I was attached to a reconnaissance troop with an unclear mission, and both times I was saved by luck if not by chance. Yet both situations occupied my dreams for years, offering variation after variation on my escape.

I knew about close calls from books I had more devoured than read as a schoolboy. One of my teachers—Littschwager by name, a man who appreciated the flights into absurdity in my compositions—had pressed a cheap, easy-to-read edition of *Simplicissimus* into my hands with the recommendation, "It's Baroque Realism, unbelievable but true, like everything Grimmelshausen wrote." I read myself silly.

So I could have taken heart from my predecessors: If Simplicius the survival artist had the fortune and cunning to steer clear of dangers lurking behind every bush for the length of a war lasting a full thirty years, and if his soulmate, Heartbrother, with his watertight argumentation could save him at the last minute—as he did at the Battle of Wittstock—from the clutches of the quick-to-sentence military judge and thus enable Simplicius to write his heart out when the time came, then why shouldn't Luck or another Heartbrother help me?

MY first opportunity to croak under machine-gun fire or be taken prisoner and learn to survive in Siberia presented itself when a troop of six or seven men led by a sergeant attempted to break out of the cellar of a one-story house. The house was in the Russian-occupied part of a village still under dispute.

How we got behind Russian lines and into the cellar of this house, which was actually more of a hut, is unclear, but breaking out of it and racing to one of the houses on the other side of the street still occupied by Germans was supposed to save us. I hear the sergeant, a beanpole topped by a cocked field hat, saying, "Now or never!"

The name of the disputed locality—it was in the sandy Lusatian region, a one-street village that stretched on and on—may never have been told us, or I may have forgotten it. Through the cellar window we could hear shots—single shots and machine-gun fire—going back and forth at intervals. There was nothing edible on the cellar shelves, but we could tell that the man living there, who had obviously cleared out just in time, had owned a bicycle shop, because he had used the cellar to hide his much-sought-after wares, quite a number of which were hanging by their front wheels from wooden racks, their tires pumped and ready, even raring, to go.

The sergeant must have been prone to snap decisions, because just after saying "Now or never!" he whispered rather than commanded, "Get a move on. Grab a bike, each one of you, and make a run for it . . ."

My embarrassed but precisely formulated response—"Sorry, Sergeant, I can't ride a bike"—must have sounded like a bad joke to him. Nobody laughed. There was no time to go into deeper reasons for my disgraceful failing: "My mother, who runs a no more than marginally profitable grocery, was unfortunately so chronically short of funds that she could not afford to buy me a bicycle, new or used, thus preventing me from acquiring a skill that might now possibly save my life . . ."

Before I could go on to laud my early-acquired natatorial skills, however, the sergeant made another snap decision: "All right, then. Grab the machine gun and cover us. We'll come back for you later . . ."

It may be that one or another of the privates, while dutifully removing his bike from the rack, tried to allay my fear. If so, his words went unheeded. I was at the cellar window taking up a position with a weapon I had not been trained to operate. The doubly incapable soldier never had a chance to fire, however, because no sooner had the five or six men emerged from the cellar, bicycles—including girls' bicycles—and all, than they were mown down by machine-gun fire out of nowhere, that is, from one side of the street or the other or both.

I think I see a wriggling, then only twitching pile. Someone—the lanky sergeant?—turns head over heels as he falls.

Then nothing moves. I may also see a front wheel sticking out of the pile, turning and turning.

But it may be that this description of the slaughter is no more than an after-the-fact, staged image, because I had left my cellar-window post before the fatal shoot-out and had seen nothing, wanted to see nothing.

I departed the bicycle shop owner's house without the light machine gun entrusted to me, but with my rifle, and made a run for it through the back garden and creaky gate. Behind and between gardens I was hidden by bushes already in bud, and having left the village still ringing with gunfire on the q.t., I suddenly came to the tracks of a narrow-gauge railway bordered on both sides by shrubbery along embankments the height of a man. They ran straight in the presumed direction of our front. Silence. Only sparrows and titmice in the shrubbery.

Not that I had learned a lesson from that sergeant for whom my inability to ride a bicycle had been nothing but a bad joke, but my impulse to follow the tracks like a prophetic directive proved to be the right decision.

After little more than a kilometer of gravel and wooden ties I saw an undamaged bridge arching the tracks. Crossing it were jeeps and trucks carrying infantry, then a horse-drawn howitzer, then small groups of unmistakably German foot soldiers dragging their feet. Blindly I joined their column, since without evidence of an enemy wound a soldier on his own with no marching orders would be a likely candidate for the noose.

I realize this survival story is hard to believe and smells strongly of artifice. In support of its kernel of truth let me point out that years later, whenever my sons and daughters tried to convince their father—deep in the woods with no one in sight—

that learning to ride a bike was child's play, he would venture no more than a quick try. Because when—in, say, Ulvshale Skov in Denmark—I let myself be lured onto a bicycle by cries like "Don't be a coward!" and "Come on, Papa!" from Malte, Hänschen, and Helene, who had been bike-trained at a tender age, the son of a mother who had unwittingly saved his life by insisting there was never enough money for one of those "wire donkeys," as she dubbed the two-wheelers, fell off.

The only person capable of seducing me into a bit of courage—and that as her partner on a Dutch tandem—was my wife Ute, who told me in the early eighties that I needed more exercise. She sat in front and steered, while I on the back seat enjoyed the sight of her loose hair blowing in the wind. Thus assured, I could let my thoughts wander without being endangered by snap decisions.

OF THE course of my days and nights—how did I get through them?—after the breach in the Oder-Neisse Line, the oft-spliced film has little to show. Neither the previously eloquent onion skin nor the transparent amber bearing a primordial insect that looks as if it belonged to today's world can be of any use. I must go back to Grimmelshausen, whom a comparable wartime chaos helped to learn fear, and conjure up the adventures of the hunter of Soest. Just as his description of the Battle of Wittstock focuses on the Dosse River and the marshlands in which the Kaiser's men come to grief—the bloodbath artfully adorned with his writer-colleague Martin Opitz's baroque word stock—so my battle scenes reflect the region of Lusatia between Cottbus and Spremberg.

Clearly the goal was to stabilize the front, starting at the very spot where I was wandering in circles, and break through the ever-narrowing ring around Berlin with newly formed units. There, so it was said, the Führer was holed up.

But the goal had spawned contradictory orders and led to a mishmash of mutually obstructive troop movements. Only the Silesian refugee columns tried to maintain a clear-cut direction: westward.

OH, how easily words came to me in the early sixties, when I was oblivious enough to think I could give the lie to the facts and pin clear-cut explanations on all sorts of absurdities. The floodgates were open, and page after page of bound words poured forth. Traditional narrative forms shed their age first in hot, then in cold word-baths. And the torture wrung cries of recognition out of defiantly tight lips. Every fart had its echo. Every point well taken was worth three sacrificed truths. And since everything proceeded according to the logic of fact, the contrary was also logically possible.

Thus, the point of the chapter concluding the second part of *Dog Years* was to make some sense out of the Führer's underground bunker, and ipso facto, of the battle for Berlin, which followed a path of total insanity. The search for a lost German shepherd, who answered to the name of Prinz and was said to be the Führer's favorite pet, suggested to me a language that combined meandering Heidegger-German—"nothingness nullifies unexposedly"—and the clumsy, noun-laden diction of the Wehrmacht High Command, whose verbal overflow washed away even the most minor objections: "As per Führer-orders, the Twenty-Fifth Armored Infantry Division is instructed to close the Cottbus-front breach and ensure against canine break-through. . . . The primordial manifestness of the Führer-dog is through-determined by distantiality. . . . The nothingness through-determined by distantiality is acknowledged in the Steiner Group space as nothingness. . . . Nothingness is coming-into-being between the armored enemy and our spearheads . . ."

But where I was, or was supposed to be—the Cottbus-front breach?—there were no spearheads, or, for that matter, recognizable military cohesion. The Frundsberg division could also have been acknowledged by the ominous Steiner Group as nothingness (though it may well have been attached to it): it had been reduced to a few hastily cobbled together remnants reacting to inconsistent orders. Everything was falling apart, nothing was proceeding as planned until—and now the film starts up again and brings me back into the picture—the lone tank gunner was given a new assignment at the whim of a higher power.

DEALT this hand by my old acquaintance Fate, I found myself in a group of twelve to fifteen men, with no heavy artillery and therefore classified as a raiding party, belonging to an ascension commando—soldiers' slang for suicide squad. Since I had managed to lose my rifle as well as the tarpaulin that had sheltered me from the rain, I was given a submachine gun of Italian manufacture, which, had there been occasion for me to use it, would have been in unsure hands.

I recall a meeting of steel helmets shadowing sullen men's and fearful boys' faces, of which mine would have been third from the left had anyone taken a picture of the lost troop.

Again we were led by an old-timer of a sergeant, this one

with broad shoulders but a less than brilliant career. Our orders were to advance and seek contact with the enemy.

Dusk was descending, and after a number of false starts we wandered onto a forest path churned up by tank tracks. The tracks had been made only hours before, we learned, by a column of Tigers and armored personnel carriers racing forward to serve as an advance guard. But hard as we tried to make radio contact with them, all that came over our walkie-talkie was gibberish and static.

The tree stock on both sides of the road was highly repetitive, pine giving way to pine, towering pines right and left. We may have had no heavy artillery to weigh us down, but we had picked up an old man along the way—his armband identified him as a member of the Volkssturm, the Home Front Army— as well as two lightly wounded soldiers, both of them, like twins, with lame left legs. The man from the Volkssturm was constantly babbling about something, quarreling with God or cursing his neighbor; the wounded men had to be helped along, half carried. We made slow progress.

After further vain attempts at contacting the tank brigade, the sergeant called for a halt. Putting to use his evident front-line savvy, he had decided to wait for the armored personnel carriers that were expected for the retreat, in the hope that they would provide transport for at least the hobblers and the Home Front bore. We'd had it for the day in any case. Luckily, he singled me out to stand watch and ordered me to keep my eyes open.

I see another picture: Myself in my own imagination. Myself under my sliding helmet. Myself obeying an order. Myself eager to do a good job.

And that, tired as I was, I did. Because it was not long before I spied a speck of light in the now night-black path running through the woods. It divided in two as it drew nearer. After delivering my required report—"Motorized vehicle, probably armored personnel carrier, straight ahead!"—I positioned myself in the middle of the path so as to be easily spotted and, according to my orders, ready to stop the tank with—since I am left-handed—a raised left hand.

My first intimation of surprise may have come from the fact that the rapidly approaching vehicle had its headlights on full beam, and when it came to a halt two steps in front of me I realized why. Only Russians would waste lights like that . . .

"It's the Ivans!" I shouted to the group at the side of the road but did not take the time to differentiate the gunners sitting cheek by jowl on the enemy tank and thus meet my first Soviet soldier face to face. I broke rank before they could shoot, diving into a stand of young pines to the right of the road, out of sight, though not out of danger.

I heard shouting in two languages immediately overlayered by gunfire, until only the Russian submachine guns had their say.

Crawling my way through the dense pine thicket and slowly increasing my distance from the road, I was shot at from right and left but not hit, which was not necessarily the case with the group around the sergeant: the old man was no longer cursing God or his neighbor or calling for various scores to be settled. The only voices I heard were Russian voices, now quite far off. Someone was laughing. He must have been in a good mood.

Because the dry twigs made such a racket, the isolated tank gunner stopped inching forward on his elbows as he had been trained to do, and played dead, as if he could escape the march of history and, with his Italian submachine gun and two magazines of ammunition, he could still be considered battle ready. Not until the enemy tank, which had been followed by others, started moving did he begin to crawl forward again, and he crawled on until the pine cover turned into a mature wood with Prussian-neat rows. No, I had no desire to go back and find only corpses; besides, the pale lights and engine noises coming from the road confirmed the enemy's advance.

I moved deeper and deeper into the woods, a half moon shining through a moderately cloudy sky, actually and suddenly— or only wishfully—which meant that the lone soldier did not bump into tree trunks very often. He was, however, so engulfed by the smell of resin that he felt encapsulated in it, like the insect that has come down to the present in my piece of amber and now claims to embody me. There it lies on the shelf with other such objects I have found, waiting to be held up to the light and interrogated. Spider, tick, or beetle, it will deliver its message if you're patient enough . . .

But what do I see when I hold up the lone tank gunner by half-moonlight and view him as an early edition of the man to come?

He looks like a character who has escaped from a Grimm's fairy tale. He is about to cry. He clearly doesn't like the story in which he appears. He would much rather resemble the title character of a book that is always so close to him he feels he can reach out and touch it. Right: he feels like the hero from Grimmelshausen's stable, the man for whom the world is a tortuous labyrinth of a madhouse that can be escaped only through pen and ink as a character named Soonother. A trick he has used since his school days: making words to help him get on with life.

So everything that happens now has been nurtured in the greenhouse of suppositions. He may have been this way or that, but all I can see is an aimless wanderer, appearing and disappearing nebulously between and behind tree trunks of uniform size, until he is finally recaptured by the image-seeker as the soldier with the helmet that keeps sliding down over his eyes.

He is still armed, still holding his submachine gun at the ready. A gas mask dangles uselessly from him like an elongated drum. All he has left in his haversack is a few crumbs from his last ration. His canteen is half empty. The Kienzle luminous-dial wristwatch, the birthday present from his father, has long since stopped.

If only he had the leather dice cup and three ivory dice that he claimed shortly after the war's end and that he and a friend his age used to tell the future when they were prisoners together at the Bad Aibling camp. The friend will be called Joseph, and he will be so single-mindedly Catholic that he will want to be a priest, a bishop, maybe even a cardinal . . . But that is another story, whose origins are lost and have no business here in the dark wood.

Now he is asleep, propped against a tree. Now he awakes with a start, though without the coat he lost at Weisswasser he is not cold. Now he casts a shadow like the tree trunks because it is day, but he cannot find his way out of the wood and stumbles around in a circle without knowing it, takes some crumbly zwieback out of his haversack, unscrews the top of his canteen, and drinks, sending the helmet back over his neck. He does not know how time passes to the minute, and has nothing to help him foretell the future, but he longs for a friend, as yet nameless, and tries in vain to be the Simplicius who can find his way out of any danger and therefore becomes the universally celebrated hunter of Soest, whose foraging expeditions yield nutritious loot like pumpernickel and Westphalian ham. Now it is dark again and an owl is calling, and, hungry and abandoned under the moderately cloudy night sky, he chews his last crumbs.

A prisoner of the dark, he learns another lesson in fear: he feels it sitting on his back, and tries to recall the prayers he said as a child—"Please, dear God, stand by my side, that I may in heav'n abide"—and maybe even calls out "Mama, Mama" and hears his mother's warning voice, luring him home from far away—"Come back, my boy! I'll give you egg yolk mixed with sugar in a glass!"—but he stays where he is, alone as can be, and then something happens.

I heard steps or something that could be construed as steps. Twigs crackling underfoot. An animal of some kind? A boar? Maybe even a unicorn.

I stood stock-still and made not a sound; he or it—the animal, man, or imaginary beast that had been stepping through the wood—followed suit.

Then a figure appeared, drew nearer, withdrew, only to come near again. Too near.

Careful! Don't swallow too loud. Take cover behind the tree trunks. Lessons from military training. Release the weapon's safety catch as the other man's safety catch is almost certainly being released.

Two men assuming each other to be enemies. Conceivably, many years down the line, an idea for a ballet or movie scene.

Like the scene that sets up the climax in every classic Western: the ritual dance before the final shoot-out.

Whistling is said to help dispel fear in a dark wood. I did not whistle. Something, perhaps the thought of my far-off mother, made me sing instead. I did not seek out a melody from among the marches we had been taught, like "Erika," or current film hits, like Marika Rökk's "No One Likes to Be Alone at Night." No, it was a nursery rhyme relevant to my situation that came unbidden to my lips, and I sang the first line over and over— "Hans left home, on his own"—until I finally heard its mate: "Went into the world alone."

I can't say how long this antiphonal singing continued. Most likely until the message behind the words—two native speakers of German are wandering through the pitch-dark woods—was clear enough to allow both sides to drop their cover, address each other in German soldierspeak, lower their weapons, and move within arm's length, then even closer.

My singing partner was equipped with a rifle, several more years, and several fewer centimeters than me. What I saw under the field cap—he had no helmet—was a puny little man, and what I heard was a Berlin drawl you could cut with a knife. The scare was over the moment he lit up: a cigarette in a sullen face that said nothing.

Later I learned that in the course of the war, starting with the Polish campaign, moving on to France and Greece, and getting as far as the Crimean peninsula, he made it to the rank of private first class. He had no desire to advance any further. Nothing could throw him, a characteristic that in our precarious situation was not long in proving its worth. He became my guardian angel, the soulmate I had seen at work in Grimmelshausen, my

Heartbrother: he led me out of the woods and over the fields and across the Russian front line.

Since, unlike me, the private first class had been to the edge of the woods and had several opportunities to observe the bivouac fires in the open field beyond, which he judged to be enemy territory, we looked for a place that was not lit by fire. That is: he looked, I remained two paces behind him.

During a halt he lathered his face by the light of the lingering moon and shaved off a three-day growth. I held my superior's pocket mirror for him.

Not until a field with a furrow leading westward into the darkness bolstered our courage did we abandon the protection afforded by the trees. The field looked freshly plowed and came to an end behind a swell in the soil, after which we followed a bush-lined country road that bridged a stream. The bridge was unguarded. We filled our canteens, drank, and filled them again. He had a smoke.

Two bridges down—could these have been tributaries of the Spree?—we saw the flicker of a fire in the distance. Laughter, snippets of words floated in our direction; shadow figures flitted back and forth in the glow.

No, the Ivans weren't singing, nor did they appear to be a pile of hopeless drunks. Half of them were probably still asleep; the other half . . .

After crossing the bridge, we heard a *"Stoi!"* and then another.

At the third *"Stoi!"*—the bridge was quite far behind us— my Pfc issued his directive: "Run, and as fast as you can!"

And so we ran, but we ran the sluggish run I ran through many a postwar dream: across a field, its clumps and clods clinging to our boot soles, falling off, sticking back on, making us look as if we were running in slow motion—though we were now under submachine-gun fire and a sky exploding with signal rockets—through an extended film sequence that finally came to an end in the cover of a ditch at the far end of the field.

The Russians, or, as we called them, the Ivans, made no effort to flush us out. The shooting ebbed, the rockets stopped. The moon took back the sky. A rabbit hobbled past leisurely, as if we were not to be feared.

So on we trudged through the fields, crossing no more bridges, and just as the sun came up we saw a village the enemy had apparently not yet occupied. It lay tranquil in the morning mist, huddled up to the church, peaceful, as if fallen out of time.

STRANGE that I can still picture the impassive or rather grouchy cavalry captain of Austrian descent who met us at the entry to the village behind a poorly guarded roadblock, and can therefore either draw or describe him complete with eye pouches and toothbrush mustache, even though we were exposed to him and his Home Front men for only a minute. He seemed anxious by nature and interrupted our detailed report with a nonchalant "Just show me your marching orders," as if that were a mere catchphrase.

Since without official papers we were virtual outlaws and court-martial fodder, he had us taken away by three old men armed with hunting rifles and bazookas, one of whom made a great show of being mayor and head of the local farmers' organization. They locked us up in the cellar of a farmhouse.

Oddly enough, though, they failed to disarm us. The cavalry officer had a little dog with a pearl-studded collar he carried in his arms and spoke to so lovingly as if nothing in this world, outside the mangy cur, was worthy of his sympathy. One of the hobbling Home Front men—to show where his own sympathy lay—slipped my Pfc an open packet of cigarettes, I don't know what brand.

Nor do I know the name of the village where, hale though hungry, we had reached German lines and would immediately, if not sooner, be summarily court-martialed. Could it have been Peterlein? Or did that sweet diminutive of a name belong to a village we passed through later?

In any case, the cellar where they kept us was lined with shelves full of bottled preserves, their labels in grandmotherly Sütterlin script: asparagus, pickled gherkins with mustard seed, pumpkin, and green peas, as well as a blood-and-vinegar ragout and goose giblets. The jars weren't even dusty. There were also bottles of cloudy apple and elderberry juice and, in a corner, a pile of potatoes with sprouts the size of a little finger.

We spooned lard with pork chunks straight from the jar and munched on the gherkins, washing it all down with the juice and stopping only when we were on the point of vomiting. Then my Pfc smoked a cigarette. He did so rarely, but when he did he did it with reverence. And like my far-off mother he was a master at blowing smoke rings. I took my gas mask out of its case and filled the case with strawberry or cherry jam. I would live to regret it.

HAVING waited two hours to be summoned to our court-martial, the likely verdict of which we refrained from discussing—we had probably slipped into an after-dinner doze because I do not re-call the interval as a period of apprehension—the Pfc tried the cellar door. It was unlocked. The key was hanging from the outside keyhole. No one was guarding us. Did we scare a cat or, if cat there was, disturb its sleep?

Through the kitchen window above the cellar we could see the roadblock. There was no Home Front man smoking his last pipe. Gone was the officer along with his dog. The village must have been evacuated in the meantime. Or its inhabitants were making believe that it didn't exist, had never existed.

The officer had either forgotten us or in a fit of melancholy had delivered us into the hands of a capricious fate. The sparrows were doing their calisthenics on the roadblock's freshly chopped pine logs. The sun was warm. You felt like bursting into song.

On one side of the block we had an unobstructed view of the fields: the enemy, the Russian infantry, was advancing in protective ranks. It all looked harmless from a distance—a bunch of figurines—but it was my second encounter with the Red Army. I couldn't make out any faces, the distance was closing step by step. Still no shot rang out. Some of the slowly advancing figures under their caps, fur hats, and helmets could have been my age. Earth-colored uniforms, baby faces. You could count them from left to right. Each a target.

Yet I did not aim my submachine gun, nor did my Pfc attempt to defend the village of Peterlein with his rifle. We made tracks, noiseless tracks. Not even if the Ivans had shot on command or out of habit would we have shot back.

We did not act out of brotherly love and deserve no credit. What kept us from aiming and pulling the trigger was more like reason, or the absence of necessity. That is why the claim I have so often made—namely, that during the week in which the war had me firmly in its grasp I never looked through a sight, never felt for a trigger, and thus never fired a shot—is at best a way of alleviating in retrospect the shame that remains. Yet something else remains: the fact that we did not shoot. What is less certain is when I exchanged my uniform jacket for one less onerous. Did I do so of my own accord?

It was more likely the Pfc who, his eye on the runes on my collar, had recommended and made possible the change of jacket. He could not have been pleased about my markings: through me, though he never put it in those terms, he had got into bad company.

What he did say at some point, either in the larder of a cellar or while lathering, or shaving, or puffing on his cigarette, was: "Listen, boy, if those Ivans nab us, you're in for it. They see those ornaments on your collar, they'll shoot you in the neck. No questions asked . . ."

How he did it I don't know, but he managed to "organize"— as the soldiers used to say—an ordinary Wehrmacht jacket somewhere. One without bullet holes or bloodstains. It even fit. That way, minus the double rune, he liked me a lot better. I came to like me better, too.

So considerate he was, my guardian angel. Just as Simplicius had a soulmate at his side whenever he was in danger, so I and my newly retouched self-image could rely on my Pfc.

AFTER is always before. What we call the present, this fleeting nownownow, is constantly overshadowed by a past now in such a way that the escape route known as the future can be marched to only in lead-soled shoes.

Thus encumbered and at a distance of sixty years, I see a seventeen-year-old with an indecently bulging gas-mask case no longer serving its original function, and a like-new tailored uniform jacket doing everything possible to join up with the units flooding back through Germany side by side with a tough slyboots of a Pfc who has seen it all and whom you'd never guess to be a barber by trade. The two of them repeatedly make their way around the "bloodhounds." There are always holes to be found. The front is not easy to recognize. But they are only two among thousands of soldiers who have lost their regiments. And what unit is so desperate that it will take them in without papers?

Then, on the road from Senftenberg to Spremberg, which is packed with horses and carts full of refugees, the two of them in the same field-gray battle dress, yet so ill-matched, take advantage of the crush to negotiate purchase of an official document, the life-giving marching orders, at an improvised assembly point, which is out in the open at the side of the road and consists of a table and a stool. There is some printed paper on the table. The war-weary master sergeant on the stool asks no questions, writes quickly, slams down his stamp. I regurgitate the tale my Pfc has drummed into me.

Now we are protected: we belong to a newly assembled combat group. True, for the time being it exists only on paper, as a vague promise, but we can see a perfectly concrete mobile field kitchen—the "goulash cannon" of soldiers' slang—set up in the meadow behind the table, its kettle steaming and sending out a soupy aroma.

We join the line. All together. Not even officers may pull rank. Come the end, fate dishes out moments of rank-free anarchy.

We have potato soup with bits of meat floating in it. The mess boy ladles each of us a scoop from the bottom, then a half-scoop from the top. The mess tin we each have buckled onto our haversacks is just the right size. The mood is neither down nor up. Typical April weather. The sun is out.

Now we are facing each other, our spoons moving in rhythm. "Hey," says somebody a few steps away, without breaking the rhythm of his spoon, "isn't today Adolf's birthday? So where's the extra ration? And the chocolate, the cigarettes, a shot of brandy for the toast! Heil, mein Führer!"

Now somebody tries to tell a joke, but gets all mixed up. Infectious laughter. A few more jokes take off. A peaceful scene. All it needs is an accordion player.

"What do they call this place?"

"Lusatia!"

That rings a bell with someone. "The brown-coal place."

In spring of 1990 I had occasion to visit some towns and villages in the area of Cottbus and Spremberg, not far from Berlin. Eager as I was to get down on paper everything that happened there recently, I couldn't keep my thoughts away from the past.

At the time it looked as though unification could, if not overcome, then during the gradual rapprochement at least compensate for one of the consequences of war, the forty-year split of Germany into two countries. The possibility, miracle that it seemed, at least presented itself. And since people thought this was no time for long-term operations, the poor East was to be brought level with the rich West, and quickly too.

I made two trips to the area, the first time staying for several days in Cottbus, where a swarm of business representatives, the harbingers of capital investment, had laid siege to the hotel, the second time, just as summer was coming in—in Altdöbern, where I found a bed-and-breakfast with a widow and her daughter. The town boasted a castle and grounds, a factory no longer in operation, a cooperative store, a women's clinic, and a cemetery in the church square for Soviet soldiers, its graves set out in neat rows. One restaurant still served Russian *solyanka*, but you could now wash it down with beer brought in from Bavaria. The currency reform was still to come, but the sale of the peacefully captured country was already under way: Western companies were flying their pennants everywhere.

But it was the environment I cared about. Wherever I looked, I saw the ravages of decades of brown-coal mining. Where the coal had been deep in the ground, as it was behind the castle, there was now a lunar landscape: otherworldly, conical hills of overburden among pools of stagnant groundwater. Not a bird in sight.

The quarry behind the women's clinic afforded a good overview, and I covered page after page with pencil and charcoal drawings. From Altdöbern I moved on to what remained of the village of Pritzen and later to the rows of chimneys and cooling towers belonging to the doomed Black Pump industrial complex.

My drawing pad—twenty sheets of Ingres paper strong— was soon full. I drew conveyor belts so deeply worked into the ground that they looked like tripe. Coal scrapers near and far, perched on pit edges like insects, provided motif after motif.

This glance into the abysses wrought by human hands showed me more than meets the eye and set words free that later, in the novel *Too Far Afield,* outlined the prospect of the easternization of the West and other dark thoughts out of the depths. At the time, however, between drawings, the film started running backward, and I was, as I am now, back on my own trail.

On the road from Senftenberg to Spremberg we must locate a time-traveling tank gunner standing next to a private first class with a Berlin drawl you can cut with a knife, staring open-mouthed at his surroundings and grimacing. I can't place the mess boy doling out the potato soup, but the private and the private first class are facing each other with half-full mess tins.

I am now being warmed by the June sun as I was then warmed by its April counterpart. I now see us spooning our soup in unison. We are standing near a street on which a column of tanks trying to advance and counterattack is being obstructed by a column of refugees advancing in the opposite direction. There is no room to maneuver on one side of the road. The earth's crust is cracking.

Down below, the brown-coal mining region stretches all the way to the quarry opposite, black gold waiting to be pressed into briquettes and fed to power stations. In war as in peace, Lusatia was a stronghold of opencast mining and remained so until the year the Wall came down and I went there and saw more than met the eye.

Then, stillness reigned over the cones of overburden and the pools of groundwater. It was quiet enough, while I sat drawing the opencast landscape in the most present of presents, for me to turn my ear back to the howling of the tank commanders, the roaring of the Maybach engines, the screaming of the refugees in their carts, the neighing of their horses, and the crying of their children, but also to the slam of the sergeant's rubber stamp and the clatter of the tin spoons—we were scraping the last bits out of our mess tins—and finally to the first explosions of the Soviet tank grenades.

Between one spoonful and another my Pfc said, "Those are T-34s."

"T-34s," said his echo. Me.

On the opposite side of the road a number of tanks had emerged from the woods and begun climbing the deep quarry. Small as toys, they stopped and fired. The traffic on the street had come to a halt, presenting the enemy fire with an easy target. The shots came closer. Because of their fixed barrels our Jagdpanther tanks had to turn before they could respond. Commands vying with screams, our tanks pushing jam-packed carts and their passengers and horses over the edge of the road into the quarry pit. They tipped over like trinkets.

Now I see a handsome lieutenant gesticulating out of an open turret as if trying to change the direction of the barrels with his bare hands; I see Silesian peasants refusing to let their possessions go; I see doll-like children on carts sliding off the road, I see women screaming but fail to hear their cries, I see grenades exploding, sometimes far off, sometimes nearby— silently they find their targets—so as not to see, I stare now at the remains of the soup in my mess tin; on the one hand, I am still a hungry man, on the other, a dumbfounded observer, a mere witness, a nonparticipant in the silent film-like action; and now, with the stroke of a pen I become the young Grimmelshausen, stringing story after story, battle after battle, through the savage years of war, there's a stranger whispering in my ear, I see myself watching everything that happens. I seem to be dreaming but I am and remain awake until the helmet, its strap now flapping, flies off my head now, this very minute, and my senses vanish.

For no more than an instant, insofar as time could be measured. What happened to me and around me a minute later flashes on and off in sharp, then eerily fuzzy images: gone the all but empty mess tin, gone too the Kienzle wristwatch.

Where is my Pfc? Where is the submachine gun, the two magazines of ammunition? Why am I still standing—or standing again?

The badly bleeding wound in my right thigh drenching my trousers. The pain in my chin caused by the helmet strap. A limp arm dangling from my left shoulder refuses to obey when I try, with the help of someone else, to lift—there he is!—my Pfc.

His legs ripped to bits. His torso apparently intact. His eyes open wide, amazed, unbelieving . . .

Then a whirl of sand dust shifts my gaze to the field kitchen, still steaming, unscathed, where it remains until we—he carried, I supported—and another wounded man are loaded into a field ambulance. An orderly climbs in. Other victims left behind, curse, one of them insists on coming with us and clings to the vehicle. . . . At last the door is shut and bolted.

We rumble along, presumably to the dressing station.

THE smell of Lysol. I must have felt safe in the ambulance. The war had taken a break. At any rate nothing much was going on, especially as we were so slow in finding the way. The Pfc lay flat on his back. His formerly smooth, pink, shiny face—the result of frequent shaves—was tinged with green, and stubble was beginning to show. He seemed to have shrunk. His legs were bandaged, wrapped in gauze.

He lay, conscious, on a plank bed, looking at me out of the corner of his eye, his head straight. He was trying to form words, and finally, in a soft version of his drawl, managed to ask for a cigarette. I extracted one out of the crumpled packet in his breast pocket, together with his lighter.

I, the nonsmoker, lit it for him, and stuck it between his lips. The lips suddenly stopped trembling. He took a few greedy puffs, shut his eyes, but immediately opened them in terror, as if he had only then understood his condition. Now I saw fear written on his face, and it startled me. Then, after an interval, during which I heard the groans of the wounded and the curses of the orderly—he was short on gauze—and wondered at my own oddly pain-free condition, my Pfc asked me, no, ordered me to open his trousers and his underpants too and reach in and check between his legs.

Having received confirmation that everything was present and accounted for, he let out a quiet groan, took a few more puffs, then dropped off, breathed calmly, looked tranquil.

Twelve years later, while committing the defense of the Polish Post Office to paper, I had Jan Bronski perform the same trouser inspection, that is, confirm the unscathed virility of the reluctantly dying porter Kobyella with his five fingers.

WE WERE separated at the dressing station: he was put in a tent, I left out in the open. When the time came for my thigh to be bandaged, I became a laughingstock for the following obvious reason: the gas-mask case, which was still attached to me, had been slit open by a finger-length grenade splinter and the contents had gushed out and made a mess of strawberry or cherry jam in my pants. From then on, my trouser seat stuck to me whenever I sat down. In time it attracted ants, which was nothing to laugh at.

The injured gas-mask case stayed behind at the dressing station. As for the splinter of the Soviet grenade, which had spared me and therefore granted the future father of sons and daughters survivor status, I would have liked to show it in all its glory to my children and theirs. You see before you a clear-cut example of what I had to go through as an enlisted man in order to have a taste of anxiety, learn the meaning of fear. Look, children. See how long and jagged the splinter is?

Not until after the thigh was bandaged did they bandage my left shoulder, which was hardly bleeding, though it was likely that a foreign object made of metal, however small, had lodged itself there. The hole it had made in my new uniform jacket was all but invisible. The dangling arm was now supported by a sling. Since the dressing station happened to be in the immediate vicinity of a marshaling yard, I retain no images of intermediary stations. As evident as the war was all around, it was suddenly over for me.

We were loaded onto the train that evening. It must have been the night of the twentieth to the twenty-first of April, because the army doctor, the orderlies, and my fellow walking wounded were making the same complaints I'd heard being bandied about the field kitchen that afternoon: Where were the extras they'd passed around every year on the Führer's birthday? No cigarettes, no sardines, no bottle of Doppelkorn per four men, no nothing. All of the soldiers—even me, a nonsmoker—found this situation more upsetting and of greater import than the fall of the German Reich so obviously taking place all around us. The moanings and groanings were peppered with curses the likes of which I'd never heard.

WHERE the freight train in which I lay with all the wounded was headed I had no idea. It made frequent endlessly long and occasional short stops and was shunted several times to different tracks. Soon it was dark out. The only light we had came from a primitive acetylene lamp.

We lay on rotten, piss-smelling straw. The man to the left of me, a member of the mountain troops with a bandage around his head, was reading a religious book by the glimmer of a pocket flashlight. He was moving his lips. The man to my right had been shot in the stomach and writhed and screamed until he writhed and screamed no more.

There was no water to be had, no orderly to tend to the pleas of the wounded. Voices and sobs, whether the train was moving or not. Sudden silences after the last groan.

My neighbor to the left prayed sotto voce. A man driven mad by pain tore his bandage off, leapt up, fell, leapt back up only to fall again and stay down. The man to the right of me had stopped moving altogether.

The night seemed never ending; it lasted in my dreams through the early postwar years. No, I had no pain as yet, but I slept fitfully, starting each time I awoke, till in the end I fell into a deep sleep, for how long I can't say.

When the freight train came to its final stop, the goods, both the quick and the dead (my neighbor with the stomach wound), were unloaded, and an army doctor checked off our names on the list, separating the seriously wounded from the rest. A glance was enough. It took no time at all.

THE ancient and miraculously undamaged cathedral town of Meissen lay bathed in the spring morning light. True to the folk song, the birds were all there. Those of the wounded who could, myself included, reached greedily for the glasses of juice passed out by representatives of the League of German Girls, who were clearly used to trains with this sort of content.

The seriously wounded were hauled away in trucks; the rest of us, propping each other up, hobbled along the path leading up to the fortress, which had been turned into a military hospital. Locals, mostly women, lined the path, and many helped the disabled. I see myself being helped uphill by a young woman.

Last year, my eldest son, Franz, a forty-something so enterprising that his goals keep changing, and my youngest daughter, Nele, who was in Dresden learning the skills it takes to be a midwife while trying to keep her affairs of the heart under wraps, undertook a family pilgrimage to the newly restored Meissen. They sent me a shiny picture-postcard view of the town with a message that could be read as a sign of filial affection: they had lit candles in the cathedral to commemorate my chance survival.

I was anything but well cared for up there in the fortress. The hospital was full to bursting, its corridors lined with emergency pallets. Exhausted doctors, harried nurses. Everything was in short supply, especially medicine. All they could do for me was put fresh bandages on my right thigh and my left shoulder, in which—it was now official, confirmed by a signed and stamped document—a small grenade splinter had been lodged. They did not deem me worthy of an operation, nor did they waste a tetanus shot on me.

We were given marching rations, enough to fill the haversack I'd managed to hang on to. The only thing gone was my watch. But I now wore a field cap, one that fit. I wouldn't have minded a change of trousers; their sticky bottom was an embarrassment.

Finally, along with a document promising the shot and another pair of trousers, I was handed new marching orders, my last, destination Marienbad. Then a military hospital center, once a spa for the rich and famous, much celebrated in literature—as an old man, Goethe had fallen in love with a young thing there, was given the brush-off, and sublimated his grief in a "Marienbad Elegy"—it lay on the far side of the Ore Mountains, deep in the Sudetenland.

While I waited for the orders—they were the only way I could prove my identity—the Pfc was pushed out of the operating room in a wheelchair. His nose more pointed. It was the first time I had seen my guardian angel unshaven. A legless torso wrapped in gauze rolled past deep in sleep, leaving behind the question of whether his coming out of that sleep was to be desired or feared.

He was rolled down a corridor whose walls were studded with armaments dating from the Middle Ages: halberds, crossbows, battleaxes, arrows, cudgels, and swords bound together, and muskets that may well have dated from Grimmelshausen's war-torn times—an arsenal of the artifacts man has discovered for dealing with his fellow man at various points in history.

I watched my Pfc go. This picture of him being silently wheeled away, which I can call up at will, balks at the question of whether he is still alive and, if so, where he is living. As for his name, he never told me, and it must remain unspoken.

Well-trained soldier that I was, I addressed him only as private first class: Herr Obergefreiter, whether we were in the pitch-black pine wood or the cellar filled with preserves. He was my superior, and whenever I strayed from the straight and narrow he called me to order using the familiar *du*, but addressing me as gunner. His intonation brooked no familiarities.

That is why I hesitate to trust my memory, which has him called Hans after the hero of the children's song I sang to him in the dark wood until he sang back, which even has him referring to himself as Hänschen and saying in the ambulance, anxious to learn the condition of certain irreplaceable body parts and his present status as a man, "Check in Hänschen's trousers." No, nothing was missing. But my guardian angel had no soulmate of his own. Without him I would have been nabbed. Whenever danger was in the air, he would say, "Watch out you don't get nabbed, gunner."

During the early postwar years and even later, as long as amputees in wheelchairs were part and parcel of our street scene or given jobs sitting at desks stamping papers, I couldn't help asking myself, Is that him? Could that puny invalid of a bureaucrat drawling out questions without looking up and issuing you the pass you need to get to Berlin-Charlottenburg, could that be my Hänschen with the Berlin accent?

I have no idea how I made it over the Ore Mountains. Some stretches by train and—since trains were then a rarity—by horse and cart through villages whose names now escape me.

Once I was sitting in an open wood-and-gas-powered truck that was puffing its way uphill when suddenly an American fighter-bomber swooped down and the truck went up in flames seconds after I jumped off and rolled into a ditch at the side of the road: I had seen the plane coming. Had the scene been shot for an action movie called *As Everything Fell to Pieces,* they would have had to use a stuntman for my part.

Then—a total blank. Nothing to attach to the plot. Somehow I managed to make progress. And never did I deviate from my marching orders. Detours were out of the question.

I spent one night in the mountains with a couple who kept rabbits behind the house. Man and wife were both teachers. I had begun to run a temperature, and they offered to look after me, give me civilian clothes, and hide me in the cellar until, as they said, "it's all finally over." Their son, whose picture, ringed in black, I saw in a bookcase, had fallen at the Battle of Sevastopol. He was about twenty years young. His clothing would have fit me. I could reach out and take down his books. Like me—I could see from the picture—he parted his hair on the left.

I didn't stay. I wanted to go where my travel papers ordered me to go, to cross the mountains in my own trousers, which after a thorough washing had ceased to attract ants. The couple stood in front of their shingle-roofed cottage and watched me disappear.

And I made it, heaven knows how, all the way to Karlsbad, that other spa with literary and—given its connection with Metternich—political connotations, and where I fell to my knees in the street and couldn't get up.

I had a fever. It may have been caused by the grenade splinters in my shoulder or the lack of a tetanus shot. My left arm was now stiff down to my fingertips, but I don't recall being in pain.

It was a good thing I had a properly stamped document, because, as I later heard, one of the infamous bloodhounds was known to go up to soldiers lying in the street and immediately check their marching orders, the only piece of paper they had. The military policeman who picked me up followed my marching orders to the letter even though both spas were designated hospital centers. He apparently draped me over the back seat of his motorcycle—I was unconscious—buckled me down, and drove me to neighboring Marienbad, where for the panzer gunner the war had indeed ended, and the fear drained out of him; it did however return to haunt my sleep, where it had taken up long-term residence.

Guests at Table

By the time the military policeman had dropped me off in Marienbad and I had been placed, still feverish, in a freshly made bed, the Führer was no more. Word had it he had fallen in the last battle for the Reich, for Berlin. His departure was taken as only to be expected. Nor did I miss him particularly, since his often cited and never doubted grandeur was as naught under the hands of the ever busier nurses, whose fingers did not stray beyond my left arm yet made themselves felt in every bone of my body.

Nor did I later—my wound cured and one of thousands in the far-flung network of prisoner-of-war camps, first in the Upper Palatinate, then under Bavarian skies—suffer withdrawal symptoms. He was gone as if he had never been, had never quite existed and was now to be forgotten, as if you could live perfectly well without the Führer.

By the same token, his "heroic death" was lost in the mass of individual deaths and was soon no more than a footnote. Now you could even make jokes about him, about him and his mistress, who had been all but invisible till then but was now good for a rumor or two. Much more tangible than his figure, wherever he may have been, was the lilac blossoming in the hospital garden in early May.

Everything that happened in the military hospital or shortly thereafter in the POW camps seemed to have escaped the tick-tock of time. We breathed inside an air bubble, and everything that had till so recently been accepted as fact now existed only approximately. There was only one certainty: I was hungry.

WHENEVER my children and grandchildren ask me for details about the end of the war—"What was it like then?"—I respond with the utmost self-confidence: "From the moment I was behind barbed wire, I was hungry."

But what I really should say is that hunger occupied me like an empty house, holding its place whether I was in barracks or out under an open sky.

It gnawed. We talk about gnawing hunger. And the youth I am trying to imagine as an early damaged edition of myself was one of the thousands who were plagued by the rodent Hunger. As part of a portion of the now disarmed but long since bedraggled, out of step German army, I was a pitiful sight, and not even if it had been possible would I have sent my mother a picture of her boy.

The initials stenciled on to the backs of our jackets in an indelible white paint had turned us into POWs. For the time being, our only activity from dawn to dusk and into our dreams, was "sniffing the steam from the cabbage pot."

Of course, much as my hunger gnawed away at me, it was nothing compared to what I later learned had been the prescribed variety in the concentration camps or our camps for Russian prisoners of war, which caused hundreds of thousands to starve, starve to death. But the only hunger I can put into words is my own; it is the only hunger inscribed in me, so to speak. I am the only one I can ask, How did it feel? How long did it make itself felt?

Once it appeared, it took over, making a noise that has stuck in my ear ever since and to which the expression "stomach rumblings" does not begin to do justice.

MEMORY likes to refer to blind spots. What has stuck turns up uncalled for, under various guises; it enjoys disguise. Often it gives only vague information. Moreover, its mesh is sometimes large, sometimes small. Scraps of feeling and thought literally fall through it.

But what was I after besides something to chew on? What moved the youth bearing my name once his faith in the final victory was gone? Only the lack of food?

And how can the gnawings of resident hunger be remembered? Can an empty stomach be filled after the fact?

Aren't there more pressing needs, such as making an over-sated public aware of the hunger in present-day African refugee camps, or giving an overall account of hunger, as I did in my novel *The Flounder,* of "how it spread in print" and refused to abate, in other words, telling endless hunger stories.

Again my I pushes its way to the fore, asking how long it lasted, this hunger I had never before been and would seldom thereafter be plagued by. Was it from mid-May to early August?

But what would be gained by defining its precise boundaries?

When after all my practice and despite all my misgivings I say "I"—meaning when I try to recall what my state of being was sixty years ago—my I of that time may not be a complete and utter stranger, but it is lost and as distant as a distant relative.

One thing is certain: I found my first camp, the one in the Upper Palatinate near the Czech border, frightening. Its guards, well nourished the lot of them, belonged to the American Third Army. With their casual ways, the Yanks might have come from outer space. At least that was how the prisoners—who numbered, if I may make a rough guess, ten thousand or so—saw them. The setting was somewhat similar to that of the old Grafenwöhr military camp: it, too, once you got past the barbed wire, had been surrounded by a wooded area.

Likewise certain are the following: I was very young at the time of my gnawing hunger, and I had until recently served as a tank gunner of the lowest rank in a division that had existed, under the name of Jörg von Frundsberg, only as a legend.

When weighed as part of a camp-wide delousing operation, during which I made my first acquaintance with a powder by the name of DDT, my skin and bones could muster no more than a hundred and ten pounds, a condition we assumed was in line with the Morgenthau Plan which had been concocted for us.

This means of punishing all German prisoners of war, the brainchild of the American politician it was named after, required the most stringent thrift of everyone affected by it. After roll call we had to avoid every superfluous move, because we were allotted a daily intake of only 850 calories, the amount calculated to be in three-quarters of a liter of barley soup with here and there a globule of fat floating on the surface, a quarter of a loaf of army bread, and a minuscule portion of margarine or cheese spread or a dollop of jam. There was plenty of water. And no end of DDT.

The word calorie had not been part of my vocabulary before I experienced my gnawing hunger. Hunger was my first teacher.

And because I knew little and had picked up a lot of misinformation and was only now—and only by fits and starts—becoming aware of the extent of my stupidity, I began soaking things up like a sponge.

WHENEVER I am asked the routine reporters' questions about the end of the Third Reich, as a representative of that soon-to-be-extinct minority still brought together under the rubric of "eyewitnesses," I turn immediately to my camp experience and the all too frugal calorie allotment, because even though I had learned of the unconditional capitulation of the German Reich—or its "collapse," a term that soon caught on—as a wounded soldier in the military hospital center of Marienbad, it seems to have registered only in passing with me, or have struck me in my ignorance as something temporary, a cease-fire of sorts. I somehow failed to perceive that the adjective *unconditional* preceding the word *capitulation* meant *final, incontrovertible.*

In Marienbad, the combination of spring weather and the nurses' physical proximity had a provocative effect on me. Fixated as I was on my pubescent discomposure, I felt more beleaguered than released. Peace was an empty concept, the word freedom still awkward. True, I no longer had to fear the military police or the gallows tree, but a fresh start of the sort I felt later as a whole new era, a license to begin again from scratch, I did not yet feel.

Perhaps the place itself had an effect on my reaction. Formerly a resort where one went to take the waters, and during my Maytime stay a backwater decked in vernal green, it was too soporific a setting for marking the monumental day as the end of one era and the beginning of the next. Then, too, white- and black-skinned Americans—like the Russians in neighboring Karlsbad—had been in the city for days, and we eagerly awaited their appearance.

Silently they came on rubber soles. What a contrast to our jackboots. We couldn't get over it. The victors' nonstop gum chewing made an impression on me, too, as did their reluctance to walk even short distances: they were always lounging in their jeeps. It was like a movie taking place in the distant future.

There was a GI posted in front of the villa that served as our hospital. We couldn't quite think of him as standing guard because as often as not he was squatting on his heels stroking his submachine gun. And we couldn't help wondering whether he was there to keep us from escaping or to keep the Czech militia, humiliated for so long by the German presence in their country, from taking revenge. When I tried my schoolboy English out on him, he, the conqueror, gave me, the conquered, a pack of chewing gum.

BUT what was really going on in the head of the seventeen-year-old youth who claimed to be physically mature and was under the care of Finnish nurses in what had once been a glorified boarding house?

For a while, nothing specific: he is only outwardly there, lying quietly in a row of beds. Soon he is permitted to stand and take his first steps along the corridor, then in front of the house. The wound in his right thigh has as good as healed; his left hand—the grenade splinter had caused his arm to stiffen from the shoulder down—has to be moved, bent, kneaded, finger by finger.

But all that is soon behind him and forgotten. What remains

is the scent of the Finnish Lottas, as the nurses were called: a mixture of plain soap and birch-sap hair lotion.

The war had taken the young women far from their Karelian forests. They spoke little and, smiling sympathetically the while, gave me the no-nonsense treatment, which is probably why its pushes and pulls left a deeper impression on the still-pimpled youth under their healing fingers than the news of the unconditional surrender of all German combat units.

Yet whenever the fateful date came up on the calendar and the eyewitness was asked what "liberation day" meant to him, he would let the question dictate the answer. Instead of reacting with know-it-all hindsight—"I was suddenly free of all my anxieties, though I had little idea of what freedom would mean for us now that we were liberated"—I should have come out and said, "I was and remained a prisoner of myself because all day every day and into my dreams I hungered after girls, and 'liberation day' was surely no exception. My every thought was of one thing and one thing only. I fingered and longed to be fingered."

This other hunger, appeasable in the short term with the right hand, outlasted the gnawing variety, which did not take possession of me until—after the satisfying and hence memory-unencumbering hospital meals of what must have been soup and goulash with noodles and, on Sundays, meatloaf smothered in onion sauce and mashed potatoes—Morgenthau's starvation rations took over our fenced-in existence.

But it may also be that the practically photographic images I had of the nurses in ultra-close proximity, or the beloved face of a schoolgirl in braids, served as votive pictures in the POW camp and assuaged the gnawing hunger a bit.

In any case, I felt the lack of both one and the other, and one hunger of the two was always wide awake. Yet when I look back on it all, I don't see myself in constant pain. Just as, though here the image is a bit fuzzy, I handled the one need manually—first with the right hand, then, as the wound healed and as was only natural for a lefty like me, with the left—I took care of the other to some extent by maintaining a supply of goods for barter. The first time I put them on the market was when we were transferred from the Upper Palatinate to a more spacious, open-air camp in Bad Aibling, where we were broken up into manageable groups and moved into fenced-in barracks. Going out to work, we came in regular contact with our guards. I offered my services as interpreter and made it clear that I had a small cache of articles available for exchange. Once more my execrable school English passed the test, enabling me to apply the business strategies I had learned at my mother's knee and strike bargain after bargain.

IT's amazing how much can fit into an empty haversack. My stock came from the two short days of anarchy vouchsafed us in Marienbad when German order went up in smoke, the Americans had not yet marched in on their rubber soles, and the insufficiently armed Czech militia failed to fill the gap and take matters into their own hands.

A space suddenly opened up for those of us no longer bedridden. We scoured the neighborhood for loot. Next door to our villa was another villa-like edifice, complete with turret, bay window, balcony, and patio. Hours before, this architecturally very busy structure had housed the district headquarters of the local branch of the National Socialist Party. Or perhaps only a branch of the party administration. In any case, now that the district leaders and other bigwigs had fled, it was just standing there open. Though it may actually have been standing there locked and somebody had helped things along with a crowbar.

Be that as it may, all the walking wounded, myself among them (as I have indicated, I could by now grasp things with my left hand), rummaged through the offices, the conference room, the pigeon-infested turret room, and finally the basement, which had a room the officials had furnished with couches and wickerwork for gemütlich evening get-togethers: group photos of party comrades in uniform lined the walls. I seem to remember having seen a Faith and Beauty poster showing girls with bouncing breasts doing gymnastics. Only the obligatory portrait of the Führer was missing. And the usual flags and pennants. There wasn't a single item worth lifting. When we got there, the cupboards were bare, literally. "Nothing to drink," cursed a sergeant, whose missing left ear is encapsulated in the omnium-gatherum of my memories.

Then on the top floor I struck gold. In the lowest drawer of a desk at which some party chief must have sat out the war in comfort I came upon a cigar box containing approximately fifty glittering silver pins, whose heads were faithful reproductions in miniature of an embossed bunker. The inscription stamped under each tiny bunker confirmed it beyond a doubt: they were Siegfried Line souvenirs, popular prewar collectors' items. I recognized them from having seen the bunkers in newsreels.

During my childhood, the fortification of the Reich's western frontier with staggered tank barriers and bunkers of all sizes provided the regular impetus for flickering pictorial reports and brash verbal commentaries accompanied by a rhythmically aggressive score. Now the nickel-silver commemoratives had a kind of heroic futility about them: they had been devised to honor the virtuous workers who built the fortifications along the French border, a labor force that after 1938 had doubtless included Sudeten German volunteers. I can still see the newsreel images: men shoveling, cement-mixers churning, huge concrete blocks.

My friends and I were thrilled to see this bulwark rising against our traditional arch enemy, France. We thought the kilometers of tank barriers blending into the rolling countryside were indomitable. We played at sighting targets through observation slits: if we didn't get sent to the submarines, then at least we could man the bunkers heroically.

Six years later, those pins must have reminded me of my prewar games and dreams as they now remind me—I can almost count them in their cigar box—of the immediate postwar years.

I found little else of interest in the drawers, though I was able to fill up my haversack with two small blank notebooks, some elegant writing paper, and a few pencils, if not the Pelikan fountain pen I had been hoping for. I'm not sure whether I managed to grab an eraser and a pencil sharpener.

Others lifted teaspoons, pastry forks, and various useless items like napkin rings. Some even took rubber stamps and stamp-pads, as if they could issue passes for leaves and business trips.

Oh yes. I also came away with three ivory dice and a leather dice cup. Did I have time for a lucky throw? Two sixes, a three, or even a five?

Later, after we had been transferred from the Upper Palatinate camp, I used them to play dice with a boy my age, the friend I had so longed to have in the dark pine wood, who now actually had a name, Joseph, and spoke a bookish, Bavarian-tinted German. It rained a lot. We dug a hole and would huddle under his tarpaulin for shelter. We talked about God and the world, about our experiences as altar boys—his permanent, mine very much auxiliary. He believed I thought nothing was holy. We both got deloused. It didn't bother us in the slightest. Like me he wrote poems, but we had very different plans for the future, which later, and then only gradually, became history. For the time being the Siegfried Line pins were more important.

AT FIRST I was only vaguely aware of the value of my sudden windfall, but once I had been transferred from Bad Aibling to a labor camp and had joined a work detail charged with felling adolescent beech trees, I was able to use my English again— "This is a souvenir from the Siegfried Line"—to find buyers for three of the shiny pins.

The guard assigned to us, a good-natured Virginia farm boy who had as yet no war souvenirs to show the folks at home, was willing to part with a whole pack of Lucky Strikes for a single pin. Back in the camp, I swapped it for a loaf of army bread. For the nonsmoker, that meant four filling daily rations.

When another guard, a black truck driver with whom, as a matter of principle, the pink-skinned farm boy exchanged not a word, traded me a rather doughy loaf of cornmeal bread for two Siegfried Line pins, an old-timer in the camp advised me to toast it. He sliced it up and cut the slices in two, then laid them out on the top of the cylindrical cast-iron stove that was kept lit even in the summer months, because come evening the men in the wood-felling commando would cook up everything they could find—thistles, dandelions and the like—into a spinach of sorts. Some even threw in roots.

An NCO who, as he put it, had chalked up some wonderful years in France as an occupier, pulled a dozen wriggly frogs out of his haversack, cut them up alive, and threw the legs in with the spinach.

The barracks, in which two rows of plank beds replaced the bunk beds we were used to, had been occupied until the war's end by forced laborers. We found Cyrillic inscriptions carved in the wood of the planks and beams, and some soldiers who had returned from Smolensk and Kiev maintained the men had been Ukrainians.

The stove had been brought here for the laborers. We pretty much saw ourselves as their successors: we, too, carved inscriptions in the planks and beams—the names of the girls we longed for plus the usual obscenities.

I hid my toasted cornmeal bread in newsprint covered with the bold-faced Stand Firm headlines of the last days of the war and tucked it away between a plank and the straw mattress to supplement my daily ration. Only with such economies could I keep my hunger within limits.

When our column returned from wood felling the next evening, there was not a trace of the bread or its packaging. The soldier who had shown me how to toast the bread and received a quarter of the loaf for his pains reported the disappearance to the sergeant in charge of the barracks, a sergeant of the traditional, disciplinarian school.

At which point all the straw mattresses and clothes of anyone who had remained in the barracks—because they had been

sick or assigned to fatigue duty instead of felling wood or clearing rubble—were searched.

The remains of the toast-cum-newsprint were found under
the straw of a Luftwaffe lieutenant first class—the camp mixed
common soldiers with officers all the way up to captain in rank—
who until then had made a show of being unfailingly jaunty.

In our unwritten laws, what he had done was called comrade
theft. There was nothing worse. It was a crime that demanded
immediate condemnation and retribution. Though personally
involved as victim and eyewitness, I cannot or will not remember whether once the verdict had been delivered by a duly ap-
pointed barracks court I took part physically in delivering lashes
with the Wehrmacht belt to the bare ass.

True, I can picture weals on festering flesh, but they may
have been painted in after the fact, because once experiences of
this sort blossom into stories, they take on a life of their own and
flaunt one detail or another.

In any case, the fury felt by the common soldier toward
every officer he had known was transferred to the thief, and the
thrashing was excessive: a war's worth of hatred was venting itself. As for me, who had until recently known nothing but unconditional obedience, having been drilled in it from my days in
the Hitler Youth, I lost my last vestige of respect for the officers
of the Wehrmacht of the Great German Reich.

Shortly thereafter the "Luftwaffe guy," who had been transferred to the infantry as a last-ditch Hermann Göring Fund con-
tribution, was moved to another barracks.

The cornmeal toast didn't taste bad, slightly sweet, a bit like
zwieback. The Siegfried Line pins were responsible for many
more portions of toast, which I would dunk in mushroom soup.

I had found chanterelles in a stand of short-trunked conifers and, versed as I was in mushrooms and Kashubian mushroom specialties since childhood, I even made a dish from agarics of the lactarius variety and, later, from puffballs, frying them like chanterelles on the stove in the dollop of margarine we received as part of our daily ration. I also came to like thistle spinach. These were the first dishes I made on my own. The private contributed salt, and I shared my mushroom feast with him.

I HAVE enjoyed cooking for guests ever since. And not only for those who bring the here and now into the house, but also for characters I have invented or called up from history. So recently I had Michel de Montaigne, the young Henri de Navarre, and—as the biographer of the mature Henri, Henri the Fourth—the elder Mann brother as guests at my table—a small but garrulous group that indulged in quotations.

We talked about kidney- and gallstones, the Massacre of Saint Bartholomew, the other Mann brother and their Hanseatic background, then back to the Massacre and the endless trials of the Huguenots, and finally the similarities between Bordeaux and Lübeck. Along the way we cursed lawyers as the plague of society, compared hard stool with soft, evoked the Sunday chicken in every French pot, and bemoaned—even as we delighted in the sweetbreads smothered in agarics that followed the fish soup—the woeful state of enlightenment after so much progress. We also debated the ever timely question of whether Paris was worth a mass. And along with the latest yield of our Behlendorf walnut tree—which accompanied the cheese platter—the topic of Calvinism as the midwife of capitalism was laid on the table.

The later Henri laughed. Montaigne cited Livy or Plutarch. The elder Mann brother mocked his younger brother's hard-wearing leitmotifs. I praised the art of quotation.

My first guest, however, the private I dished up the chanter-elles to, told me about the temple ruins on Greek islands, the beauty of Norwegian fjords, the wine cellars in French castles, the highest mountains in the Caucasus, and about his trip to Brussels—where he swore the best *pommes frites* were to be had. He had marched through half of Europe—that's how long he'd worn the uniform, how battle-tried and border-resistant he was. After our plates were empty, he regaled his host with the old-time march, "A Little Town in Poland."

Just as the bulletins of the Wehrmacht High Command had helped to enhance my knowledge of geography, so my guest's wartime experience had furnished him with the chatty cosmo-politanism served up to us during the sustained period of peace at the home slide shows of manically shutter-clicking tourists. And did he not say then, "I want to travel everywhere with my Erna, later, after the gunsmoke has settled"?

TRUE, the mushroom dish and thistle spinach made a cook and host of me, but the prerequisites for the pleasure I still take in combining this stew with that, of stuffing this with that, adding this or that ingredient to get the taste I'm after, and imagining living and dead guests as I cook—the prerequisites were already present in the early period of gnawing hunger, when the wounded soldier, healed, was torn from the nurses' gentle hands and when, having taken the cure in Marienbad, he was sent to the Upper Palatinate hunger colony.

Among ten and more thousand prisoners of war and after seventeen years of eating my fill—we had seldom had to tighten our belts at home—I learned what it is to be hungry. Hunger, because it had the first and last word, was a source of gnawing pain, but also a source of sparkling inspiration: the more my stomach shrank, the more my imagination grew.

Not a single one of the ten thousand starved to death, of course, but the want of food gave us an ascetic appearance. Even those not so inclined underwent a spiritual transformation. My new spiritual look must have suited me: my enlarged eyes saw more than was before them, choirs rejoicing beyond the senses. And since hunger brought home the maxim "Man does not live by bread alone" not only as camp cynicism but also as consolatory bromide, many of us felt an increased desire for spiritual food.

Something happened in the camp. Activities designed to do away with the collective, oppressive tedium arose out of the blue. The listless wandering, the sleepwalking came to an end. The vanquished were pulling themselves together. In fact, total defeat liberated forces that had gone into hibernation during the long war years and were now awakening, as if victory were still possible—though in a different sphere.

The occupying powers tolerated the activities, which they regarded as proof of what seemed the Germans' inborn gift for organization.

We organized ourselves into groups and sub-groups, each with its own field to hoe, fostering general education, art appreciation, philosophy, the renewal of faith, or practical knowledge. Everything ran according to a timetable, everything was thorough and punctual.

There were courses in Latin and classical Greek and Esperanto. There were study groups for algebra and for higher mathematics. From Aristotle via Spinoza all the way to Heidegger, there was room for high-flown speculation and profound meditation.

Nor did professional training get short shrift: future shopkeepers were initiated into double-entry bookkeeping, civil engineers into statistics, lawyers into subterfuge, economists of tomorrow made familiar with profit-oriented laws of the marketplace and tips from confident stock market speculators. All this with a view to peace and the potential it had opened up.

Then there were the Bible circles. And a popular introduction to Buddhism. And because a number of pocket-size musical instruments had survived the losses otherwise sustained during the retreat, a harmonica orchestra gathered daily for outdoor rehearsals and gave performances attended even by American officers and foreign journalists. The band's repertory of the Soldiers' Internationale, "Lili Marleen," recent hits, and concert pieces like "A Petersburg Sleigh Ride" and Liszt's Hungarian Rhapsody was always warmly applauded.

There were also several singing groups, including an a cappella chorus that regaled a small band of music lovers with motets and madrigals every Sunday.

All this and more was available on a daily basis: we had time to burn. In the Upper Palatinate camp we were not permitted to work on the outside; we were not even allowed out to clear rubble in nearby Nuremberg. There was nothing for us to do but sit around in our tents, barracks, and spacious stalls—the camp must originally have been the garrison of a cavalry regiment—bravely learning to battle hunger and its gnawings.

Few opted out of our program, only those who took pleasure in lamenting their lot and grieving over battles lost. Some even thought they could win the battles—the tank encounter at Kursk or even the Battle of Stalingrad—after the fact with their sandbox tactics. Many more, however, signed up for more than one course—taking, say, stenography in the morning and Middle High German poetry in the afternoon.

And what made a scholar out of me? Given that I had pretty much turned my back on school since the handsome uniform of the Luftwaffe auxiliary graced my frame, the sensible thing to do would have been to go for mathematics and Latin, my two weak subjects, and to develop my knowledge of art by attending the lecture series "Early Gothic Sculpture in the Naumburg Cathedral." I would also have profited from a therapy group dealing with the widely spread camp phenomenon of "Behavioral Disturbances During Puberty." But hunger drove me to a course in the art of cooking.

I found the tempting announcement on the notice board in front of the camp administration building. It stood out because of the stick figure wearing a chef's hat. This wildest of all courses was to meet for two two-hour sessions daily in the former veterinary ward. Bring your own writing paper.

How fortunate that when pilfering the silver Siegfried Line pins to barter with I had not disdained the dice cup and ivory dice or, even more important, a pile of standard typewriter paper, two small notebooks, and a handful of pencils.

ALTHOUGH my memory is porous in one or another area and I no longer know, for example, whether my adolescent fuzz needed shaving during my camp stay or even when I first acquired a razor and shaving brush of my own, I need have no recourse to my usual stratagems to evoke the stark, all but empty room of the veterinary ward. The walls were of white tile, rimmed at eye level with a blue glazed border. Although I can say nothing about most of the pedagogical accessories, I can see the blackboard opposite the wide window and imagine it serving the instruction of future army veterans with illustrations of all things equine— the intestinal tract, the hocks, the heart, the hooves, the bite— and questions about the quadruped's illnesses and habits: How does one treat colic in a horse? When do horses sleep?

Confident as I am about the room's appearance, I am not certain whether it was left vacant after our two-hour "Cooking for Beginners" sessions or whether other subjects—classical Greek, say, or civil engineering—were taught there. Perhaps the blackboard was the site of the first profit-margin calculations of the coming Economic Miracle, or early intimations of fusions in the coal and steel industries, or the popular current practice of hostile corporate takeover, though the versatile space may as easily have been used for church services of one or another denomination, the high, pointed windows giving the rectangle of a room with its slight echo and Lysol rather than equine smell a sacred quality.

In any case, the place has served me repeatedly as a backdrop for scenes that go off in all kinds of directions: I have never lacked for characters. In *Local Anesthetic*, for example, the story of what took place there is sketched out rather than told in all its glory by the teacher named Starusch, who transfers the "Cooking for Beginners" course to the camp at Bad Aibling—to Upper Bavaria, in other words—and leaves out the blackboard.

What follows is an attempt at using believable facts to refute this fictitious account, in which a faceless Herr Brühsam appears as the master chef. After all, I am the one whom hunger drove to take the abstract cooking course.

I CAN see him clearly, the master chef—one of a kind, though his name escapes me. I see him standing at the blackboard, gangling and emaciated, a middle-aged apostolic figure in military dress who demanded that his pupils call him Chef. But there was nothing militaristic in the curly-headed graybeard's demand. His eyebrows were so long you wanted to comb them.

The first thing he did was give us a rundown of his career. He had gone from Bucharest to Sofia to Budapest and had arrived in Vienna a chef much in demand, though he dropped the names of luxury hotels in other cities as well and claimed to have been the personal chef of a Croatian or Hungarian count in Zagreb or Szeged. He even cited Vienna's Hotel Sacher as proof of his artistic qualifications. I cannot be certain whether he also cooked for illustrious passengers in the dining car of the legendary Orient Express and thereby witnessed the intricate plots and complicated murders that even detectives with the proper literary credentials and devilishly clever sleuthing abilities had trouble untangling.

What I do know for certain is that our master chef was active only in southeastern Europe, that is, a region of many peoples where razor-sharp distinctions apply to more than cuisines, yet mixing is also in evidence.

If his background information was to be trusted, he came from far-off Bessarabia. This made him what was called at the time a trophy German, who, like the Germans from the Baltic countries, had been called *heim ins Reich,* "home to the Reich" as a consequence of the nonaggression pact between Hitler and Stalin. Though what did this young ignoramus know about the consequences, evident to this day, of the Hitler-Stalin Pact?

Shortly after the war broke out, as everyone—even I—knew, Polish peasants from the hinterlands of my native city, starting in the Kashubian region but reaching as far as the Tuchel Heath, had been turned out of their farms to make room for the Baltic trophy Germans. Their broad accent was easy to imitate, it was so close to our Low German; besides, for a short time I had shared a school bench with a boy from Riga.

But our master chef's Deutsch—or Deitsch, as he pronounced it—was like none I had ever heard: he had trouble with the definite article, for example, and used Austrianisms— *bisserl* for *bisschen* ("a little"), *Kapuster* for *Weisskohl* ("cabbage"), and when making a point at the blackboard, waving his arms eloquently in the air, he spoke through his nose like the movie star Hans Moser.

This master chef—demoted, as he put it, "from gunner to goulash-cannon" and destined to remain a private to the bitter end—may have seemed a sadist out to torture his famished pupils with visions of exquisite dishes like prime rib with horse-radish sauce, pike croquettes, shashlik, wild rice with truffles, and glazed breast of pheasant with wine-cured sauerkraut, but to him we were meat-and-potatoes Philistines in need of enlightenment. Coarse pleasures of the palate he relegated to the margins of his elucidations, which emphasized the principles of cooking, though they also tended to feature the slaughter of the animal to be consumed.

We, the famished, took it all down. Page after scribbled page. First you put . . . then you add . . . let it simmer for two and a half hours . . .

If only I had managed to hold on to even one of the two notebooks of my Marienbad inheritance. But of all the voluble two-hour sessions, attended by more than one venerable pater-familias alongside us whippersnappers, only two or three survived on record, though survive they did, down to the last drop of rendered fat.

He was a master of evocation. Single-handedly he would hurl force-fed dreams under the knife. He could squeeze flavor out of nothing, whip the creamiest soups out of air. Two or three of his nasal words would soften any stone. Were I able to invite the critics who have grown old with me to sit down with him at table, I would ask him, as guest of honor, to enlighten them on the miracle of freehand imagination, that is, white-paper sorcery, but incurable know-it-alls that they are they would list-lessly lap up my chickpeas stewed with lamb chops and reach immediately for their literary cholesterol counters.

"MY TOPIC for today," he said by way of introduction, "is pig," and with a sure hand but much screeching of chalk he covered the board with the outline of a full-grown sow. Then he divided the beast into Roman-numeraled parts. "Number one is tail, best appreciated when cooked in your usual lentil soup."

He proceeded to the legs, from the trotters up to the knee joint—that, too, suited to simmering in soup. Next he went from the knuckle of the front leg to the haunch of the back leg, then from the neck to the loins, ribs, and stomach, peppering his commentary with irrefutable bits of wisdom: "Neck is juicier than rib." "Filet of pork should be wrapped in dough and baked in oven." And other tips I follow to this day.

He advised us, who had no more than a ladleful of watery cabbage or barley soup to look forward to, to slit each joint of pork across its length and breadth with a sharp knife so that the fat would come out and "make nice crispy crust."

At that point he let his gaze wander, looking each of us in the eye, sparing no one, me included, and said, "I know, gentlemen. My mouth is watering as much as yours," whereupon, after a carefully measured pause during which each of us heard himself and the others swallow, he announced out of pity and in recognition of our common need, "But enough about fat. Let us now turn to throat-slitting."

Even though the notebooks are gone, the onion primes my memory and helps me to recite the master's hammered-out adages. In retrospect I see how he used pantomime too, demonstrating with his arms the urgency of collecting the blood while it was still warm ("Hot blood's good blood!"), the importance of stirring it tirelessly to keep it from clumping ("You must stir, keep stirring!").

We would sit on stools and boxes or the tiled floor stirring the blood to the left and right and crosswise in imaginary troughs as it poured steaming out of the imaginary stab wound and gradually diminished to a trickle. We could almost hear the pig's screeches dying down, feel the heat of the blood, breathe its smell.

Going to slaughter feasts in later years was always a disappointment for me: the reality of it lagged far behind the master's evocations. It was mere butchery, a pale echo of his words.

We learned to reduce the blood by boiling it with marjoram-seasoned oats and to stuff the newly cleaned intestines with the resulting mushy paste so it could be bound into sausages. His last bit of advice for the sausage filling was "Remember, gentlemen, thirty grams of raisins to every five liters of blood."

My taste buds were so primed in anticipation that I have gobbled down oatmeal-and-blood sausages with mashed potatoes and sauerkraut ever since, and not only because I was constantly hard up in the fifties and it was a cheap meal: even today in the unavoidable Paris-Bar in Berlin I savor the French *boudin*. The North German dish of pork preserved in blood thickened with shredded kidneys is one of my favorites. And if I have guests, various and sundry card players from various and sundry times in my life, I enjoy putting this coarse fare on the table.

Oh, the pleasure of a double-or-nothing hand followed by steaming fried or boiled sausages, of watching the tightly tied casing burst or be slit open and the raisin-and-oat filling, thick and lumpy with blood, ooze out. Yes, that Bessarabian chef in the Upper Palatinate camp conditioned my taste buds for life.

"BUT one more thing, gentlemen," he said, "another possibility. We are not through with pig yet."

Just as Salome points her long finger at the head of John the Baptist, so he pointed his at the pig's head he had drawn with chalk and numbered, the way he numbered the neck, haunch, and curl of a tail. "Now we make delicious pig's-head brawn, but please, gentlemen, no gelatin from factory . . ." It was a matter of principle that the brawn should generate a jelly of its own from the fatback, snout, and earlobes. He then proceeded to celebrate the process whereby the pig's head is split in two, placed in a large pot, covered with salted water, and simmered for a good two hours with cloves, bay leaves, and an unsliced onion for flavoring.

During the late sixties, the days of protest, when anger, rage, and fury were as cheap as headlines and sauerkraut, I wrote a long poem titled "The Jellied Pig's Head," in which I had everything stew in the traditional spices but added a "knife tip of clotting, thickened, leftover rage" and healthy portions of the indignation that had run wild because people felt so helpless against government-sanctioned violence, and of the anger that had led to the ranting red banners of the revolutionaries of '68.

When it came to the more prosaic deboning of the head, however, the pupil followed the master. Using both hands, our chef mimed how to remove the meat and fat from the bone and the snout from the cartilage once they had cooled and how to scrape the jelly from the jelly-rich ear flaps—his every gesture purposeful. He made fast work of the jawbone, scooped the congealed brains out of the brainpan, emptied the eye sockets, held up first the tongue, after detaching it from the gullet, next the large lump of a cheek, after freeing it from its layer of fat, and then, while skillfully cubing the entire spoils, launched into an enumeration of what constituted the simmering stock that the lean meat from the breast or neck was swimming in: finely chopped leeks, sliced pickled gherkins, mustard seeds, capers, grated lemon rind, and coarsely ground peppercorns.

Next he added pinches of green and red paprika—"but not hot kind"—and brought everything—the cubes of meat and mounds of seasoning—to the boil again, whereupon he ushered the ceremony to a solemn close by pouring what might have been holy water from a phantom demijohn but was in fact vinegar into the nearly full pot: you needed a lot of vinegar because it lost its punch as the brew cooled. "Now, gentlemen, we pour into earthenware bowls, put in cool spot, and wait and wait with patience we have plenty of."

For an extended pause, during which the ideal of a jellied pig's head generated a jelly of its own, without factory gelatin, and onetime soldiers crammed Latin words and mathematical formulas in the balmy spring air outside the former veterinary ward, he looked each member of his audience, each victim of his magic, in the eye. Before any skepticism on our part could break the spell, he blinked a few times as if he, too, were awakening from a calorie-rich dream, and said in his nasal, movie-star voice, "Is ready now, firm now in bowls. You can cut with knife. Dinner is served, gentlemen."

After another pause and another round of blinks, he turned to the future: "Is good for breakfast also. When things will be better and enough pigs are in market again."

OF EVERYTHING that went astray I miss my notebooks the most: I would be more believable if I could quote from them.

Or was I too taken up by the master's performance of the rites—the simmering, the deboning, the detaching and cubing of the meat, the piling up of the seasonings—to take it all down?

Was the writing paper from my Marienbad stock, which I used for scribbling poems dealing with another variety of flesh and for sketching the wizened faces of veteran soldiers, too elegant for mundane recipes?

The answer is not long in coming: looking back, I see my pencil flying across lost paper of one variety or other, with or without erasures; I hear myself swallowing saliva, as the other pupils in the course must have done, to stifle the permanent sound of the rodent Hunger. Indeed, the master's lessons became so much a part of me that later, when, as that fortune-teller of a Bessarabian chef foretold, "enough pigs were in market again," I not only wrote a poem in celebration of jellied pig's head but also regaled my guests, living and from times past, with pots brimful of natural jelly. And I rarely missed the chance to regale the company—I once invited the publishers of the folk-song collection *Des Knaben Wunderhorn,* the Brothers Grimm, and the Romantic painter Philipp Otto Runge—with the tale of the abstract but hunger-stifling cooking course, in one or another of its variations.

I enjoyed varying the chef's origins: sometimes he came from the Hungarian Banat region; then I had him born in Austrian Bukovina, in the city of Czernowitz, where he would claim to have met the young poet Paul Celan, who was still Paul Antschel at the time; from Bukovina, his birthplace would move to Russian Bessarabia.

Sometimes I served sautéed potatoes with the brawn, sometimes plain black bread. My various guests—who included dignitaries from afar, the European Social Democratic Big Three (Brandt, Palme, Kreisky), to say nothing of friends from the Baroque, like Andreas Gryphius, who liked to call everything vanity of vanities, and Martin Opitz, before the plague got him, and Grimmelshausen's Mother Courasche and Grimmelshausen himself, when he was still Gelnhausen—seldom left anything on their plates. Sometimes I served the brawn as a first course, sometimes as the main course, but the recipe never varied.

The master also had much to say about the nature and virtues of sows, boars, and suckling pigs during those fast-moving two-hour sessions: we learned that where he came from they were all fattened with corn cobs but that there were also oak woods planted specially to supply them with acorns; that acorns made for firm and not overly fatty meat, but that the fat layer was not to be looked down upon, because it could be rendered in a pan into dripping and cracklings; that pig's liver, pig's heart, and pig's lung could be put through a meat grinder and—like the blood during the slaughtering process—turned into sausages ("But please, gentlemen, add marjoram!"); and that the smoking of ham and bacon was a high art.

When we all, myself included, believed we had attained the requisite degree of piety and verbal satiety, he said by way of conclusion, "Now, gentlemen, we are through with pig. So day after tomorrow I talk about something different. My topic for day after tomorrow is poultry. But let me say in advance: No goose without mugwort!"

Was it really only two days later that his adage became the epitome of a delectable stuffed goose for us all? It was more likely that days and days passed before I was back in the tiled room of the former veterinary ward that still reverberates in my memory, days good for nothing but the endless story of the ruminant Hunger, apart from rumors that sped through the camp dropping their young.

The rumor that all prisoners from the eastern part of Germany would be handed over to the Soviet occupation forces struck fear in the hearts of many. Then there was the one about how entire Cossack regiments that had fought on our side had been turned over to the Russians by the English and were committing group suicide—anything to escape Soviet revenge. There were also rumors of a mass release of prisoners, occasionally combined with talk of shipping the youngest inmates off for reeducation: to America! They'll knock the Hitler Youth out of you, the older soldiers jeered.

But the rumor with the longest run on the "latrine-vine" was the one about a long since planned, now approved, and soon to be enacted rearming of all unarmed prisoners of war. And with American equipment: "Sherman tanks, and so on . . ."

"Makes sense," I heard a sergeant reason. "From now on we're in it with the Amis"—we had begun calling Americans the "Amis" by then—"against the Ivans. They need us too. They won't get anywhere without us . . ."

Lots of men agreed with him. Things would start up again with the Russians—it was as clear as day. They should have figured it out before the Ivans marched into Poland, but it took them until now, when Adolf's out of the picture and also the other bigwigs, Goebbels and Himmler and so on, or under lock and key like Göring.

"Right. Our experience at the front as bulwark against the Red Tide. We know what it is to fight the Ivans, especially in winter. The Amis have no idea . . ."

"Count me out. I'd make myself scarce. Two years at Leningrad, the Pripyet marshes, the Oder front. I've had it!"

Even this prophetic view—prophetic in that a very few years

later, once Adenauer here and Ulbricht there had bought into the victors' systems, the Germans were rearmed and had two armies instead of one—faded in time, though without ever fully disappearing; even as this longest-lived latrine-vine legend circulated and had its believers—some officers started polishing their medals—it could not contend against the camp-wide need for education, both general and specialized, for biblical edification, for culture. Neither I nor any of my fellow pupils wished to save the West—or anything else for that matter—in American uniform. We peaceably succumbed to the culinary anesthetic for our gnawing hunger.

WHICH is probably why I recall that the two-hour goose session, immediately or shortly after the session devoted to making the most out of the pig, was especially beneficial to my later culinary development. Looking back, I see myself on the one hand as a boy out to gratify his diffuse desires and on the other as a seasoned cynic experienced in mangled corpses swinging from trees. Having burnt my fingers, I had no tolerance for any faith, be it in Führer or God. The only authority I was willing to recognize besides the private first class who had responded to my "Hans left home" was that emaciated, graying man whose eyebrows called out for a comb: he had the power to stave off my hunger, if only for two hours, with his words and gestures.

That is why our chef—who must have turned other ingredients into sausage, brought other animals under the knife, and shown us how to make various fishes and crablike creatures into delicacies—has remained so evocative a presence in my life that even now when I lard a leg of lamb with garlic and sage or skin a calf's rough tongue, he is there, peering at my fingers.

That is why his masterly supervision meant so much to me, for instance, in the late sixties, when the revolution was making itself felt—at least on paper, with exclamation marks—and when, preparing a Martinmas goose for the philosopher Ernst Bloch in my Niedstrasse flat in the district of Friedenau in Berlin, I was faced with a choice between apple or chestnut stuffing. The pupil, inoculated as he was with the admonition "No goose without mugwort!," went with the chestnuts, the master's recommendation. Bloch got half of the breast, a wing, plus the wishbone on his plate, the latter prompting him immediately to a lengthy disquisition. He praised the chestnut stuffing and told Anna, me, and the four astonished children a seemingly never-ending tale about "unfulfilled men," from Thomas Müntzer to Karl Marx and from the latter's messianic message to Old Shatterhand, the hero of Karl May, German Western writer extraordinaire, now thundering like Moses from Mount Sinai, now humming a Wagner motif, now evoking the oral origins of literature, now clearing the straight and narrow of some stumbling blocks in a whisper, and finally, after picking apart a fairy tale—was it Hansel and Gretel?—raised the chewed wishbone into the air, ordered a light to shine on his prophetic countenance, invoked his oft-cited principle, and launched into a paean to tall tales in general and in particular.

The children at the table—Franz, Raoul, Laura, and little Bruno—listened open-mouthed to our unusual guest, with the same faith in his words as I'd had in those of my master, the Bessarabian chef, when he recommended an exotic spice like mugwort for any and all goose stuffings.

———

SUDDENLY he was gone. No more chef. No one to appease our hunger with his "But please, gentlemen" gesture. Word had it he'd been transferred by order of the top authorities and had last been seen sitting between two military policemen in shiny white helmets.

This was immediately followed by the rumor that General Patton, who headed the Third American Army and whose speeches brimming with Russophobia had fanned the latrine-vine speculation that we would be rearmed and sent to a new eastern front, yes, this oh-so-farsighted general had commandeered our internationally renowned chef as his own personal chef so as to feed himself and his high-ranking guests in the style to which they were accustomed.

And when General Patton reportedly lost his life in an accident, a new spate of rumors started circulating: he had been murdered, poisoned most likely. And since his personal chef and our master of imaginary cuisine had been involved in the plot, he, the chef, had been put under lock and key together with a slew of other agents and shady characters. The trial against the conspirators as well as all relevant documents, had been declared top secret on the advice of a German expert. Throw it all together, and you have the makings of a novel or a film.

What the disappearance of the master and putative chef of General Patton meant for me at the time was an immediate increase in hunger pangs, but now after all these years I have a yen to do a script for that thriller. The southeast European cuisine puts General Patton into a cocky, war-mongering mood, which in turn puts my master teacher in danger because the loud-mouth general's war lust is of concern to more than the NKVD:

Western intelligence agencies, too, feel the need for remedial action. Patton is talking too loudly, too much, too soon. Patton has outlived his usefulness. Patton must go. Why not then by means of a goose whose stuffing is seasoned with a spice quite different from mugwort . . .

Such more or less are the terms in which my script would test the rules of the Cold War game and give a minute account of the birth of Organization Gehlen, the hotbed of the already active German intelligence. It would also benefit the German film industry.

NOT until the POW camp on the territory of the former Grafenwöhr military training ground had been partially closed—it was late May—and we had been transferred in trucks to the open-air camp of Bad Aibling in Upper Bavaria, where we were housed in holes in the ground under tents for several weeks, then split up and sent to work camps—not until then did my hunger abate. It was then that I managed to beef up my calorie-poor Morgenthau ration by trading with the shiny silver Siegfried Line pins.

I traded them for American cigarettes, which was quite lucrative because I was not yet tempted by tobacco and could trade the cigarettes for bread and peanut butter. A large can of corned beef has lodged itself in the tow-rope of my memory. Some hefty chocolate bars as well. And I think I was given an impressive supply of Gillette razor blades, though surely not for my own use.

Once, while still at the Bad Aibling camp, I got a bag of caraway seeds in exchange for three Camels and chewed them in memory of the caraway sauerkraut recipe of my missing master, though I saved some for the friend I'd made during those endless rains under the tarp, when we told each other's fortunes with the three dice. I can still see him—Joseph—and hear his unfailingly soft, even gentle voice. I can't get him out of my mind.

I wanted to be this, he that.

I said, There are many truths.

He said, There is only one.

I said, I don't believe in anything anymore.

He saddled one dogma onto the next.

Joseph, I cried, you sound like a grand inquisitor. Or are you aiming higher?

He always beat me at dice, quoting Saint Augustine when he threw them, as if he had the *Confessions* in Latin at his side.

And so we shot the breeze and rolled the dice for days on end, until he was sent home—because he lived in Bavaria, nearby—but I, with no address to return to and thus homeless, was first deloused and then sent to a work camp.

TALK there turned on two events, which affected us POWs in different ways. One was the dropping of two atomic bombs on Japanese cities I'd never heard of. We accepted this double strike because the other event had a much more immediate and tangible effect on us: in late summer Morgenthau's slimming cure was called off. We now received more than a thousand calories. We could even count on two or three ounces of sausage a day.

This meant we were arguably better fed than those outside the barbed wire, who brought their hunger to the black market. We heard that the citizens of Augsburg and Munich had been mobilized to clear the rubble and that civilians had to stand in military-like ranks to get what little the bakers and butchers had to offer. They were rationing out peace in smaller and smaller portions; we captives of the camp were doing better and better: we had grown used to our situation, felt safe behind our fence.

Many prisoners of war, especially those who had lived in what were now Russian- and Polish-occupied territories, even feared being released. I may well have been one of them. For want of news—had Mother and Father managed to flee Danzig with my sister or had they drowned on the *Gustloff*?—I pictured myself as parentless, homeless, uprooted. I wallowed in self-pity and tried on various roles, the little orphan boy, for instance. Especially at night on my straw mattress.

Fortunately I had friends my age in similar circumstances. But what we missed more than Mama and Papa was something dreams of female contours could not provide. It was enough to make one queer. And sometimes—no, often—we reached for one another, touched, fumbled.

THEN the situation improved again. Practicing my school English on every possible occasion to make it more American, I got myself assigned to a work detail responsible for washing dishes in the U.S. Air Force company kitchen attached to the barracks of the Fürstenfeldbruck airfield. We were in charge of potato- and carrot-peeling too. And we were delivered every morning by truck to our land of milk and honey.

A group of DPs, as the displaced persons of various nationalities were called, had also found work there, washing and ironing. The group was made up of a half-dozen young Jews who had been smiled upon by fate and escaped death in one or another concentration camp. They wanted to go to Palestine, but had not received permission.

Like us, they were astounded at the quantity of leftovers—mountains of mashed potatoes, bacon fat, meat left on chicken carcasses after only breasts and legs had been served—that ended up in the trash day after day. Since we observed the waste without a word, our common feelings could only be surmised. Can it be that the mirror in which until then I had seen only a spruced-up image of our victors had suddenly developed a crack?

The one thing we had in common with the Jews our age was that we all ate the leftovers. But that's where the similarity ended. Supervision was relaxed, and we engaged in verbal battles with them whenever we had a break, though they spoke Yiddish or Polish to one another and their German was mostly limited to *Raus! Schnellschnell! Stillgestanden! Fresse halten! Ab ins Gas!*—linguistic souvenirs of an experience we did not want to acknowledge. Our vocabulary was pieced together out of "barracks German": You bow-legged dogs! You bed wetters! I'll make you toe the line, the lot of you!

At first the Amis laughed at our war of words. They were white GIs and called the men in the neighboring company niggers. We and the young Jews passed this over in silence because we had other fish to fry.

Then the Amis took a pedagogical tack, but the American "education officer," with his spectacles and soft voice and freshly ironed shirts, did not get very far with us; we, myself included, refused to believe the evidence he put before us, the black-and-white pictures of Bergen-Belsen, Ravensbrück . . . I saw the piles of corpses, the ovens; I saw the starving and the starved, the skeletal bodies of the survivors from another world. I couldn't believe it.

"You mean Germans did that?" we kept asking.

"Germans could never have done that."

"Germans don't do that."

And among ourselves we said, "Propaganda. Pure propaganda."

A mason who went with us on a brief reeducation tour of Dachau—we were classified as young Nazis—said after we had been led through the camp from one station of the cross to the next, "Remember the shower rooms? And the shower heads? For gas supposedly. Well, they were freshly plastered, the Amis installed them afterward . . ."

It was some time before I came gradually to understand and hesitantly to admit that I had unknowingly—or, more precisely, unwilling to know—taken part in a crime that did not diminish over the years and for which no statute of limitations would ever apply, a crime that grieves me still.

Guilt and the shame it engendered can be said, like hunger, to gnaw, gnaw ceaselessly. Hunger I suffered only for a time, but shame . . .

IT WAS neither the education officer's arguments nor the overly graphic photographs he showed us that broke through my obstinacy; no, I did not get over my block until a year later, when I heard the voice of my former Hitler Youth leader Baldur von Schirach, I don't remember where, coming from the radio. Those accused by the Nuremberg tribunal of being war criminals were entitled to take the floor one last time before the verdict was read out. In an attempt to exonerate the Hitler Youth, Schirach asserted its ignorance, claiming that he and only he was aware of mass extermination as the final solution of the Jewish question.

I had to believe him. I continued to believe him. But as long as I served as dishwasher and interpreter, I was obstinate. We had lost the war all right: the victors had more soldiers, tanks, and planes, never mind calories, than we had. But what about the pictures?

When we argued with our Jewish coevals, they shouted "Nazis! You Nazis!"

We responded, "Get out of here! Go to your Palestine!" But then we would laugh together over the crazy Americans, especially the education officer, whom we embarrassed with questions about his country's contemptible treatment of the "niggers."

Once tired of quarreling, we would change the subject to women, first calling them whores, then putting them on a pedestal. Because the surviving sons of murdered Jewish parents were as hungry for their picture of womanhood as we POWs were for ours. And we both found the Amis and their pin-ups ridiculous.

Once or twice one of the Jews, who was called Ben by the others, would silently push a tin can chock-full of thick meat fat and juices in my direction just after inspection and before we climbed into the backs of our trucks. It was against the rules to take leftovers back to our camp.

I REMEMBER Ben as having curly red hair. I gave a talk about Ben and Dieter in March of '67 in Tel Aviv. I had been invited by the university. I was thirty-nine at the time and had the reputation of being a troublemaker because of my tendency to bring out into the open what had too long been swept under the carpet.

My lecture was entitled "A Talk About Accommodation." I gave it in German because the audience consisted mainly of Jews of German origin. Part of it dealt with Ben and Dieter, the kitchen and laundry crews, and the education officer who tried to arbitrate between the estranged parties.

I called the education officer Hermann Mautler. He had had to flee Austria in '38, had emigrated to the United States, had earned a degree in history, and believed in reason. The story I inserted into the talk for the audience of survivors was the story of his failure, and when I read it today, at a distance of nearly four decades, his failure strikes me as related to my failures.

True, I made up the name Hermann Mautler, but the fragile person whose real name I no longer know is more vivid to me than the obstinate youth I am trying to recognize in an early self-portrait. Because the Dieter in my story is only a part of me.

How do stories remain fresh? Since they are invariably unfinished, they require more than the usual quotient of invention. They always wait for the chance to move forward or backward. Like the story of Joseph, the Bavarian youth who was released early from the Bad Aibling camp and with whom I spent several long days squashing lice, chewing caraway seeds under a tarp in the rain, and telling fortunes with dice. A gentle know-it-all. His story must keep being told, because though we had very different plans for the future, he, like me, had written poetry from the time he was an altar boy . . .

Only the story of Ben and Dieter must come to an end, because the kitchen crew in question was replaced by a group of older soldiers in the autumn just after I turned eighteen. The Jews stayed on a bit longer, probably until they managed to find a way to get to Palestine, where the promise of Israel as a sovereign state and war upon war stood ahead of them.

The education officer may later have written a book about the problems of camp inmates of various origins during puberty and about his glorious defeat. As for me, a change of camp granted me something I did not know. It was called freedom.

By the time I was transferred to the Lüneburg Heath early in the winter I was low on Siegfried Line pins but still well stocked with razor blades. We traveled in army trucks over empty autobahns through rolling, then flat, landscapes that stretched out peacefully before us. We were being transferred, we were told, only to be released. An occasional bombed autobahn bridge or burned-out tank reminded us of the horrors we had survived. No sooner had we arrived than we moved into barracks in the Münster camp.

The English guards took an interest in one of my remaining items for barter: the tiny Siegfried Line bunker pins. But they eventually stamped my papers, disinfected me, gave me my final ration, and released me into the British Occupation Zone. There I found a vast rubble-lined reservation, and there I was to try on that unknown quantity, freedom.

It is disappointing at first sight: peeling the onion makes the eyes water. What would be legible to clear vision is clouded over. My amber captures its inclusion with greater definition: it appears for a time to be a mosquito or tiny spider. But then it can bring something else to mind, like the grenade splinter encapsulated in my left shoulder as a souvenir—so to speak.

What do I retain from the war and my camp experience besides episodes that have been bound together into anecdotes or wish to remain variable as true stories?

First, incredulity, when the concentration camp pictures startled me with their black-and-whiteness; then, speechlessness.

Also the lessons fear and hunger taught me. And the ability, thanks to the cooking course with no equipment but blackboard and chalk dust, to summon up what I fervently desire, even the unattainable, with all its smells and noises. I also learned to invite dinner guests from distant places and times, friends I miss, who died young or who speak to me only from books, friends pronounced dead yet very much alive.

They bring news from another star, carry on their quarrels at table, or seek redemption in pious-sounding tall tales because they have been frozen into medieval stone images.

Later I expanded my time period and wrote *The Flounder*, in the course of which I welcome guests from every century to my table, serving Skåne herring during Dorothea's Gothic times, the tripe the Abbess Margarete Rusch made for her father's final meal, the meal before he was executed, the cod in dill sauce Agnes cooked for the ailing poet Martin Opitz, the potato soup Amanda prepared for Ollefritz, as well as the mushroom garnish Sophie used to stuff the calf's head that Napoleon's governor, General Rapp, escaped by the skin of his teeth, and the kidneys in mustard sauce Lena Stubbe served August Bebel when she showed him her *Proletarian Cookbook* . . .

In the days of gnawing hunger I paid close attention to my master. As soon as the ingredients were available at a reasonable price, I put air soups, cloud dumplings, and weathercocks on my menu. The I that disappeared in those early years must have been an empty vessel. Among those who filled it, a Bessarabian chef deserves a place all his own. What I would give to make a place at my table for the gentleman who said, "But please, gentlemen . . ."

At and Below the Surface

No MORE barbed wire to dictate horizontal and vertical lines of sight. With only the lightest of luggage, including two pounds of bartered tea, he or I was transferred into a state called freedom, limited though it was to the British Occupation Zone.

But who had granted freedom to whom? How to make use of this gift? What did it promise, this two-syllable word that could be explained, expanded, or extenuated, even negated, by any number of epithets.

Snippets of memory strung together—now this way, now that—but always with gaps. I trace the silhouette of a person who happened to survive, but no, I see a smudged yet otherwise blank sheet of paper that is, could be, or would like to be me, the imprecise outline of an existence to come.

Someone who still parts his hair on the left and is still five foot six and a half. Someone in dyed military garb who now shaves his down once a week and sees the freedom offered to him as a hard road to travel. Yet he takes the first step.

Besides, ideals come to call—he is an earnest, contemplative young man seeking meaning among the ruins—that are falteringly rejected.

For now, at least, I can't seem to come up with a picture of my condition at that point. The facts are too few and unclear. I am eighteen. By the time I am released, I am no longer underweight. I am louse-free, I wear rubber-soled American boots, and I look all right in the mirror.

Whether life in the camps has cured me of my youthful grimacing is uncertain. My only possessions are the exotically packed English tea that the as yet nonsmoker has hoarded in exchange for cigarettes, silver pins, and the enormous supply of razor blades. Apart from a few odds and ends and scribblings, they are all my haversack contains. And what of the picture my inner life displays? It seems the godless Catholic was familiar with all the virulent questions of faith and at the same time did not give a damn. To suspect an atheist lurking within would have meant to ascribe another religion to him.

He meditates. Nothing quotable results. Outwardly a few things have not faded: the German-army trousers, a U.S. Army windbreaker, lined and dyed a rusty red. A woolen cap—it, too, U.S. Army issue—provides olive-drab warmth. He looks nearly civilian. Only the haversack is still field gray.

To BE released, I had to give an address. It was provided by Philipp, a friend my age, along with greetings to his mother. He was a good-looking boy with an angelic face, dimples, and a contagious smile. Like me, he had the gift of frivolity, the kind that had made volunteers of us.

He had to stay behind at the Münster camp and was later shipped to Britain with a labor detachment. I was allowed out because an x-ray (praise be to Roentgen) had shown my bean-sized grenade splinter to have encapsulated in my left shoulder.

It has remained there to this day, my little souvenir analogous to the beetle outlasting time in its amber prison. When, trying to show off—first to Anna, now to Ute—I pulled back my left arm, left-handed as I am, to throw a stone or a ball, it would send me tangible signals: *Hey! Stop! Let me sleep!*

So, unlike Philipp, I was considered unfit for work below ground in the Welsh coal mines. I promised to assure his mother he'd be home soon. That is how my first officially registered residence as a free man came to be Cologne-Mülheim, a pile of debris with an occasional miraculously surviving street sign stuck to what was left of a façade, or hung on a pole sticking out of the rubble, which was also sprouting lush patches of dandelions about to blossom.

Later, while scavenging the American and French occupation zones like a stray dog for food, a place to sleep, and—driven by that other hunger—skin-on-skin contact, I was led or misled by similar street signs past other ruins and over rubble harboring missing persons.

Awake or dreaming, I am still treading these makeshift paths between damaged masonry, pausing on a mound of debris for a better view, my teeth grinding, the stone and mortar dust in the air . . .

MY FRIEND'S mother, a nimble woman with dyed or natural blue-black hair and a cigarette always dangling from her lips, gave me an unceremonious introduction to the black market. The euphemistically named four-fruit marmalade and artificial honey, American peanut butter and gramophone needles, flints and flashlight batteries would cross the kitchen table for me to weigh or count. I could also cash in my razor blades on the side. I soon had money. From morning till night there was a stream of customers with items to trade. Furs—I recall a silver fox— were worth their weight in butter.

Philipp's sister pranced through the daily round of transactions like a graceful doll, as if before an imagined public. She was the image of her brother. She wore silk stockings, changed hats regularly, smelled of spring, but could be fondled only in long-fingered dreams. Can it be that—floating past like an angel—she stroked my hair?

By way of compensation I would slip off to the movies. I can still see the local film palace intact among the ruins. In peace as in war, its main attraction was *Romance in a Minor Key*, starring such onetime favorites as Marianne Hoppe, Paul Dahlke, and Ferdinand Marian, now in disrepute because of his role in *Jew Süss*.

Romance in a Minor Key had served to stimulate desires, some years before, when I was in the Luftwaffe auxiliary. Whenever "An Hour Between Day and Dreams" summoned Hoppe to the screen . . . she in front of a shop window . . . she struggling with temptation . . . she alone with her grief . . . her immaculately scrubbed face . . . the jewel on her neck . . . her fleeting smile . . . her beauty, her everlasting beauty . . .

The heartthrob of my youth died only three or four years ago. She was over ninety.

LIKE the hungry outside Cologne's Hohe Strasse shops, my questions now form a line:

Did the aimless black marketeer who bore my name use his

machinations as an excuse to extend his time away from the classroom and postpone his final examinations? Did I think of apprenticing myself to a craftsman, and if so in what trade?

Did I miss my father, mother, and sister so terribly that I made regular trips to the offices that posted refugee lists?

Were my sufferings limited to my own person or did they extend to the state of the world? More specifically, did I partake in what was beginning to be called, with and without quotation marks, German collective guilt? Can it be that my grief encompassed only my loss of house, home, and family and nothing more? What other losses might I have mourned?

The onion gives the following answers, though not without blank spots:

I made no attempt to enroll in an academic institution in Cologne, nor was I tempted by an apprenticeship.

I submitted no application to the bureaus in charge of registering refugees from the eastern part of the country or whose houses had been destroyed in bombing raids. I still had a clear picture of my mother, but did not miss her terribly. I wrote no homesick verse.

Nor did I feel any guilt.

Thus the aimless wanderer amidst ruins and rubble appears to have been concerned with himself alone: no other concerns can I remember. Or did I flee with ineffable pain to the sanctum of the Cologne Cathedral? The colossus and its two towers looked rather the worse for wear when the city that had grown around it lay flattened and in ruins.

What I know for sure is that in the spring Philipp's sister— I may have been getting on her nerves—helped me find work on a farm in the Lower Rhine district of Bergheim-Erft. It must have been in the spring, because I can see myself after a bit of last-minute training stumbling behind a plow or leading a horse by the halter while the farmer made the furrows. In the fields from dawn to dusk. There was enough to eat. But then there was the other hunger, which neither mush nor must could still, the one that fed my need, enlarged it, enflamed it.

I shared a cramped room with a retarded farmhand. There was an East Prussian girl working on the farm as a milkmaid— she and her elderly father, who was good for nothing more than force-feeding pigs, had been officially foisted on the farmer— but the farmer, who besides pigs kept twelve cows and four horses, had commandeered her for himself. The only thing he did with his wife was go to church. Sunday after Sunday. He was a good Catholic.

On the proscenium of my mind I pictured Elsabe, for such was her name, standing large and heavy-boned by the garden fence or in shadow by the farm gate or brightly lit between two milk canisters. Wherever she stood, walked, bent, an image arose. So compelling was the stable smell she emitted that between thinning turnip rows and chopping firewood I penned a good ten rickety-rhymed poems in its wake.

There was little that was lyrical about my surroundings: farm after farm in the sunlight, one big blur of countryside in the rain, flat except for village steeples.

The snoring farmhand by night, the farmer's shouts by day, and through it all visions of a dozen cows milked by a goddess with ash-blond eyelashes. It was too much for me. I moved on, ravenous, though I had eaten my fill. The hunger that remained, a densely written onion skin be my witness, was of a different nature.

———

I WENT as far as the Saarland, where the address given me by another Münster camp crony secured me a genuine feather bed in the attic of a small house where he lived with his mother, who treated me like a second son.

It may sound cozy, but the Saarland was harder hit by hunger than other places. The French occupation forces seemed to punish all Saarlanders retrospectively, not simply those who had voted in favor of returning to the Reich in the plebiscite of '35.

My pal and I—I never knew his name: we all called him Kongo—he wanted to join the French Foreign Legion and liked to picture himself fighting rebellious Berbers under the desert sky—took crowded trains into the countryside, all the way to the mountainous Hunsrück region, which seemed like the end of the world to us.

Train journeys of this kind were quite common, and were known as "hamster trips." Farm to farm, we bartered the rest of my English tea, razor blades, and the ever sought-after flints I had been given as payment on the Cologne black market for potatoes and cabbage. There were times we came away empty-handed. But I had more to offer than items that could be weighed or counted.

One day I did a frivolous but sympathetic palm-reading for a visibly pregnant peasant woman who happily shared table and bed with the French "foreign worker" assigned her during the war. So pleased was the woman with my reading—I had prophesied that her husband would remain absent if not forever then at least for the foreseeable future—that she rewarded me with a hunk of smoked bacon in addition to my honorarium of a slab of sheep's-milk cheese. The man had been reported missing in action at the Eastern Front in 1943, but was still very much in evidence in a framed photograph.

Where had I acquired this questionable art? Was I born with it? Had I learned it at the knees of the Gypsy women who went back and forth over the Free State's borders and did more than sharpen scissors and mend kettles for the good people of Langfuhr? No, it was probably in the Upper Palatinate, in the camp where I killed time and stayed a very real hunger by taking the abstract cooking course: there must have also been a course in palmistry that attracted the likes of me.

Whether my skill was inborn, Gypsy-taught, or camp-learned, I must have been pretty low on scruples to have made a positive professional prediction in deepest Hunsrück: the more rewarding the woman's life line was for her and the retiring French peasant who shared her table and bed, the more rewarding— that is, calorific—they were for me. And yet bacon was not the most important reward I reaped from the trip to Hunsrück. The peasant woman's sister-in-law, who had been bombed out of her Ruhr residence and found refuge and work on the farm, did me a service whose worth went beyond the usual measure of weight or quantity.

Much as my friend Kongo dogged her footsteps, he didn't get anywhere with her: once he came staggering out of the sheepfold, scratched and cursing. Yet soon enough he was all smiles again: he was a broad-shouldered, good-natured sort, who took things as they came.

The war had been too short for him: he was a great adventurer. That was probably why he stayed with me. My first play, a two-acter entitled *Flood* that premiered in the mid-fifties at a

Frankfurt student theater, featured a character very much like him, a soldier back from the Legion whom his comrade-in-arms calls Kongo. The two of them have been to Laos and Indochina and are now playing the prodigal son . . .

I had a glimmer of what was to come on the way to the nearest station. The sister-in-law helped us transport in a handcart the things we'd squirrelled away: a sack of potatoes, cabbage, a slab of sheep's-milk cheese, a hunk of bacon, and perhaps a bag of runner beans.

The moon lit our way through the fields, the path rising slightly at first, then sloping for the remaining three or three and a half kilometers. Distances and times are only approximate in the memory.

Kongo pulled the cart and would not let either of us take over, so we brought up the rear, silent at first, then chatty. Walking side by side but not holding hands or anything, we talked about films and discovered we both liked a young actress by the name of Hildegard Knef, soon to become one of German cinema's brightest stars. The film, which I happen to have seen again on television recently, was *Under the Bridges*.

Since the local to Bad Kreuznach wasn't due in for another two hours or so, Kongo lay down on a bench in the waiting room. He immediately fell asleep. We stood outside by the shed whose flaking sign was the only indication it was a station. The moon or the clouds were scuttering along. What was there for us to see, to say, to do or even wish?

Suddenly the young woman, or girl, as I saw her, asked me to accompany her with the handcart, not because she was afraid, just because . . .

It must have been early summer and the moon was almost

full. The haystacks on either side of the path, which ran through a newly mown field, had suggested nothing to me on the way there. They lay evenly spaced to the edge of the woods, which set off the sky like a dark band. Sometimes clouds shadowed their order, then lit them with a silvery brilliance. Perhaps the piled-up hay had made us offer after offer on the way to the station. I had the feeling the scent of the freshly mown hay had grown stronger.

No sooner was the station, along with the sleeping friend and the haul, a stone's throw away—or did we walk farther?—than I abandoned the cart and she took my hand, and the two of us drifted from the path to the nearest haystack.

I must have been the one who let himself be drawn into the hay. Inge has remained clear in my memory, in more than a few details, and not only because she was the first. Her broad, flat, almost full moon of a face was sprinkled with freckles, but they didn't count in the hay. It is fairly certain that her eyes, which she didn't close, were green rather than gray. I remember her hands as large and coarse from work in the fields. But they knew how to come to my aid.

Of course the hay smelled sweet beyond compare. As I was too eager, because starved, she had to teach me not to rush, not to buck, to use my fingers, use them all and gently, the way she did. There was so much to discover. Moist and fathomless. All there, waiting to be touched. Soft and round. Yielding. The noises, the animal sounds we made.

Then the scent of hay overcame us. Intoxicated, we reached for more. Or was once enough? I only hope the novice proved a good learner.

And then? Afterwards? Did we whisper in the hay, or was it only me? I've no idea what whisper words could be found in a haystack. All I know is that Inge spoke matter-of-factly: The familiar story of war. The bombed-out row house on the outskirts of Bochum, the fiancé who had fallen in action two years before in the Balkans "because the partisans were everywhere." As a miner he was exempt from military service, she said, but then they sent him straight to Stalingrad and even put him in the engineers. They sent him to Gross-Boschpol for training, then to the front, and later, as he had written, to the mountains, to build bridges . . .

She said more, but it's gone now, as is the name of her fiancé, which she kept repeating, out of habit, out of intimacy, as if he were lying next to her.

And was that really me, whispering this and that in the haystack? Profundities about the firmament? About the moon's comings and goings? I probably tried to be original and lyrical, because whenever something threw me off course I used to wax poetic, in rhymed verse or free.

Or did I stutter when she asked me out of concern or simple curiosity what I wanted to be, when I grew up, so to speak? Did I say there in the hay, "An artist. No two ways about it!"?

Of the fleshy glow of skin under skin the onion knows nothing. Only gaps in a garbled text. Unless I myself try to decipher what appears illegible, and put together a rhyme . . .

In my memory, overloaded with constantly shifting debris, I made Inge laugh, or wanted to make her laugh, goodness knows how. She did not try to make me laugh. The novice at her side, under the almost full moon, had suddenly grown animal-sad not knowing why, and no amount of stroking and coaxing could bring him out of it. What is more, he could no longer tolerate the scent of the mown meadow.

Our haystack lay flat by the time we stood up, she searching for her knickers, I fumbling with my fly buttons. We plucked the hay off our clothes—each from our own, presumably—though I probably helped her to put the haystack back in order. Seen from afar: a couple working their fields by night.

After that, the bleak feeling of isolation was gone. Not that there was any singing or humming as I helped Inge bring our bed in line with the other haystacks. Four busy hands.

I am uncertain whether she said "Send me a postcard" when she told me her family name, which ended in the Polish -kowiak or -ski like the names of our Ruhr Basin soccer players.

And that was that. Or was it? Maybe a tiny pause. Then off we went in opposite directions, she with the empty handcart.

I must have been the one who didn't look back, even this first time. What had happened lay behind me. "Don't turn around" is a line in a children's song and the title of a poem I wrote later, much later.

But on the short, or was it actually long, way back someone sniffed the fingers of his left hand, as if to ensure what it had held a few minutes before a place in his memory.

Inge's scent and the haystack's still clung to me as I sat in the waiting room next to my sleeping friend, whose face she had scratched. Kongo was still grinning cheerfully as we rode in the direction of Bad Kreuznach with our "hamster loot," but he made no dirty remarks . . .

EVEN now, the hasty departure weighs heavily on me. Why the rush? You'd think I was running away out of fear. It lasted until the train finally came. Time passed unused.

Too late, I tell myself: You could have had the girl named

Inge in the next haystack too and—you'd have been hungry again soon—the one after that. What was the point of going back to low-calorie Saarland? The Hunsrück—godforsaken, Catholic, and hilly as it was—would eventually have come to seem like home, material for a long TV mini-series.

Your pal Kongo would soon be gone, taking the potatoes and cabbage, the slab of cheese, and the counterpart of your skill at palm-reading with him: he intended to go to Algeria or Morocco because he hadn't had enough war and wanted to go to the dogs in the name of La Grande Nation. You could have done an occasional optimistic palm-reading for the peasant woman, to help her sleep and have an easy delivery. And if one day the husband missing in Russia should in fact turn up on her doorstep . . . A late homecoming . . . The man outside . . .

In my mind I have often turned to haystacks left and right, less because of the young woman with the broad, flat face lit by the moon and dusted with countless freckles than in search of self, the vanished I of earlier years. Yet I never got further than the sound and the smell of my first, much too hasty attempt at making one flesh of two, an endeavor also known as love.

THEN gaps, interference. Nothing that smacks of conquest or even adventure. All that remains, nailed down, is the season: early summer, '46.

I'm constantly on the road, first in the Weserbergland, then along the Hessian border of the American Occupation Zone, and finally, legal again, with the Brits in Göttingen, after having spent a few days with the family of another comrade, a peasant boy with a slight speech impediment, in the area of Nörten-Hardenberg.

No more haystacks, though. No more profitable palm-readings. Aimless, restless, a fixed abode no temptation. And yet I must have registered with the police here and there to gain access to the all-important ration cards.

What was I after in Göttingen? Not the university, that's for sure. What kind of school record could I offer? I hadn't seen the inside of a school since the age of fifteen. Teachers put me off. That is why primary school teachers like Fräulein Spollenhauer in the "Timetable" chapter of *The Tin Drum,* the gym teacher Mallenbrandt in *Cat and Mouse,* and the teacher Starusch in *Local Anesthetic,* were destined to fill pages of my manuscripts. See how important my teachers were to me. One of my plays, too, a play called *Thirty-Two Teeth,* deals not only with dental hygiene but also with pedagogical hysteria.

Even though I had been taught to strip down the ninety-eight carbine and reassemble it in no time flat into a battle-ready weapon; even though I could operate the fuse mechanism of an eight-point-eight anti-aircraft gun and, trained gunner that I was, the gun of a tank; even though I had been drilled in the art of seeking cover at lightning speed, saying "Jawoll!" and marching in formation; even though I learned to "organize" food, to sniff danger, to steer clear of the military police bloodhounds, and even endure the sight of bodies blown to bits and bodies hanging on a procession of trees; even though I pissed my pants out of fear and learned to sing in the woods, to sleep standing, to lie my way to safety, to invent roasts and soups without fat, fish, meat, or vegetables, to people my table with guests from distant times, and even to read fortunes from palms, I was a world away from the exam that would have admitted me to the university.

One day in front of Göttingen Station—it was a habit of mine to roam the precincts of bustling stations—I met a classmate from my former life. I am not sure whether I sat on a bench next to him or behind him at the Conradinum or Saint Peter's or Saint John's.

He kept at me until I agreed to cross the city, which had been largely spared, to where his mother, but no grown sister, lived in emergency quarters for refugees from the east.

They were all in a row, Nissen barracks, tunnel-shaped, vaulted, corrugated iron constructions, with washing hung between them. Barley soup with cabbage stalks was all she had to eat, a cot the only place she had to sleep. Her eldest son had fallen in the battle for Monte Cassino Abbey, her husband, whom the Russians had arrested and then dragged from pillar to post, was reported missing. It was the job of the remaining son to make up for what she had lost.

After a few days I let him, my putative benchmate, take me to a school that specialized in helping its charges brush up on what they had forgotten or missed during the years they'd been away. You could get back into the school routine there, he said over and over, and then try your hand at the *Abitur*. Because, he said, passing that exam was as important to me, who still carried a haversack, as it was to him, who sported a real briefcase, artificial though its leather was. Without the *Abitur*, you were worth half as much. Plenty of others were in the same boat. "When will you understand? Without the *Abitur* you don't count!"

I barely made it beyond the first period. The first period was Latin, and Latin is Latin, what you'd expect. But the second period was history, my onetime favorite. Its extensive spatial and temporal territory supplied vacuums galore for my imagination to fill in and populate with characters I'd dreamed up, most of whom wore medieval garb and engaged in endless warfare. What is man? A mere particle, partner, fellow traveler, cog in the cogwheel of history. A colorful ball being kicked around—that is how I saw myself back in the schoolroom again.

Although a good deal of what happened during my years on the road, my *Wanderjahre,* is gone forever—for example, the number of students who followed us from the Latin class to the history class, though I do remember they were all war-years older than we were—I can still see the history teacher as if it were yesterday: short, wiry, close-cropped, no glasses, bow tie, scurrying up and down the rows of benches, turning on his heel, then coming to an abrupt halt, as if on the irrevocable command of the *Weltgeist,* and opening the class with the classic "Where did we leave off yesterday?" only to answer immediately "Ah, the Ems Dispatch."

I'm sure that was what the curriculum called for. I didn't want to be stuck with Bismarck and his machinations. What did I care about the Franco-Prussian War?

My crash course in what is called war experience was more recent: I had completed it the day before yesterday.

I was still experiencing its repercussions in my dreams and nightmares. I hadn't come to rest anywhere.

What had a war that forged a united Germany out of blood and iron, to offer me?

What did I care about the Ems Dispatch?

What had to be chewed over, what dates nailed into my memory?

What span of time—mine?—would that pedant skip, deny, gloss over as an embarrassment?

It was as if the ominous dispatch had delivered a cue: I stood, reached for my ever ready haversack, and, ignoring the professor's reproach, left not only the classroom for ex-servicemen wishing to make up for lost time, no, I also left school and its musty conservatism-on-principle forever. I may even have relished the leave-taking.

As for my classmate, who doubtless completed his *Abitur* and was therefore able to go through life a totally worthy person, I never saw him again. But since my publisher and his printing press are located on Göttingen's Düstere Strasse, the city is still worth a trip, for more than one reason.

ALTHOUGH the fine points of the previous episode are fuzzy, another meeting, which took place immediately thereafter, is as sharp as can be.

I was in the station waiting room. Where was I heading? Had I any travel plans?

Did I feel the call of the south? Up and away, illegal or not, into the American zone, where I might ferret out my pal Joseph in some Bavarian burg between Altötting and Freilassing and tell our fortunes again with my dice?

I look around the waiting room of Göttingen Station helplessly: all the seats are taken. Suitcases and bundles everywhere. The stale air of overcrowding. Finally, a spot. The man next to me is a man I might well have chosen to sit next to, the kind I feel an affinity with: the eternal private first class in his dyed Wehrmacht uniform. I could have guessed his rank even without seeing the two chevrons on his left sleeve.

I seemed destined to meet up with his kind. This fellow— like the other Pfc, who led me out of the wood in the guise of Hans-who-left-home, though this one was taller and more brawny, more rugged than him—this fellow was somebody you could trust. You can count on somebody who doesn't need to make it to corporal, I said to myself. Crafty, cunning, sly, he will always come out on top. Advance, positional warfare, hand-to-hand combat, counterattack, retreat—if it had to do with military operations he was at home with it. He would find the breach, he would get away, wounded or not. You could rely on him.

His wooden leg stretched out in front of him, he was smoking a pipe filled with an indefinable substance only distantly related to tobacco. He looked as if he had survived not only the most recent war but also the Thirty Years' War and Seven Years' War: he was timeless. He wore his field cap on the back of his head.

"So, my boy, don't know where to go, do you?" marked the start of our conversation.

You couldn't actually see the wooden leg, but you could tell it was there under the cloth, and this became significant before long. "What do you say we have a look at Hanover? It's got a station too. Maybe we'll find something there."

So we got on the next local and jolted our way through ten or fifteen stations. After a bit of shoving we found seats in a full nonsmoking compartment, which didn't interfere with my Pfc's pipe in the slightest. Smoke poured from it.

Puffing away, he pulled a heel of bread and hunk of sausage out of his haversack. He said the sausage came from Eichsfeld, which, everybody knew, made the best in the country.

With a paratrooper knife he sliced it into finger-thick pieces, more for me than for him. He was loath to take the pipe out of his mouth. He wanted to feed his pal, as he called me.

It was air-cured blood sausage, if I remember correctly, though it had an aftertaste of pork. In any case, he smoked while I chewed and gazed out at the hilly countryside passing by us on both sides and thought my own jumbled thoughts.

An old woman sitting opposite us in a prewar pot of a hat complained of the pipe, pointed at the "no smoking" sign, coughed by way of demonstration, then resumed her laments, even shouting for the conductor and urging her fellow passengers in her affected Hanover accent to join her protest against the "indecent fumes." My pal, who called me pal, raised his knife menacingly—it was glistening with fat—and, holding on to his pipe in his free hand, froze in that position for an endless few seconds. Then, jabbing the blade through his trouser leg into his right thigh, where it remained, quivering, he laughed a spine-tingling laugh.

Horrified, the woman fled the compartment clutching her hat. Her place was immediately occupied by a man who had been standing in the corridor. The onetime private first class loosened the knife, snapped the blade shut, dropped it back into the haversack, and tapped his pipe a few times. We were pulling in to Hanover.

WHAT remains are Fortune's candid snapshots, which the memory archives. The silent sausage-chewer can still see the quivering knife sticking out of the wooden leg, though he cannot be quite certain whether the incident took place during the train trip from Göttingen to Hanover or during a journey in the opposite direction, to Kassel and on, all the way to Munich, where I went to visit my Bavarian friend Joseph in Marktl am Inn or some other dump—the friend with whom the year before I'd munched caraway seeds and rolled dice and argued about the Immaculate Conception. I didn't find him at his parents' house: he must have been off in a seminary somewhere, surmounting scholastic obstacles, passing examinations with flying colors, while I . . .

The incident could just as easily have featured another "pal" with a wooden leg—there were so many. Blood sausage or pork, flick knife or fixed blade, on the way there or back: what memory stores and preserves in condensed form blends with the story in whatever way it is told, and has no interest in origins or other such questionable issues.

The fact remains that the private first class sitting next to me in Göttingen Station waiting room with a perfectly possible wooden leg had advised placeless me by the time we pulled into Hanover to present myself at the office of the potash manufacturers Burbach-Kali Limited and ask for work. "They need men for underground. You'll get special ration cards—all the butter you can eat—and a roof over your head. What do you say, boy?"

Two pals standing in front of Hanover Central Station next to an Ernst-August-Crown-Prince-of-Hanover-on-a-horse monument riddled with bomb splinters.

The younger pal did what the older pal advised, because whatever he was like at the time or whatever the time had made of him, one experience had marked him: he mistrusted anyone who claimed adult status, with one exception: the unmistakable type of the private first class. It was a type he had known since a man, a barber by trade, had led him out of the woods and across the Russian front lines. When T-34 tanks fired on the street along which troops were retreating, the Pfc's legs had been shot to pieces, which made his survival highly unlikely. My waiting room pal got off with a wooden leg. He knew what to do or not to do and where. His advice was worth following.

Besides, I liked the word *underground*. I liked the idea of crawling through the bowels of the earth, where nothing could change abruptly, isolated, swallowed up, out of sight, long forgotten. I was even willing to work deep under the earth's crust, to sweat at hard labor. I may have hoped to find something underground that was invisible by the light of day.

Out of gratitude for his tip, I gave my friend the rest of my cigarette coupons before I followed his advice, because I still had no taste for cigs, which had the power of a stable currency at the time. They were my riches, my ready cash.

So I went to the office, was seen immediately, asked for work, and was hired on the spot by Burbach-Kali Limited, as a "coupler boy." The mine where I was to work, the Siegfried I Mine, was located near the village of Gross Giesen, in the Sarstedt district. I was given work clogs and carbide lamp when I got there. I felt right at home. I had been "top man" in a bunk bed for years.

The village lay about halfway between Hildesheim and Hanover in a flat region perfect for sugar-beet cultivation. On the southwestern horizon the hills of the Weserbergland loomed blue. Out of the early-summer green of the plains arose the winding tower of the pit, the stone mill, the boiler house with its locker-room annex, the villa-like administration building, and, towering above all else, the slag heap, partly poured into a white cone shape, partly strewn about, the daily recipient of new loads of refuse rock from dumpers running on a cable railway. Up they climbed chock-full, and down they rolled once emptied. The swell and fade of their screech has remained in my ears, and even today I keep watch for the whitish slag heaps rising up over the cultivated flatlands, visible from the train that takes me from Ratzeburg via Lüneburg and Hanover to my publisher, Steidl, in Göttingen. They have outlasted their time and become part of the landscape: the pit along with the entire Siegfried I Mine were closed down and cleaned up decades ago.

THE barracks slept six men per room. The canteen food was filling if somewhat tasteless, and the ration coupons for miners allowed for ample extras: sausage, cheese, gobs of butter, and eggs for breakfast or before the late shift. We got a special portion of milk daily to prevent black lung and clogs to wear underground. In the locker room we changed, hoisting our street clothes up to the ceiling in bags, and took showers after our shifts.

As a coupler boy I worked on a mine floor 950 meters below the surface. Electric-powered dumper trains either empty or full of potash ore ran along kilometers of tracks, away from the vents of the higher floors and to the hoist of the main shaft, which also came, at the ring of a bell, to take miners to and from their shifts.

My job was to couple the dumpers, full or empty, then uncouple them at the main shaft, and to open and close the weather door on the trip to the roof galleries, where the salty ore was dynamited and broken down. It meant a lot of running through drafty tunnels, a lot of tripping over tracks, a lot of bumped knees.

I had been taught the tricks of the trade by other coupler boys. When the trains slowed down, I had to jump off the last dumper, jog alongside the train, pull aside the artificial-leather flaps of the weather door, let the train pass, shut the weather door, run after the last dumper, and jump back onto it. Usually the driver of the electric locomotive on my shift gave me enough time, but once or twice I missed the train and had to catch up on foot. Alone, it was a long haul.

The rush involved makes it sound like grueling work worthy of those special rations, whereas in fact it was not all that strenuous because the power supply would go off during nearly every shift, and outages of an hour or two were not unusual. Outages were part of day-to-day existence, and people simply accepted them.

At such times we would sit it out near the main-shaft hoist or, if the outage caught us while we were on our rounds, in one of the gigantic roof galleries, which were big enough to store all our present and future atomic waste and let it shine and shine . . .

Later I set the last chapter of *Dog Years* in a former potash mine taken over by scarecrows, which were being manufactured for export on all levels of the mine, including the roof galleries. Either frozen in particular poses or else mobile, thanks to a built-in mechanism, they were decked out as reproductions of human society and meant to convey human desires and sorrows, and as merchandise they had their price. They could be ordered direct from the factory and sold well worldwide. And since man is said to be created in God's image, God could be said to be the protoscarecrow.

The only light we had during the outages came from our carbide lamps, which made giant, ghost-like shadows on the towering roof-gallery walls. Out they came from newly dug tunnels, from the now silenced vibrating chutes, from the depths of the earth: miners, blasters, inspectors, face workers, and coupler boys like me with their drivers—a mixture of quickly trained, mostly young workers and old-timers, some approaching retirement age, all brought together by a power failure.

It was never long before their babble came round to politics and voices grew louder and more argumentative until the fight that was brewing failed to break out only because the current had gone on again, the galleries had lit up, the chutes had started rattling, the trains humming, and the hoist had jerked into action. Then the dialect-tinged quarrel died down and everyone returned to work, silent or swallowing their last words, their shadows in the beams of the swaying carbide lamps, growing smaller and smaller.

For me, who, as if struck by lockjaw, did no more than listen and pick up arguments and counterarguments passively, indiscriminately, these power-free periods made up for lessons missed in school. Despite the heat—we sweated even when idle—I tried to follow the debate. I didn't catch much, felt stupid, *was* stupid, wanted to question the old-timers, but didn't dare. I kept feeling torn because various factions would take shape in the course of the discussion. Roughly speaking, there were three opposing groups.

The smallest of them represented Communist class consciousness. Its members predicted the imminent demise of capitalism and the victory of the proletariat, and had a pat answer to every question and a predilection for clenched fists. The pit foreman, who belonged to their ranks, was an amiable enough fellow above ground, where he had a detached one-family house not far from the mine, and I occasionally took his eldest daughter to the cinema.

The second and largest group was big on Nazispeak and claimed to be trailing the culprits responsible for the collapse of the old order. Its members would hum the Horst Wessel Song and indulge in speculations and maledictions of the "If the Führer were alive today, he'd round up the lot of you . . ." variety.

The third group tried to tone down the dispute with increasingly shabby compromises. On the one hand, it opposed the expropriation of companies like Burbach-Kali Limited; on the other, it called for the nationalization of major industries under trade-union supervision. This group, which would lose ground for a while and then rally, was referred to disparagingly as social-democratic and even, by the Communists, as social-fascistic.

Even though I had trouble making sense of the issues that infuriated them so, I realized, coupler boy and idiot on the fringe that I was, that when push came to shove the communists inevitably teamed up with the Nazis to shout down the Social Democrat remainder. Mortal enemies as they were, they made a red and brown front against the Socis.

It was so predictable as to be maddening. Every time the power went out, out came the factions. I had trouble siding with one or another. Lacking firm beliefs, I was besieged from all sides and could have taken any direction.

The driver of my locomotive, a former face worker who had been injured in a blasting accident, was a Soci; he explained the odd-bedfellows alliance to me as we were leaving the locker room after our shift one evening. "The same thing happened just before Hitler came to power in '33: the Commies and the Browns ganged up on us. Till then the Browns were out to liquidate the Commies; then they switched to us. And that was the end of solidarity. When will they ever learn? All or nothing, that's what they want, and they hate us Socis because we'll take only half if need be . . ."

Far be it from me to claim that this carbide-lamp lecture in ideology enlightened me to the extent that it fashioned my first postwar political views, but it did help the coupler boy to see how a malignant partnership had stymied a regime that both elements, Communists and Nazis, had denigrated as "the system" and how it had eventually laid that regime low.

Even though I didn't become a sophisticated Soci below the surface, I did imbibe some more of its principles above the surface when my locomotive driver took me to that former rubble heap, Hanover, one Sunday morning to hear the head of the Social Democratic Party, Kurt Schumacher, speak to an open-air audience of ten thousand.

No, he didn't speak, he screamed, the way all politicians—not only Forster, the Nazi Gauleiter in the Danzig Maiwiese—screamed. And yet the future Social Democrat and unflinching supporter of ontheonehandontheother took to heart some of the words that the frail figure with the empty, fluttering sleeve thundered down to his ten thousand adherents in the blazing sun.

His years in Nazi prisons had made an ascetic of him. He was a stylite gone public. He called for the renewal of the nation, for a social and democratic Germany to rise from the ruins. His will was firm, his every word a hammer striking iron.

Repelled by his delivery though I was, I was convinced by Comrade Schumacher.

Convinced of what? With what consequences? It was not until many years later that the coupler boy of yore—after a number of misguided attempts at utopian discipline—began to fall into step with the Social Democrats in the sense of Willy

Brandt's "policy of small steps." And it was not until years later, in *The Diary of a Snail*, that I prescribed crawling shoes for the ills of progress. The snail's track, not the fast track. A long road paved with the cobblestones of doubt, Dr. Doubt being the nickname I chose for the *Diary's* protagonist.

But even below the surface my political encapsulation, that empty shell, developed cracks. I would try taking sides. The private tutoring offered me by the Siegfried I Mine had varying results: as erratic as the play of light and shadow in the steeple-high roof galleries, I favored this and opposed that, I championed one side, then the other, closing my ears only when the neversaydie Nazis tried to win me over.

Below the surface, whenever the issue of merging the Communists and the Socis into a single party in the Soviet zone came up, I would parrot my locomotive driver, who warned against compulsory unity and always proceeded slowly and prudently when his coupler boy was opening and shutting the weather door to give him time to jump aboard the last dumper; at the surface, in the postwar low-calorie reality, I would be fed quotations from the *Communist Manifesto* by the pit foreman and affable father of three daughters.

They had varying degrees of success with me. The fact that I was a good listener must have encouraged their efforts. But when I conjure up the coupler boy today—that is, in a time of the absolute supremacy of capital and in full consciousness of my utter lack of power—when I lure him next to my stand-up desk and force him, a born dodger, through an ever more rigorous third degree, putting him more and more on the spot with my trick questions, what I piece together out of the subordinate clauses of the young man in dungarees is that what actually

lured him to the one-family house with its porch and garden was
the inspector's eldest daughter: she won him over without a word
of propaganda.

THOUGH no beauty, she was not without charm. She had dragged
her left leg since childhood. An accident? She never spoke about
it. Or did I simply close my ears to her laments about the cause
of her misfortune?

There was a breathy, raspy quality to her speech, and she
spoke quickly, as if there wasn't enough time. I see an oval, elongated face, close-set brown eyes, straight dark hair, an always
thoughtful and hence wrinkled brow. She was intelligent and
could form logical, well-thought-out sentences. Her spirited
hands gave her words a second voice. One of her favorite words
was *precise*: to be precise, a precise way of talking, thinking . . .

She was training to be a secretary in the office, and typed up
a few of my hastily rhymed poems on the office typewriter. That
made them read fluently and look important, ready for print, if
only visually, especially because she had quietly corrected my
spelling mistakes.

We spent as much time as we could together. Her leg didn't
bother me. The face and spirited hands were attractive enough.
She would stand at the entrance to the mine, small and small-
breasted, waiting for her father and probably for me as well. So
dainty and light she was that I could lift her flat body to the appropriate height and enter it standing, as soon as we came back
from the movies in Sarstedt and had a few minutes on the porch,
or inside the door, to become one flesh.

I was not allowed upstairs into her maiden's chamber; she refused to go to my room with bunk beds. But she was concerned

about me and always let the final feature on our movie bill run its course, even if I was the only one who felt like it. And I obeyed her request to be careful.

But more vivid than our moments on the porch were the times we spent on the paths between the sugar-beet fields. Her precise speech. Calling everything by its name. Face-to-face with the towering slag heap shimmering white against an overcast sky, we went on and on about the movies we had been seeing: *Gaslight*, a bloodcurdling tale of foggy England; *Murderers Among Us*, starring Hildegard Knef.

We also talked about God, who didn't exist. We outdid each other in tearing apart the articles of faith. Two pupils of existentialism who did not yet know or had barely heard of that newly fashionable concept. Both had dipped into *Thus Spake Zarathustra* and snapped up lofty philosophical monstrosities like "essentiality" and "facticity." There were no haystacks in the area.

When after the first frost the sugar-beets were ready for harvest, we would hurry into the fields after dark with sacks and baskets and short-handled hoes. We weren't the only ones harvesting by night. Our enemies were peasants with dogs.

In the laundry room of the pit foreman's house—his wife had died during the last year of the war and he often seemed at a loss when it came to his three daughters—we would peel and dice the beets, then stew them into a syrup in the kettle meant for washing clothes. I can still remember the large wooden ladle I used for stirring and the smell and taste of the sticky, cloyingly sweet paste and the three-part laughter of the sisters as they cut up the beets. We poured the syrup into the bulbous bottles specially reserved for it, and turned what was left in the kettle into malt lozenges, having added a little anis.

We sang while we worked. The father had taught his daughters some workers' songs. Neither the time he had spent in the concentration camp nor his experience in a penal battalion at the front had dampened what he was proud to call his class consciousness.

What were the daughters' names? One of the girls—I can't quite remember which—was called Elke. Our discussions could get pretty heated. But during the syrup-making sessions we steered clear of politics.

SHORTLY after my nineteenth birthday, also the day on which the sentence condemning war criminals to be hanged was carried out in far-off Nuremburg, and which I celebrated with a few of my pals on the 950-meter floor just before the sugar-beet harvest began—I located the name and address of a distant relative who had found refuge in Lübeck with his wife and daughters. Did I write immediately or after some hesitation?

In towns and villages all over the occupation zones, the corridors of municipal buildings were hung with the names and dates of the missing and, often enough, the dead. The Red Cross and other organizations were responsible for their distribution and maintenance of the lists. Small photographs of children were displayed to one side. Refugees and people driven from their homes in East Prussia, Silesia, Pomerania, the Sudetenland, and my native city, Danzig, soldiers of every branch and rank, the evacuated and the bombed-out, millions of people were looking for one another. Mothers needed to find sons and daughters they had been separated from during their flight; infants without names needed to find parents. Often pictures of small children were captioned only with the name of the place where they had been found.

Seeking and finding. Women still hoping for the return of their fiancés or husbands. Girlfriends and boyfriends missing each other. Everyone was missing someone. I, too, scoured the lists, posted weekly, for signs of my parents and my three-years-younger sister.

Against all reason I still pictured them at home—Mother never budging from behind the counter, Father mixing dough in the kitchen, sister playing with her braids in the living room—I couldn't or wouldn't imagine my family away from home: evicted, without the familiar furniture and oleographs, far from the tile stove that heated both living room and bedroom.

Was the radio still standing on the sideboard and who listened to which station? What had become of Mother's glass-fronted bookcase that had actually been mine? Who was leafing through the albums full of meticulously pasted cigarette card pictures?

Anyway, either immediately or after brief hesitation, I wrote to the distant relatives, who had once lived in Danzig-Schidlitz. But before I heard back from them, one of my barrackmates, who was from Upper Silesia, got married. The bride, a widow, came from the local village.

SHE stands before me in all her glory, a blonde always good for a laugh. First she is in curlers, then in a wedding dress made of parachute silk that had been acquired in exchange for hundred-weight sacks of potash salt. Another coupler boy and I had to serve as witnesses because nobody in the village would do it. The bridegroom, who spoke the Polack German that was to be expected of a Kattowitz native, played a mean harmonica and performed a song with endless stanzas, of which I can recall only the lines "If there's a flea/on Antek's knee,/He wants to run,/And find a gun."

The celebration in the war widow's one room got rather boisterous. There were only the four of us: nobody from Gross Giesen, the surrounding villages, or Sarstedt—no relatives, no neighbors had come. Neither the sister nor even the parents of the bride had deigned to sit at the same table with what to their Lower Saxon understanding was a foreigner, hence a ne'er-do-well. And once a foreigner, always a foreigner.

We drank an inordinate amount, as if to quench the thirst of the missing guests. The groom, the witnesses, and—most of all—the bride were determined to whoop it up, have a grand old time. We washed down our pig's neck with alcohol out of tumblers. I don't remember who drank more, who less. There was plenty of potato schnapps and whatever else was available on the black market, even egg liqueur. We downed so much of the suspicious liquids that all four of us could have ended up blind: there had been reports of collective poisoning as a result of family celebrations, the cause being methyl alcohol in otherwise watered-down schnapps. But we just kept toasting the bride's health and loudly cursing the absent guests.

At some point the four of us tumbled into the marriage bed of the onetime war widow. Not blind but blindly. What transpired then amongst so much flesh no onion skin wished or wishes to recall. The bride, perhaps, is the only one who knew, felt, or sensed what did or did not happen during the rest of the night and with whom definitely, with whom probably or definitely not, and with whom many times over.

On the wall at the head of the marriage bed hung an oil painting depicting either two beautiful swans, a couple, or a lone stag belling.

By the time we awoke the next morning, no, it was closer to noon, the blond newlywed had laid the table for breakfast. The room smelled of fried eggs and crisp bacon. She was smiling her blond smile, beaming it at her husband and the two coupler boys, all three of whom were staring past one another into space, hardly speaking, and when they did, it was about the next, the late shift.

SUCH was the depressing and fuzzy end of a wedding night, at the surface in the lee of the pit tower and with a view from the bedroom window of the slag heap dominating the countryside, which resulted rather than happened. Below the surface, during the outages, miners went on with their disputes. Tired of hearing the same things over and over, I kept my distance. I seemed to have sweated out my one-time Young Nazi sympathies once and for all and wanted nothing more to do with that troublesome past dragging along behind me. But I found none of the miners' hackneyed ideas alluring, even though in the place where the only valid idea had once bound everything with everything, a gaping hole opened up.

What could fill this void, invisible though it was?

The basis for the coupler boy's self-rescue operation appears to have been an unremitting, if diffuse search for meaning during the periods of enforced silence when, removed from his argumentative comrades and lit only by his carbide lamp, he memorized the vocabulary and iron-clad rules of a dead language, thereby becoming a scholar in the end.

This absurd situation has remained so clear for so long that I can still hear myself conjugating verbs. There can be no doubt: the coupler boy trying diligently, doggedly to improve his miserable Latin 950 meters below the earth's surface is none other than I. As in his school days, he still grimaces as he reels off his *qui quae quod, cuius, cuius, cuius . . .*

I mock him, I call him a figure of fun, but nothing deters him: he is out to fill the void if only with the slag of the language his pal in the Bad Aibling camp knew so well and called world-dominating for all eternity. Joseph had even claimed to dream according to its incontrovertible rules.

I was most kindly lent a grammar and a dictionary by a retired gymnasium teacher who resided in the bishopric of Hildesheim, mercilessly destroyed at the tail end of the war, and who in exchange for the nonsmoker's cigarettes tutored me in her attic room.

I had met her by chance, where I can't remember. She wore thick glasses and would sit, cat in her lap, in an armchair upholstered in wine red. "A little Latin never hurts," she would say.

Whenever I had a day off, I would hop on a bus for Hildesheim. She never offered me more than a cup of peppermint tea after the sessions.

BUT then a series of postcards from relatives close and distant brought my reversion to scholarship to an end. The message was always the same: Your parents and sister survived the war and the expulsion from Danzig with no visible damage. They have recently managed to move from the Soviet to the British Occupation Zone. They had been living in Mecklenburg and crossed the border with only two suitcases. After a brief stay in Lüneburg, where your grandparents had found refuge, they have been sent to the Rhineland, near Cologne (the north had long been overcrowded) and housed on a large farm in the Bergheim-Erft district.

The far-flung relatives had other things to say as well. About the ravaged city they came from—"Our Danzig is no more"— and all the terrible things they had suffered. Their response to the "reputed crimes" they couldn't have known about was: "But not a word about the injustices the Poles visited upon us."

They also wrote about the violence they had endured, about the missing, the dead. They reported that Grandpa complained all the time. He couldn't accept losing his carpentry workshop: "the circular saw, the planing machine, all the door- and window-mountings he had stored in the basement."

And they complained about the general poverty, which was steadily increasing: "Those expelled like us are the worst off. Nobody wants us. And we're as German as anybody here . . ."

It must have been the Gross Giesen mayor's office that gave me my parents' Rhineland address. In any case, I took off by bus one day after the early shift without quitting my job. It would have been shortly before Christmas or rather early in the new year. Something had held me back until then. Was it the pit foreman's affectionate daughter?

The roads were covered with snow and the snow kept falling. My luggage included a kilo of butter I had saved up and two big bromine bottles, lifted from the mine laboratory, of beet syrup, my share of the harvest. No, I don't remember any tears from the pit foreman's eldest daughter or words of farewell to the rapidly departing coupler boy from her father. Even so, another piece of pit property must have made its way into the duffel bag

I was using as a suitcase, because when more than twenty years later I was traveling through the region to help set up voter initiatives in preparation for the elections to the Bundestag—the issue at hand was Brandt's "New East-Bloc and Germany Policy"—and told the Social Democrat candidate after a rally in Hildesheim about my underground past and the outage debates, thus revealing how far back Social Democratic uncertainty began to color my political outlook, he must have found my résumé a bit too artfully constructed, a kind of complement to an episode in the novel *Dog Years,* and had a look at the rolls of the still highly profitable Burbach-Kali Limited, which stated that someone bearing my name had left the Siegfried I Mine "having absconded with a pair of the company's clogs."

Potash is no longer mined there and more rape is grown than sugar-beets, but the white slag heap still rises out of the flat fields and shows no signs of disappearing, a reminder of a time when sugar-beet theft and power outages were the order of the day, grueling work meant special ration coupons, a clever girl corrected a fledgling poet's spelling mistakes, freedom went on trial in verbal battles, and a stupid coupler boy received an education in the pit of the Siegfried I Mine.

From Hanover I took the train to Cologne, from Cologne the bus again through a now familiar Lower Rhineland, accompanied all the way by frigid weather. No one who experienced it has forgotten that early winter: it began in late November and went on and on, bringing heavy snows and relentless frosts. Rivers froze, water pipes burst. Coal and coke distribution broke down. There were no warm public places. The freezing starved, the starving froze.

The winter of '46–'47 was especially deadly for children and elderly people living alone. Coal supplies were looted, trees cut down, tree stumps uprooted. Tugs laden with coke stuck in the frozen canals had to be guarded day and night. Humor became ersatz fuel. That perhaps explains why the municipal theaters of Hanover and Cologne were performing *A Midsummer-Night's Dream,* the actors cavorting lithely and the audiences clapping wildly to keep warm.

The lack of heat and calories notwithstanding, life went on. I too, who had recently escaped from the warmth of 950 meters below ground, now froze in the unheated train, the cold, wet bus.

All the passengers froze, but I felt worse hit than any of them despite the preventative pit-heat and coupon-calories I had garnered as a coupler boy and the mittens the pit foreman's eldest daughter had knitted for me as a going-away present.

Perhaps the physical cold was exacerbated in my case by the inner fear, lurking just behind the joyful anticipation of a family reunion, that the encounter with Father and Mother would be disappointing, and because the parents and the sister had grown distant, the cold would be even more piercing, and the son and brother would stand before them a stranger.

Meanwhile I held tightly to my duffel bag and its contents, the kilo of butter I had saved up, and the bottles of beet syrup.

I DID not announce the return of the prodigal son: I wanted it to be a surprise. But when I stepped off the bus, who was waiting at the Fliesstetten stop, as if wanting to surprise me, but Mother, Father, and Sister? They were on their way to Bergheim to get refugee papers stamped. A coincidence?

Later, Mother would say it was Fate. She firmly believed it. Everything that occurred, fortune and misfortune, my very survival—in fact I should have been dead—she put down to Fate: it all happened according to a higher will, providence. Besides, a Gypsy woman had predicted the return of the son: "Mama's pet" would come laden with gifts, she had said, which could only have meant the butter and syrup.

The son was horrified. There they stood, in coats now too large for them. The mother looked careworn. The father had managed to save his felt hat all through the war. The sister, without her braids, a child no longer.

They tell me I greeted her with a "Look at you, Daddau! You've become a young lady." And since whenever there is room for doubt she remembers things differently than her brother, "closer to the truth," she says, she insists to this day that the fortune teller existed. "Honestly. She *predicted . . .*"

Not long ago on a visit to our estranged native city with a few grandchildren, the two of us were walking along the beach between Glettkau and Zoppot lost in brother-sister talk about this and that, including the new pope, when suddenly, while the children were inspecting the foam of the waves for amber, she said, "Even though we couldn't give her anything to eat—we didn't have anything—the Gypsy woman read Mama's palm just before you came and promised, 'Your darling son will be home in three days.'"

SOME two years earlier—though it seemed a lifetime—in September of '44, when Danzig still had all its towers and gables, Father had accompanied me to the Central Station. He had carried my cardboard suitcase in silence. His round party badge was pinned to his suit jacket. I, still sixteen, stood next to him on the platform in knee-length trousers and a jacket already too small, my induction letter was in the breast pocket. Mother had refused to see her son be packed off to Berlin and, as she believed, to his death. Now Fate had brought us back together.

We embraced, compulsively, over and over. Wordlessly, or with meaningless phrases. Too much, more than could be put into words, had happened in the course of a time that had no beginning and could have no end. Some things came up later, others were too horrible for words.

The repeated violence done to my mother had muted her. She was old now and ailing. Little of her liveliness and wicked tongue remained.

And was that shell of a man my father? He who set such great store by dignity and self-possession.

Only my sister seemed unharmed by what had happened. She seemed almost too mature, looking up at me, her "big brother," with bright, inquisitive eyes.

IT WAS not until then that I began to see what had not been sufficiently clear during the last years of the war, in the hospital, in the POW camps, and in my desultory, ambulatory freedom, when my only concern had been myself and my dual hunger. Everything was different, everything altered by loss. No one was unscathed. Not only houses had been reduced to ruins. In hindsight the crimes coming to light with peace, the flip side of war, were making victims out of perpetrators.

The people standing before me had been expelled from their homeland as individuals, but among millions they were of mere statistical value. I embraced survivors who, as the saying went, had got off with a scare. They went on with their existence somehow, but . . .

We knew nothing about one another. "Our boy is back!" my father cried out to the people getting off the bus or getting on the bus to Bergheim. But I was no longer the boy he had seen off at Danzig Central Station, when all the churches of a city built for all eternity tolled their bells in farewell.

The officials in charge of relocation had moved my parents and sister in with a farmer. This kind of thing was usual at the time, because volunteers willing to take in refugees and those expelled were few and far between. Especially where no damage was visible—where house and stable would continue to pass from father to son and not a hair on the head of either father or son had been touched—the farmers refused to accept the notion that defeat, instead of the much ballyhooed final victory, applied as much to them as to the wretched refugees.

Only because he had been forced into it by the authorities did the owner of the farm let my parents stay in the partitioned, cement-floored room, a former fodder kitchen for force-feeding pigs. Complaining got you nowhere. "Go back to where you came from!" the man would reply, cocksure of himself and his land and as Catholic as the farmer I'd run away from the year before. People here had always been suspicious of, even hostile to, outsiders and what they now called interlopers; there was no reason to change now.

The general cold was made worse by the cement floor, which had no cellar underneath. The small supply of winter potatoes had suffered from frost damage. When thawed, they caved in if you poked a finger at them, and when cooked, peeled or not, they were watery and waxy and cloyingly sweet to the tongue.

The pigsty stank, and the wall of the fodder kitchen was coated with ice.

We slept in one room. The sister with the mother in one bed, the son with the father in the other. We were even more crowded than in my childhood, when we'd also slept four to a room, in the Langfuhr two-room flat, but then we'd had the white tile stove. Here there was only a cast-iron stove in the anteroom. We would gather around it in the evening, pressing as close as we could, saying what could be said, then escaping into eloquent silence.

We fed the fire with briquette pieces that Father brought home from work in his rucksack. He had found a job in the porter's lodge of the local open-cast brown coal–mining operation, where his neat, legible penmanship served him well. He kept track of who came and went during shift changes and signed visitors in and out. The briquettes were payment in kind. When my parents finally found a place to live, in Oberaussem, a village near his work, they were allotted an even larger quantity of "black gold," both oblong pieces and briquettes.

The place where my father was now working was an industrial plant that pumped massive amounts of steam into the air from a line of chimneys. It was called Fortuna North as was later a chapter in *The Tin Drum*, in which a corpse is reburied in the cemetery of the mining village Oberaussem, and as the corpse comes to light piece by piece Oskar Matzerath delivers his variant of Hamlet's question: "To marry or not to marry?"

IT MUST have been a week after my, if not homecoming, then surprise arrival, that my father returned from work laden with briquettes and what he termed "glad tidings." "I've found a terrific trainee position for you. In the administration. On the top floor, in the executive offices. It's nice and warm there . . ." He said more, and not without pride, unaware of the higher expectations of his son. His sky-blue eyes were not sparkling.

Perhaps he tried to buck me up with the slogan often quoted in the business sections of the high-circulation newspapers: "The future is in brown coal!" And irrefutable arguments like "You should be glad to land a job like that without having finished school." But at the time my well-meaning father must have been disappointed when the only thanks he received from his son was a laugh. Yes, the prospect was so remote from my dreams that it sounded funny, and I'm afraid I made fun of him.

"Me, a paper pusher? Ridiculous! Within three weeks I'd take off with all the official documents. You don't want to make a crook out of me, do you?"

Whereupon the thankless son spelled out precisely what he had his heart set on.

But what precisely did I want? Can it be that the prospect of an office job my father so lovingly threatened me with was what gave a precise direction to my desires?

With a stack of rhymed and rhymeless hemistiches—some in the fair copies the pit foreman's daughter had typed up—plus a good dozen drawings of solid-looking "pals" from my days as a POW plus any number of my graphic representations of either miniature or monumental figures of all sorts, naked and garbed, standing long-legged, fallen to the ground, keeling over in grief, as well as some half-animal, half-human form with a figurative turmoil in their heads—and since for as long as I could remember my inner world had been rich in characters—I wanted to become a sculptor, someone who turns mere clay into forms which, because of their tangible presence, dominate space.

Something along those lines was what, no longer laughing, I told my father, who immediately broke into thundering tirades against "starving artists" and "obsessive notions." It was a side of him I had seldom seen.

Nor was he off the mark in his warning or, rather, prediction of my immediate future: "Choosing a profession that can land you in the poorhouse in the best of times, let alone when nobody knows what the morrow will bring. Get that out of your head!"

As for my mother, who, gazing at the unplastered walls around us, never stopped bemoaning the fact that she hadn't removed her oleograph of Böcklin's *Island of Death* from the wall of the Langfuhr flat, taken it out of its frame, rolled it up, and tucked it away in their luggage, who, sober businesswoman though she was, revered all art as divine, who saw her brothers, all of whom had died so young, live on in a son snatched from the jaws of death by Fate, my mother shared her husband's concerns on the one hand but on the other could not give up the dream that her darling boy would one day create something beautiful, beautiful and melancholic, something combining the sad and the beautiful. It was a hope that always brought a smile to her lips, one that she nurtured deep within her whenever I and my high-flown plans and rose-colored promises came under discussion.

Before long a smile came to erase the anxiety that stemmed from the horrors she had experienced, but sitting at the briquette fire knitting stockings out of undyed sheep's wool for the peasant woman's children in exchange for rye flour and oat flakes, she did venture to ask about a prospect that at the time could be reasonably belittled as pie in the sky. "Tell me, my boy, do you really think you'll be able to live off your art?"

In a newspaper—or could it have been in an illustrated magazine—I found an article saying that the Düsseldorf Academy of Art, which was not too far from where we were, had begun offering instruction again. The article dated from the previous summer and included a picture of a professor of sculpture with bangs by the name of Ewald Mataré surrounded by students.

Another picture showed a piece by the master, simple in form, a cow reclining in the grass, something my mother could like. "But what makes you think they'll accept you at a bona fide art academy if you haven't finished school? They'll just laugh at you! You'll never get in."

That didn't bother me. Nothing bothered me. Decades later, when my sons and daughters started off on their various straight and roundabout paths—Laura, for example, ignoring her father's advice and choosing to be and remain a potter rather than, talented though she is, an artist—I would recall how recklessly I wrenched myself free of the constrictions of our emergency digs, a potential breeding ground for the conflict between father and son, without giving it a second thought.

Thus ended a brief guest appearance that had caused everyone to suffer, particularly "Papa's pet," my sister Waltraut, whom looking back I see as pretty, cheerful bordering on inane, and apparently free of inner strife. The dimple that appeared the moment she smiled. The shoulder-length permed hair that had replaced the braids. What would become of her? She looked so young and innocent. There was no sign whatever of what she had seen or possibly suffered in Danzig "when the Russians came." It wasn't something we talked about.

After two weeks of family life I was trudging through deep snow in the gray light of dawn, with little luggage, the flakes now whirling, now floating onto my duffel bag. My goal was Stommeln station, four kilometers away. Only the telegraph poles guided me. Progress was slow on the road to satisfying my third hunger, the hunger for art.

THE THIRD HUNGER

FROM an early age it was impossible to deal with, whether by practicing ascetic moderation and limiting myself to black-and-white or by yielding to the addiction and staining every piece of paper in sight. Not even stuffing myself with books to the point of verbal nausea could stave it off. There was never enough. I was always greedy for more.

The ordinary hunger everyone knows could be alleviated for hours by turnip soup with a few sparse globules of fat or even by frost-damaged potatoes, and the desire for carnal love, that panting, unbidden, unyielding onslaught of ever self-renewing lust, could be deadened by a chance encounter or a few flicks of the wrist. My hunger for art, however, the need to make an image for myself of everything standing still or in motion and thus of every object that throws a shadow and even of the invisible, the Holy Ghost and Its Intimate Enemy, that ever evanescent capital—if only by adorning the papal financial headquarters, the Banco di Santo Spirito, as a temple of the obscene with portal figures—this desire to conquer all with images was insatiable, accompanying my conscious self by day and my dreams by night, even as I fed it with promises when I decided to study art—or what I in my limited view considered art. But for a time, the circumstances of the winter of '46–'47 stood in the way of my wishes.

Having made the trek to Stommeln station through knee-deep snow, freezing and sweating at the same time, having bought a one-way ticket and believing thereby that I had run away from my newly found family, I had to accept the fact that at the end of the endless slow-train journey no one was waiting for me in Düsseldorf with open arms.

And having asked my way through the city, which had been bombed, though not so badly as Cologne, Hanover, or Hildesheim, to the massive building of the Academy of Art—there were no trams whether because of the snow or a power outage—I found the dark box on the edge of the Old Town open but no one in the porter's lodge to call out a friendly "Welcome!" or "We've been expecting you!"

First I knocked on doors, pressed door handles, wandered past locked studios along corridors upstairs and down.

I can still hear my steps, see my breath disappear into the multistoried ice cellar the building had become. To keep from losing strength and heart, I probably carried on a dialogue with myself: Don't give up! Hold out! Think of what your friend Joseph once said: "Grace doesn't just fall into your lap . . ." And all at once, when I was about to leave, I met Art in the person of an old man who looked like nothing so much as a silent-film cliché of an Artist. I could see his breath too.

Not until two years later did I learn more about him. The man who came up to me wrapped in a black cape with a black scarf wound around his neck and a broad-brimmed black felt hat on his head appeared to be in his mid-fifties. His name was

Enseling, he was a professor of art, and he could count on full
retirement benefits. He was probably there to go to his studio,
where life-size and terrifyingly white naked plaster-of-paris figures of both sexes stood freezing. Though he may simply have
wanted to exchange the cold of his apartment for the cold of the
Academy.

"What is your business here, young man?" he inquired
immediately.

"I want to be a sculptor," I blurted out. Or did I say something like "I've decided to be an artist"?

Give me a moment to think back, to consult the onion. The
issue at this crucial juncture was whether to act or to desist. No,
more: to be or not to be. What does the onion say on its sweating skin?

I may have burdened the figure clad all in black with the
knowledge of art gleaned from the cigarette cards of my youth,
but no matter how often I conjure up the staircase meeting it
must be permanently frozen, it yields no quotations. All I can
hear is the professor's sobering response, "We are closed due to
lack of coal."

At the time it sounded final. But someone, who was definitely me, refused to be disheartened or shaken off. I must have
reiterated my desire to become a sculptor with such vehemence
in that echoing room, that the professor, whom only young
eyes could have seen as an old man, apparently believed in my
hunger.

He asked questions. My age, nineteen, seemed either neutral
or acceptable. He swallowed my oh-so-significant birthplace
without commentary and wasted no breath on religion. The fact
that when in school I had done some model drawing with the

well-known equestrian painter Fritz Pfuhle, who gave evening courses at the Danzig Institute of Technology, did not elicit so much as an *a-ha*. Nor was he interested in hearing about the timely end of my more than sufficient war experiences. And— luckily—he asked no questions about the *Abitur,* the exam that opened all doors.

Instead he gave me clear directions—take a left, then a right, and on the right-hand side of the street—to the nearby Hindenburgalle employment bureau.

He told me I should apprentice myself as a stonemason and stone sculptor. It was a trade that never wanted for work. There was always a call for tombstones.

He concluded, my beardless prophet of an occupational counselor, by intoning, "Once you've finished your training, young man, you can apply for admission. We shall certainly have coal by then."

No ifs or buts. I, who since the war's end had shied away from any orders except the advice of the battle-scarred private first class, I, the war child badly burned and therefore inexorably attuned to contradiction, I, who had learned over time to suspect any and all promises, I—or whoever I was at the time— followed his directions, though not blindly. The words of the prophet had provided me with the only way to proceed, and no one could possibly have argued me out of it. He spake. I went.

Oh, if only I had such clear-cut directions to give my grandchildren today, when, just having finished or just about to finish school they ask me what road to take where: "Make sure you do this, Luisa, before you . . ." "Whether or not you have the *Abitur,* Ronja, you . . ." "Lucas and Leon, my advice to you . . ." "And so, Rosanna, if you started later, you . . ."

Anyway, within a half-hour I had succeeded in procuring an official document with the handwritten addresses of three stone-cutting operations, all of which, given their clientele, were in the vicinity of the municipal cemeteries. There was nothing bureaucratic about the process. School records were not required.

MEMORY is strangely moody: the snow suddenly melts, the frost abates; the outages are over, and the trams run again.

I decided to stick with the first firm I went to see, near the Wersten Cemetery, because in the workshop of the master Julius Göbel I found an old stonecutter by the name of Singer chiseling away at a splendidly muscular Christ with a head facing left. The Christ was part of a bas-relief on a broad stone wall and so true to life you couldn't take your eyes off him.

But it wasn't so much the athletic diabase Jesus that attracted me as the prospect of learning the craft from his maker. I said yes even though Göbel, who wore formal attire rather than the garb of the guild and rarely put his hand to a stone or a chisel, made it clear I would do nothing but straight-line work during the early stages of my training.

Looking more like a sweet-talking tomb salesman than a master mason, Göbel showed the future artisan the finished products lined up in front of the establishment waiting for grief-stricken customers. An apprentice was sweeping the already melting snow caps off their tops.

The names and dates of the dead were still to come. Matte or polished to a high gloss, meter-high, pillow-shaped, or wider than long, their prices varied. The bereaved who came to buy had more than Göbel's line at their disposal: his Bittweg establishment bordered on several others, their wares similarly displayed. There was a brisk business in the fleeting quality of human existence, the euphemistic phrase used in the trade for death, even in times of need.

Göbel would list the varieties of marble and granite and show us the differences between sandstone and limestone. He would bemoan the shortage of malleable material and point to a pile of cast-off tombstones in a luxuriant weed-bed, their antiquated inscriptions in need of removal before they could be reused. He would refer to each part of a tool by its name and complain that a Swedish-made flat chisel with a specially tempered steel core, known as widia, had been unavailable for years for want of hard currency.

LATER, much later, when I was finally able to get it word by word out of my system, I wrote an entire chapter about tools like bush hammers and embossing- and drove-chisels, about Silesian marble and Belgian granite, travertine and dolomite. I couldn't have done it had it not been for my somewhat ghoulish professional experience. After all, the lifeblood of literature is nothing if not a stray button, the horseshoe of an Uhlan's mount scraped free of rust, human mortality, and, therefore, weathered tombstones.

The Tin Drum—a book whose contents made waves before it ended up between covers, from the moment it learned to walk—is constantly crossing the wanderer's now straight, now winding path to art and the narrow track between literature and reality, *Dichtung und Wahrheit.*

In it, for example, I released Korneff, senior journeyman, from Göbel's employ and set him up in his own small-time workshop so he could show the hunchbacked hero of my first novel how to take a coarse but malleable slab of stone and turn it into a polished meter-high monument over an individual grave by using a straight-edge, chisels both pointed and toothed, and a gouge. That loquacious hero, Oskar Matzerath, who has come to detest black marketeering as a means of existence, is as eager to learn as I was when, though without a hump and other novelworthy life experiences, I began my training.

One never knows what will make a book. For example, the transformation of lived life, life in the raw, into a text undergoing constant revision and coming to rest only between covers, can come from a tombstone belonging to an unsightly pile of tombstones shunted off to their side, their time having passed. Because master craftsman Göbel so willed it, the deeply carved, wedge-shaped inscriptions had to be so radically removed that the stone's face contained no trace whatever of a man by the name of, say, Friedrich Gebauer, born 1854, died 1923. Various tools then served to make the diabase into a shiny surface, in which the name and dates indicating a new lifespan could be carved in cuneiform, eternal until the officially determined statute of limitations ran out again. Renewable carved stone becomes the basis for the limited span of our afterlife. Names move on, inscriptions—such as: "Death is the Gate to Life"—do not need to be removed, chiselled off.

Just as I have described the interplay between material declared dead and material revived, so I could go into the interplay among flesh-and-blood persons. For now, let me limit myself to one, my journeyman Korneff, though I am uncertain what his name really was. What is certain is that he suffered from boils. His neck was particularly susceptible to them and was notched with thick scars. Every spring, and thus in the spring of '47, he developed abscesses the size of dove's eggs that you could almost feel by looking at them and that would yield a good schnapps glass of pus. As soon as the boils began to sprout, the brazen apprentices would parade up and down Bittweg singing, instead of "Spring's come again, parting is pain," "Spring's come again, Korneff's in pain . . ."

I also know for a fact that Göbel, whose firm is called Wöbel in the novel, proclaimed the name of the enterprise in capital letters on his sign. More businessman than craftsman, he was instrumental several years later in giving a number of new buildings travertine façades and marble floors with the help of a stone sawmill he had purchased in nearby Holthausen. His rapid rise during the initial stages of the German economic miracle would make an interesting novel.

When I signed the apprentice papers, I was attracted to Göbel's firm for another reason: besides the laughable monthly salary of a hundred marks, which is the amount the miserly small-timer Korneff paid his trainee Oskar, I was promised a hearty meat-and-vegetable soup twice a week, with second helpings guaranteed.

Göbel's wife would cook masterfully seasoned soups in the house just next to the workshop. I remember her as a cow-eyed matron with a crown of braids in the style of the Reich women's Führerin. It looked good on her. Childless though she was, she deserved the Golden Mother Cross awarded in earlier times to mothers of particularly large broods, so attentive was she to the needs of those at her table.

When selling tombstones to peasants from the Rhine's left bank, Göbel charged ten kilos of legumes, a side of pork, and several unplucked chickens above and beyond the cash price.

For a double tomb of Main River sandstone Frau Göbel could expect a sheep, whose ribs and flabby stomach would end up in her soup. And a child's pillow-sized tombstone would bring two Saint Martin's Day geese, of which we especially savored the smaller pieces—wings, neck, heart, stomach—in a rich broth.

She fed us all, everyone who ingested the stone dust of the workshop: three sickly apprentices, a pair of Silesian journeymen brothers who specialized in text-carving, the senior journeyman Korneff, the stonecutter Singer, and me, the self-confident neophyte whom one of the Silesian brothers immediately advised not to think so highly of himself, not as an artist at least.

Later he told me about Breslau, undamaged at first, fiercely fought over at the end of the war, then totally destroyed. What he deplored more than the untold dead dumped by cleanup crews into mass graves was the missed opportunity to make their tombstones.

The Silesian brothers knew their literature. They could recite the epigrams by Angelus Silesium and would carve them into stone: Be to the spirit true, For when the world doth fade, And Fortune fadeth too, The spirit's not gainsaid.

So I BECAME an apprentice with the firm of Göbel & Co. The question now was where to live. The duffel bag and faithful haversack spoke volumes about the trainee's homelessness. But since a trace of my mother's Catholicism still clung to me, and I could call the Only True Church by its name when asked about my religion by Herr Göbel, help was soon on the way. He put a call through from his office to God the Father apparently, and having recommended me as a disciple of the Faith, secured for me, on the spot, a place to sleep, if not in paradise then in its local branch, the church's Caritas House, in the Rath district of town.

From the Bittweg tram stop, where, as I have pointed out, a number of stonecutting establishments bordered on one another, including the firm of Moog, which specialized in sandstone and basalt and appears in *The Tin Drum* as C. Schmoog, my future home was within easy reach by tram: I had only to change at Schadowplatz. It was as if, thanks to my mother's intervention, a guardian angel had descended and seen to everything without my having to lift a finger.

AT THIS point memory makes gratis offers by the dozen—so much happened at once—and leaves the choice to the narrator: Shall I stick to stonecutting or run through my inner life piece by piece? Is this the time to do a survey of the Danzig cemeteries in anticipation of my late novella *The Call of the Toad,* or does it make sense to move in straightaway?

The Düsseldorf-Rath Caritas House, not far from the badly bombed Mannesmann plant, was run by the Franciscans. Two or three fathers and a half-dozen friars operated an institution that had at one time cared for wandering artisans, then more and more for the homeless and lonely old men. The monks are even said to have taken in a serial killer by the name of Kürten during the twenties. And because the need for it had never abated, the building complex, which emerged from the war miraculously unharmed, still set off only by low walls and a fence, had outlived every regime change, remaining an effective enclave of good works: in peace, as in war, it was always full.

The prior of the establishment was Father Fulgentius. He was middle-aged, wore a habit, and had a gruff look about him, but instead of quizzing me on my belief system, he rummaged around in a musty used-clothing box: he thought the new-comer, the young man in the dyed uniform, should have a set of civilian clothes to wear. I also needed proper overalls for Göbel's workshop: the coupler boy had given his underground gear too severe a beating.

I was allowed to outfit myself from head to foot. The Prior even fished underpants and two shirts out of the box so I could change regularly. Then there was a sweater that had clearly been knitted out of multicolored ends of wool but that kept me warm for a long, long time. Last but not least, Father Fulgentius forced a blue tie with red polka dots on me. "For Sundays," as he put it—a bald hint at the possibility of my attending the Caritas Chapel services.

It all matched. As for my new self-image, I must have looked fabulous, because what do I see when my memory opens like a wardrobe door but a pair of trousers ironed for feast days and my first postwar jacket—with a distinct herringbone pattern.

The dormitory of the main building, which owed its solid-ity to the architectural practices of the 1880s, was at best a vari-ation on the usual. My sleeping accommodation was, as it had been when I was a Luftwaffe auxiliary, a Labor Serviceman, a tank gunner, a prisoner of war, and finally a coupler boy, the upper deck of a bunk bed. The bed was one of five in a window-less room, which, as became evident by evening, was inhabited by students and apprentices either slightly younger or a few years older than me. And like me they lusted after girls and talked endlessly about women and their fleshly attributes. In better days they could have taken one or another willing young lady to the nearby Grafenberg Woods, but in the winter of '47 the woods, like everything around, were frozen solid.

And by the way, the paths crisscrossing those woods led to the sanatorium where several years later a patient would ask his male nurse, Bruno, for five hundred sheets of innocent paper, a request that had its consequences.

NEXT to our room, windowless because trapped in the middle of the building and never free of the smell of young men, yet nice and warm, was the cell of a serving brother, whose monk name I have forgotten, though I have retained every feature of his lanky frame, always rushing off somewhere in his habit.

We looked upon him as an angelic apparition: even when he was overseeing the most mundane of operations—the distribution of bread rations, for instance—his eyes, forever red, seemed to be gazing on the Virgin Mary. He also had a ring of keys hanging from a rope around his middle that announced his comings and goings from two corners away. I never saw him sitting. He was constantly on the go. He ran here, he ran there as if answering a call. No one knew how many locks he presided over.

This friar, who seemed so timeless that we cannot pin an age on him, kept an unobtrusive but ever friendly eye not only on us, who were denied "female visitors" by signs nailed to our doors, but also on a large room full of permanently wheezing old men, as many as a hundred of them, though no fewer than seventy, cot after cot of the dying and self-renewing clientele that made up the Caritas mission.

He could peer into the dormitory any time day or night through a trapdoor-like window in his cell and so keep track of his superannuated charges, whether frail or lifeless, or collectively overcome by coughing fits, or engaged in a sudden squabble. As we drifted off, we could hear him talking through the opening, lulling the men to sleep as if they were children, his intonation retaining a trace of his Westphalian roots.

Sometimes the nameless monk let me look through the opening. What I saw, the multifarious fragility of human existence, has so retained its immediacy that I can see myself and hear my by now incurable smoker's cough in one of those seventy to one hundred cots: a serious case in the friar's care. And sometimes when against all rules I crawl under the covers and light my pipe, he scolds me through the opening, gentle yet insistent.

The door to the old men's refectory, to which only he had access, was on the other side of our dormitory, and the refectory's high windows looked onto a courtyard that in summer enjoyed the shade of chestnut trees. The benches under the trees were always taken by the old men, most of whom suffered from permanent coughs or asthma.

Every morning two kitchen monks placed a large pot of semolina porridge on the table in our room. It was made with powdered milk contributed by Canadian Franciscans. Despite loud and repeated complaints about its burnt aftertaste it never improved. On some days it didn't linger very long; on others it clung stubbornly. My gums never forgot it.

After us, the old men were fed the morning gruel. The kitchen monks ladled it out through a cafeteria window. They, too, spoke to the men as if they were children.

Caritas House having provided me with cheap room and board for years, I can state that up to and even beyond the currency reform, which so changed everything, my breakfast consisted of semolina-and-milk porridge, two slices of whole-meal bread, a bit of margarine, and, depending on what was available, plum jam, artificial honey, or a gummy cheese spread.

Sometimes on Sundays and regularly on high church holidays, like Corpus Christi, we got a hard-boiled egg as well. On Sunday noon we would have meatloaf or chicken fricassee followed by jello or vanilla pudding. The evening meal was similar and similarly forgettable.

On workdays each student on his way to lectures or apprentice on his way to work would pick up a small tin pot that could be snapped shut, known as a Henkelmann, containing a portion of soup too nondescript to reveal its ingredients.

The kitchen kept our food ration cards, but we ate our fill; the only cards we received were for clothes and cigarettes.

So SUPPLIED, I went to work day after day. Compared to the general poverty outside Caritas House, I was in good shape but for the fact that my secondary hunger made itself felt, habitually and with special insistence, the moment I got on a tram.

I would board the invariably crowded vehicle near Caritas House and take it, ringing its way from stop to stop, as far as Schadowplatz, where I changed to the tram for Bilk and the Wersten cemetery.

I never got a seat. Half-asleep and wide-awake, silent and talkative, passengers of both sexes stood jammed together. I smoked, I watched, I listened to the babble of the Rhineland dialect. I smelled threadbare clothing and looked at the women who because of the war outnumbered the men. Half shoving, half shoved, I would insert myself between young girls, find myself forced between old women. Even when I wasn't wedged between them, my trousers would rub against female clothes. With every stop, with every start of the tram, cloth and cloth, flesh and flesh beneath the cloth moved closer.

Winter coats and quilted jackets steamed, but when spring came, thinner clothes rubbed together. Knee met knee. Naked underarms, hands stretching up to the straps, too close.

No wonder my penis, which had a mind of its own and excited easily, was either half erect or fully throughout the half-hour ride. Nor did it relax when I changed trams. It made my trousers tight. And not even my intensive thinking about neutral topics could lay it to rest. Satisfied by the morning porridge, the one hunger had ceded to the other. And did so day after day.

I was always embarrassed, constantly worried somebody would notice the bulky thing and take it as an indecent offense or, worse, call indignant attention to it.

But none of the skirted, bloused passengers I stood too close to ever got upset. No one whispered umbrage into the ticket-collector's ear with her eyes fixed on me. Only the owner of the rebellious willie was aware of the revolt in his pants and of his inability to put it down.

In time, the passengers came to know one another by sight. They arrived punctually for a tram that was generally there on time. They would venture a smile, quickly erase it, and try again. They would nod, and though still strangers, get closer and closer.

From the giggles and chatter of the women and girls, I knew or sensed that they worked in department stores, telephone exchanges, offices, or on the conveyor belt at the Klöckner plant. I pushed my way determinedly between working women and seldom rubbed against housewives.

When autumn came, the morning crush landed me between two students from the acting school, both in floral dresses. Quite affected and not worried about being overheard, they went on about Hamlet and Faust and the current celebrities of the Düsseldorf stage, the famous Elisabeth Flickenschildt and the even more famous Marianne Hoppe, but most of all Gustav Gründgens, the shady master of the art of disguise, the embodiment of traditional stage discipline, and my idol since I first saw him on the silver screen when I was a schoolboy.

Hearing all that gossip, I suddenly felt the hunger for art awakening next to the other one. It made me want to chime in with my ideas on Grabbe's *Comedy, Satire, Irony, and Deeper Meaning*, which I believe was part of the repertory that season. But I just mutely moved closer to the future actresses, flat-chested and bony as the calorie-poor times had made them; they, caught up in their enthusiastic babble, were unaware of what my over-active imagination had in mind for them: both together or one right after the other.

Both tried to look like Goethe's Gretchen or Kleist's Kätchen von Heilbronn, and both practiced bits of monologues they were working up. They had mastered Flickenschildt's trilled *r*, but they lacked the sophistication to get Hoppe right, the bubbling flow of her delivery. We never exchanged a word. I later saw Sartre's *Flies* directed by Gründgens in a makeshift theater, and thought I spied my rubbing partners in the chorus wearing insect costumes.

But most of the time it was the office girls or telephone operators I rubbed up against and who rubbed up against me and caused me such blissful torment. I barely remember the faces, but one of the girls I came too close to had eyes wide apart that looked impassively past me.

Not until I was face-to-face with the rows of highly polished tombstones in front of Bittweg's stonecutting establishments, waiting for names and dates, did my regular morning half-hour arousal die down. Likewise the aftertaste of burnt porridge.

I would hand over my Henkelmann full of nondescript soup to the master's wife, and she would warm it up in a pan of hot water at noon together with the canteens of Singer the sculptor, Korneff the senior journeyman, the Silesian text-carvers, and the sickly apprentices.

Only on Tuesdays and Fridays did I leave for work without my Henkelmann. Those were the days of the delicious and nutritious meat-and-vegetable soup. They had their price, however, a price exacted promptly in equal measure from the apprentices and myself.

NEXT to the area where the stones were stored was a shed where the master's wife, who came of peasant stock from the left bank of the Rhine, and a great animal-lover, kept five Leghorns and a goat that was supposed to give milk and that required a daily supply of green fodder. The goat had a shaggy white coat and a pink udder. Its facial expression was not free of arrogance. Whether it actually gave milk I am uncertain, but the moment I ask the onion I see an udder full to bursting demanding to be milked by the master's wife.

Day after day the apprentices and I took turns leading the goat on a string to a spot where there was a supply of weeds. There was no green fodder to be had among the tombstones on display, because the Leghorns had the run of the place which eventually gave me a subject for a poem entitled, "Fowl in the Central Cemetery"—but there were plenty of weeds on the other side of the fence.

When everything green along Bittweg, down to the nettles, had been grazed clean, the only meadow left was the tram tracks heading toward Wersten and on to Holthausen. There was enough for days along both sides.

The apprentices, or lads, as Korneff called them, were perfectly happy to see to their obligation even if it deprived them of a good part of their lunch break. One of them, a boy with glasses who had a hard time with the stonework, and later switched to the post office, where he is said to have made quite a career for himself, would stay out longer than required, much longer than the break, looking for food.

For my part, the more I had to do with the goat, Genoveva by name, the more it rankled. In itself, and because of the spectators. The thing is, the buildings of the Municipal Clinic stretched along the tracks behind a row of trees. It is not unusual, after all, for hospitals to be located in the vicinity of cemeteries and stonecutting establishments. There was always a lively flow of pedestrian traffic to and from the main gate, and it consisted of more than visitors. Nurses, alone or in cheery groups, walked under the trees. Ah, how they twittered! The sight of me, young man with stubborn goat, raised more than just a smile.

I had to endure all kinds of remarks, mostly mocking. My work clothes, with their coarse, stained material, and the stubborn beast, always tugging in another direction and bleating its lungs out, made a laughingstock of me, or at least that's what I thought. I attracted barbs the way Saint Sebastian attracted arrows.

I was too shy at the time to fling them back at the nurses in their starched white uniforms. Instead, I merely blushed, and the moment the wicked tongues were out of sight, kicked Genoveva the goat.

When you think you've been pilloried, you long for revenge. Usually it falls flat or, as in my case, takes ineffectual forms such as the swallowed insults and curses that should have been mating calls.

My noontime forays had the following consequence: my hero Oskar Matzerath, who at about the time I was out feeding the goat was having growing pains and had therefore been admitted to the Municipal Clinic, succeeds at first go in getting one of the nurses attending him to agree to an assignation, and no sooner is he released as cured, than he takes her out for coffee and cake. I could not even bring myself to speak to a nurse, let alone ask her out. I was merely the tragicomic sidekick of a mulish goat with a dangling udder.

Oskar knew how to make the most of words; I seemed always at a loss for them. He, who could market even his hump, had dozens of ideas in store; all I could come up with were awkward and hence misleading gestures. The most ancient tricks in the art of seduction flowed gracefully from his lips; I was heard swallowing, swallowing words.

If only I had been as brazen as Oskar! If only I had had his wit!

It didn't help that I seemed dogged by bad luck. Because the one time I had a pleasantry ready, for a nurse with a Madonna-like face, who was out walking on her own, and some words of flattery in reserve, my goat, my albatross, began to piss loud and long.

What do I do? Look the other way? Seek support in the tombstones lining the street opposite the tracks? Make believe it wasn't happening?

All in vain. The milk-goat's piss went on and on. Some pair we made!

I might feel the blood rush to my face even now were it not for another memory, one capable of bringing Genoveva's flow of urine to a halt: it was not long afterward that I did finally score, though in a very different arena: the dance floor. My favorite halls were the Wedig and the Löwenburg. I was in demand as a dancer. And that young man's limber-legged victory paid off a second time a few years ago, in the poetry of an old man who thought himself limber enough for "Last Dances"—if only for the length of a *tango mortale*.

DANCE-MAD weekends. On workdays, though, I continued, under Korneff's guidance, to practice delivering blow after even blow with the mallet we called a club, and hewing and chiseling surfaces on rough limestone and Belgian granite. Soon I was able to make a groove around a piece of Silesian marble big enough for a child's tomb. I even attempted an egg-and-dart edging for the stone of a professor emeritus.

Old man Singer taught me how to use a three-legged instrument called a pointing machine to transfer point after point from the plaster-of-paris model of Christ on the Cross to the still formless chunks of diabase while I kept hewing away. A moveable needle measured the deepest and highest points on the model of the body, as the machine shifted back and forth between plaster and stone. The surface had to be not only hewn but also gouge-grooved to ensure the accuracy of the needle's readings. Anyone who tried to cut corners would be caught in the act by Singer, peering over his glasses. Singer, who had chiseled at Hamburg's Bismarck monument in his youth, taught me to give stone a face.

I developed calluses: my skin grew hard under the stippling iron. My muscles grew hard as well, which was good for display purposes. I looked like a manual laborer and in the coming years nursed the belief that if need be, in the case of political backsliding—for instance, a return of censorship and an official ban on writing, I could support my family as a stonemason, a thought that soothed me and gave me self-confidence. Because as everybody knows, the tombstone business is brisk even in the worst of times. Death takes no holidays. Göbel's supply of tombstones, single or double, was always in demand.

So away we chiseled, swallowing the dust that billowed up from the Belgian granite, as sulfurous as an old man's fart. The final polish was provided by a grinder. Over the weekend, the dust settled: Saturdays and Sundays were for dancing.

THIS is how it started. The monk watching over the hacking graybeards and us, the bunk-bed youths, the friar rushing about with flapping habit and clanging keys, would stand stock-still in the open door of his cell on Saturday afternoons, looking on in pious reverence as we made ourselves presentable.

I would climb into the black trousers I had fished out of Father Fulgentius's used-clothing box. In the laundry room, the monk serving there had ironed sharp creases into them. These in combination with my herringbone jacket must have given me the air of a professional gigolo. Unfortunately, there was no mirror in our ten-bed room.

An engineering student who was getting on in years, who fit my private-first-class image but eventually became a manager for Mannesmann, where he made a fortune in tubes during the economic boom, taught me how to tie the medium-large knot. Some gave their shoes a mirror shine, others smoothed down their hair with sugar-water. Everybody got all spruced up.

And through it all our reverent monk would stand there, hands in his habit sleeves, looking on motionless, until we whooped off to the dance hall as if we had just discovered buried treasure.

I had an easy time of it: I'd been a dancer for as long as I could remember. At various non-church festivities at Zinglers Höhe or Kleinhammerpark, Langfuhr's popular garden restaurant, I was there before and after the beginning of the war, not only as spectator and note-taker for future works. Whenever the local petty bourgeois gathered in civvies or shit-brown uniforms to take the floor, the thirteen-year-old boy I was at the time, led by lonely soldiers' brides, learned to dance: the Rheinländer, the one-step, the foxtrot, the English waltz, I even learned the tango, young, and was therefore considered desirable on the dance floors of the postwar years. The Dixieland band that played "Shoeshine Boy" and "Tiger Rag" and "Hey Bob a Re-bop" could also be persuaded to strike up a tango.

There were dance joints all over the place: in the cellars of Düsseldorf Old Town, in Gerresheim, and in nearby Grafenberg, a suburb bordering on the woods whose sanatorium later gained a certain notoriety, thanks to a patient with a memory mania, and whose meandering paths the overheated dancer found refreshing when escorting this or that telephone operator to an inviting bench, or the much desired mossy patch of ground.

Change your partners and blind-man's bluff—imprecise memories of touching lost in more black holes. No names to name except for a busty Helma, who asked me to dance at the Löwenburg one night when the lights dimmed and a ladies' choice was announced, and who clung to me after a foxtrot.

It was a dance-crazy time. We, the defeated, couldn't get enough of the twelve-bar liberation offered by our transatlantic victors. "Don't Fence Me In . . ."

We needed to celebrate our survival and forget the chance scenes staged by war. What was shameful or horrific we left to lurk below the surface. The past, and the hills rising above its mass graves, were leveled on Saturdays and Sundays to the dance floor.

It was only after many years that I could have the Grafenberg sanatorium occupant dance a one-step to the tune of "Rosamunde," that Oskar was allowed to call things I had passed over in silence by their names, to put into words what I had suppressed as burdensome. Yet even now, a half-century later, horrors come knocking at the door, demanding to be let in.

Memory rests on memories, which themselves go back to memories. In that, memory resembles the onion, which, as each skin peels away, reveals something long forgotten, all the way down to the milk teeth of early childhood. Then comes the knife and fulfills another function: chopping the skins, it provokes tears that cloud the sight.

YET I have no trouble picturing myself on the benches under the chestnut trees that supply the Caritas House courtyard with shade. I sit there each time with a different old man, trying to get his face down on paper. I do pencil sketches of the misty, impassive eyes and tear ducts, the dry ears, frayed and crumbly around the edges, the constantly muttering mouth. I draw the forehead, a furrowed field, the bald spot enshrouded in a fleece of sparse hair, the gently throbbing skin above the temples, and the neck, the shiny, wrinkled leather.

With the special luster of soft lead I can give a three-dimensional quality to the jaw and the ridge of the nose, the pendulous lower lip, the receding chin. Folds transverse and vertical form the forehead; the pencil lines swell and disappear in the shadows behind the lenses of his glasses. Two craters: nostrils sprouting gray hair. Endless gray tones between black and white: my credo.

From childhood I have drawn with pencil. Close-ups of gloomy, crusty brick walls. Eraser at hand until it crumbles into nothing. Later, much later, I sang the praises of this, the pencil's orderly, in a cycle called "My Eraser and the Moon, Both Waning."

The old men would sit on the benches of Caritas House in half-profile, heeding my order to keep their eyes focused on an object. I kept them for one or two hours, during which many of them had asthma attacks. Their whistling breath. Sometimes their babble was threaded with World War I, Verdun, the inflation. I rewarded them with cigarettes, my personal currency, two or three of them, which they would smoke right after the sitting—or after a lengthy coughing fit—down to the last draw. Still a nonsmoker, I always had the wherewithal to pay them: I gave precedence to drawing from live models and was careful not to deplete my supply. Only once did an old man with a wildly wavy mop of hair offer to sit gratis "just for art's sake," as he put it.

———

THE artist under the chestnut trees, however hard he worked, missed a guiding hand. What I would have given to be able to show a few of the woodpaper pencil drawings the stonecutter's assistant thought were reasonably successful to the art teacher who was doing her compulsory civilian service soon after Stalingrad, when the total war began. I was fourteen or so when she gave a class at Saint Peter's. Every Saturday she was expected to deal with a group of rude, visibly bored oafs, some of whom managed to put down hairy cunts or stick figures with ridiculously long willies on paper.

Those too dull even for this she left to their own devices, that is, to playing skat or sleeping their way through the double period; the rest she provided with lessons in perspective. There were only two or three she cared about, the ones she felt had a sliver of talent.

I was one of those who enjoyed her attentions. Not only that, she invited me to visit her at her garden studio in Zoppot. She was married to a lawyer much her senior, a quartermaster behind the lines on the Eastern Front, and lived in a cottage surrounded by weeds. I went to see her there I can't say how many times.

In short pants or in the long pants of the Hitler Youth winter uniform, I would take the tram to Glettkau via Oliva and walk from there, all anticipation, either along the dunes or down where the waves rolled in, but instead of looking for amber amid the seaweed washing ashore, I would turn left, just before Zoppot's first villas, past hedges just beginning to bloom or, in late summer, full of rose hips. The garden gate squeaked.

She was from Königsberg, but it was at the Danzig School of Technology rather than at the art academy in her hometown that she had found her teacher, Professor Pfuhle, the well-known equestrian painter, the one whose evening course I later attended.

She wore her hair straight and short, in the style of the twenties, and it goes without saying that the schoolboy bearing my name was what you might call distantly in love with her. But there were no furtive glances, no touching. She got close to me, turned my head, in a completely different manner.

On the "smoking table"—she was a chain-smoker—she had placed, unintentionally or by design, a pile of art journals and catalogues as old as I was, or older, some in black-and-white, others in color.

So the schoolboy leafed through them and saw forbidden paintings by Dix and Klee, Hofer and Feininger, sculptures by Barlach—the monastic scholar reading—and Lehmbruck's large kneeling woman.

I saw other works as well, but what exactly? All I remember is the thrill they gave me. I was fascinated by these things I'd never seen before—fascinated and terrified. It was banned, the lot of it, as "degenerate art."

The newsreels had shown the moviegoer what the Third Reich considered beautiful: sculptors like Breker and Thorak outdid one another producing larger-than-life marble heroes. Lilli Kröhnert, chain-smoker, whose squint put me off a bit, the young woman with the bobbed hair and the faraway husband, my beloved teacher, who always had another Lehmbruck to show me but also made reference to sculptors tolerated by the regime, like Wimmer and Kolbe—Lilli Kröhnert ran the risk of being turned in by this pupil she took to be not without talent. Betrayal was the norm. An anonymous tip was enough. In those years, ideologically zealous pupils were not beyond sending their teachers—witness the case of my Latin teacher Monsignor Stachnik—to concentration camps.

Lilli Kröhnert survived the war. In the early sixties, when I was touring Schleswig-Holstein with my five-year-old twin sons, Franz and Raoul, and stopped in Kiel to give a reading from *Dog Years,* I got together with her and her husband—he, too, had come out of it alive—in neighboring Flensburg the next day. Still the chain-smoker, she smiled when I expressed my gratitude for her daring art lessons.

If only she could also have given me pointers when I, still the nonsmoker, sketched coughing old men with soft lead and paid them in cigarettes . . .

AFTER my primary hunger was stilled by tasteless Caritas soups that nonetheless left an aftertaste and my other hunger, which, though intensified by my workday tram rides, was tempered by affectionate dance partners over the weekend, there remained the third, my lust for art.

I see myself in cheap seats in Gründgens's theater—was that the year they did Goethe's *Tasso* or was it the following year?— and intoxicated by the flood of images from the exhibitions of Chagall, Kirchner, Schlemmer, Macke, and who else?

At Caritas House, Father Stanislaus fed me Rilke, Trakl, a selection of Baroque poets, and the earliest Expressionists. I read everything he had managed to safeguard in the Franciscan library through the Nazi years.

And accompanied by an approachable teacher's daughter— the two had fled Bunzlau together—I tamed my lust for everything stimulating to the ear in addition to the eye at least for the length of an evening at the Robert Schumann Hall.

But my reading mania coupled with the passive consumption of artistic products merely heightened my hunger and drove me to produce art of my own.

I turned out poems by the yard. My lyrical metabolism working overtime. And instead of working harder for Göbel, I did my first small sculptures in limestone: two female torsos, an expressive girl's head. I also went on filling up Pelikan pads with whatever my asthmatic old men had to offer in exchange for tobacco: page after page of the most varied, scarred, burned-out, dried-up, skin-and-bone faces. Stubbly or bearded, eyes blinking or tearing, they were the true faces of age. Whenever I rewind time, and the benches under the chestnut trees in the bright spring, summer, or autumn light flash into sight again, I watch myself sketching on my pad those half-awake faces awaiting death.

Since the result of the nonsmoker's efforts has gone astray, I am uncertain whether I also perceived my roommates as models. Or it may be that Father Fulgentius, prior of Caritas House, he of the sullen and pockmarked countenance, or Father Stanislaus, the Rilke lover, an aesthete who trod softly and enjoyed quoting passages from "Die Trutznachtigall," by the Baroque monk Spee von Langenfeld, also made their way into my pad. I so wish there were a page on which our ever watchful friar, the one whose gaze was always expecting a Marian miracle, had been depicted as an angel. Though among the missing multitude only the sketches of the old men are a certainty.

AFTER a year with Julius Göbel, Korneff the senior journeyman, and Singer the stonecutter and his three-legged pointing machine, after weeks and weeks of vegetable soup and of leading

Genoveva the milk-goat ever farther for her weeds, the trainee thought it was time to move on.

Away from the bleating beast, from the punctured plaster torsos of athletic Christs on the Cross, from the *contrapposto* of marble Madonnas on crescent moons, from the glossy shine— forbidden by law—of polished granite and from the roses I sculpted into medallions on children's tombs. I never wanted to see another Leghorn pecking between tombstones.

I was attracted by a larger firm, Moog, at the far end of Bittweg. They dealt primarily in sandstone, tuff, and basalt fresh from the Eifel quarries. They weren't likely to do new inscriptions for giant old slabs. They wouldn't give me a goat to tend.

Still, it wasn't easy to say good-bye to Korneff and his journeyman charm. In the spring we had cemented a number of one- to three-body tombs and their pedestals onto foundations in cemeteries swarming with birds. We had also seen to the reburial of corpses desirous of switching graves. Working with him made working with death more or less bearable. He had a wicked tongue.

Since Korneff later had the chance to lug around marble and diabase with his assistant Oskar Matzerath all the way to the "Fortuna North" chapter, to witness those reburials, and to hand over the Henkelmanns full of nondescript soup at the cemetery crematorium at noon to be warmed up (a piece of advice he gave to me as well as to Oskar), we shall assume that we have exhausted the theme of tombstones and cemeteries, except perhaps with respect to the issue of literature and reality: who put what in whose mouth; who is the better liar, Oskar or I; whom should one believe in the end; what is missing both here and there; and who guided whose pen.

Given that Herr Matzerath was never an employee of the Moog concern, however, I hope I may now proceed with the late birth of my early years without further ado.

Entertaining as it may be to sweep up the eggshells of one's own incubator children, the dustpan usually shows remains of questionable origin: the pedant's details or once discarded ideas waiting to be revived—for example, the rumor that no sooner had I left Göbel's concern with Master Singer's blessing than Genoveva and her rope jerked themselves loose from the apprentice in charge of her midday expedition and that instead of going out into the world she uttered her final bleat under a tram on its way to Bilk. Göbel's wife, the cow-eyed matron, is said to have opined that it was out of grief at my departure that Genoveva flung herself under its wheels.

DURING my first months with the firm of Moog I took part in a project with the apprentices and journeymen that instead of beautifying the surrounding cemeteries was meant to deal with the war damage still very much in evidence in the city's parks and also in the Hofgarten.

Where sandstone figures had been decapitated or turned into one-armed invalids by bomb fragments our job was to provide the goddess Diana or the gorgon Medusa with an appropriate new head based on photographic or plaster models, to restore lost limbs and cloven angel's wings. But Moog was also commissioned to create whole new putti with cute little hands, rolls of fat, dimples all over the place, and luxuriant locks. The forward-looking Herr Moog had clearly found his way to the authorities' hearts.

And so we spent our days repairing war damage, patching and mending. From the apprentices, each of whom came from a long line of stonemasons, I learned that a false blow of the hammer in stone was irremediable unless it could be hidden by a clever ruse. The recipe for a putty that was neither too thick nor too thin I owed to Master Singer, who had entrusted it to me—he considered it a professional secret—as a going-away present.

As for true art, the cause of my continuous hunger, I got my first idea of what it entailed when an anonymous client commissioned several copies of a ninety-centimeter torso. Herr Moog acted conspiratorial as he removed the woolen blanket in which it had been wrapped.

It was clearly the work of the once widely recognized, even acclaimed sculptor Wilhelm Lehmbruck, whose art had been banned from all museums during the Nazi period and whom I had met as a schoolboy, if fleetingly, in the banned art journals my teacher Lilli Kröhnert had shown me. She had called him one of the truly great.

Nobody at Moog's actually mentioned the name, though there were rumors about its lineage. "Hey presto!" one of the journeymen joked. "First one, then three."

So many sandstone sculptures were being made. The order must have come from an art dealer who trafficked in copies that he sold as originals on the black market. In those postwar years there were plenty of gullible buyers, either native nouveaux riches or the imported American variety. It was a time of fakes.

In any case, the three copies in bright sandstone were snapped up before they could be put on display.

The armless torso went from mid-thigh to the crown of a slightly turned head. The tilt of the pelvis gives the *contrapposto* effect. A Lehmbruck of the middle period, shortly before the outbreak of World War I, probably done in Paris.

As usual, we transferred the many points we had penciled on the surface of the plaster model to the stone using the three-legged machine with its moveable needle.

Our work was supervised by Master Moog himself. The apprentices from stonemason families may have known plenty of tricks, but the moment Moog the heavyweight put in an appearance all tricks went by the board. He would raise his overlapping eyelids with two fingers, check every detail, and let first one, and then the other eyelid fall. He looked like a Buddha. He never resorted to the needle attached to the end of the swiveling metal arm, he never missed a single error.

To my shame I must admit that I made quite a few blunders on the calm yet mobile surface of the torso's back. These had to be reworked, which meant that the stone layer between the shoulder blades had to be evened out, but what had been removed from the surface was gone for good.

I WONDER who is enjoying my Lehmbruck, one of the copies, today. The client of the anonymous dealer of yore or, if it has since been resold, a new owner. But I would give anything to be able to ask Wilhelm Lehmbruck, who took his own life shortly after World War I, to forgive me my trespass.

I really should use my at times successful method of issuing a "subjunctive" invitation to him, whom Lilli Kröhnert praised as incomparably great, and to the painters Macke and Morgner, who fell in battle at Perthes-les-Hurlus and Langemarck, respectively, to break bread with me at my imaginary table.

We would fall into conversation about current events—how enthusiastically we went to war—then only about art. What has happened to it since. How it survives every attempt to ban it, yet once the external constraints are removed has on occasion contracted into a dogma or vanished into the abstract.

We could then laugh at the junk assembled for installations, the fashionable shallowness, the restless videomania, the event-hopping—the beatified scrap metal, that is, in the overfilled void of the ever contemporary art business.

Then it would be my privilege as host and cook to treat my guests on their leave from death to a fine meal: a bouillon of cod heads seasoned with fresh dill, for starters; next, a leg of lamb larded with garlic and sage, lentils simmered in a spicy marjoram sauce; and to top it all off, a fine chèvre with walnuts. With brimming glasses of aquavit we would toast one another and rail at the world.

From Lehmbruck, the dour Westphalian, we would have only the briefest of pronouncements; from August Macke, who liked to talk, an account of light patterns and other adventures on the short trip to Tunis with Paul Klee and Louis Moilliet in April 1914, a few months before the war broke out; and Wilhelm Morgner would let us in on what sort of paintings he would have done—abstract, perhaps?—had he not been in the trenches in Flanders and . . .

But no word about Lehmbruck's unhappy love affair with the beautiful actress and child-woman Elisabeth Bergner. They say he took his life on account of her, but I doubt it. It was the war, which in his head, in many heads would not end . . .

After the meal I would surely find an opportunity to thank

him, the chance master of my apprenticeship who set the standard by which I learned to fail . . .

AND then? Then came the currency reform. Nineteen forty-eight, a date separating the before from the thereafter, putting an end to everything and pledging a new start to everyone, devaluing what was and giving what was soon to be new value, letting a trickle of nouveaux riches filter through a mass of starving poor, pulling the rug out from under the black market, promising a free market and thereby giving both wealth and poverty long-standing status, consecrating money and making consumers of us all and giving business a general shot in the arm—witness the case of the Bittweg stonemasons, whose prices until then had been determined by barter, trade in kind.

Shortly before the momentous date Moog received a contract for the face-lift of a bank building still the worse for its war wear. The moguls were ashamed of their façade. The coming event was to be greeted with a beautified exterior, on time and on budget.

The sections of the shell-lime blocks damaged by bomb fragments had to be chiseled out and filled with rectangles of malleable shell-lime, cemented in perfectly flush with the surface. What was our client's name? Let's say it was the Dresdner Bank, newly rebaptised the Rhein-Ruhr Bank.

Only one photograph from this period survives. It shows a young man high up on a steel scaffolding looking out at the world as if he owned it. To signal his profession, he holds a wooden stonemason's mallet in his left hand—he is left-handed—and a stippling iron in his right.

A colleague must have snapped the picture. A chiseled indentation in the background makes it clear how strong the natural-stone exterior of the building is: although its interior was completely destroyed by fire, the tall building survived the hail of bombs, and is now greedy for fresh capital and renewed profits.

The young stonecutter stands alone because the board of directors of this monetary bastion, which had served all systems in power, including one of organized crime, did not wish to be photographed; they wished to remain behind the scenes. They were content with having all external damage removed from the bank's façade. They were interested in re-establishing their reputation, at least externally.

The gaunt young man in the peaked cap and work clothes perched self-confidently on the scaffolding, master of all he surveys, is none other than me, shortly before the currency reform. An action self-portrait.

The bank's upper floors I stand before, small yet recognizable, in this black-and-white photo, were not yet ready for use because fire damage had yet to be taken care of, but the main hall on the ground floor was due to be opened to the public shortly.

On the story above we stonemasons sat through the lunch break spooning our Henkelmanns empty. Since there was a hole covered with boards in the ceiling between the ground floor and ours, we could see through the narrow cracks.

And so several days before the Great Day I saw the new currency—both banknotes and coins—being sorted, counted, bundled, and packed in rolls on long tables by the employees making ready for the wonder-working cash gush. And so I became a witness.

What we would have given for slightly longer arms—or fishing rods. The newest articles of faith, so near and yet so far. We would have turned, well, not bank robbers but Robin Hoods, stealing from the rich to aid the poor.

At that point my hourly wage at construction sites was ninety-five reichspfennigs an hour. With overtime, my weekly income came to about fifty reichsmarks. Before long they were worth nothing.

Did I have any idea that down there in the main hall of the Dresdner Bank, and at a thousand and more distribution points all over the country, it was the future that would be paid out, a future that would thenceforth have its price?

SUDDENLY everything, nearly everything was for sale. Yesterday's shabbily stocked shop windows now boasted articles long hoarded. Items came out of nowhere to attract the new currency. All the shortages suddenly seemed to have been manufactured, to be a deceptive relic of the past. And since everything belonging to the past had lost its worth, everyone looked bravely—hard as it might be—to the future.

I don't know what I bought with the forty new deutschmarks hard cash each citizen received in the name of a blinking justice. Genuine Faber Castell pencils and a new eraser, perhaps. Or was it a Schmincke watercolor set with four-and-twenty little bowls?

No, most of it probably went to tickets for a trip to Hamburg I had invited Mother to take with me. She wanted to visit her sister Betty and Aunt Martha, the wife of my father's eldest brother, Uncle Alfred, a police officer who had lived with his cousins in a Hohenfriedberger Weg row house and was now somewhere in the north, in Stade, not far from Hamburg.

The Hamburg ruins stretched far and wide, like the ruins in Cologne. It wasn't till I looked again that I saw the tall chimneys that had remained standing while one after another apartment building crumbled floor after floor to the ground.

Surprisingly enough there was a theater open, and since my mother had always been attracted to theaters, to plays, operas, and operettas—she once took me to a production of Hans Christian Andersen's fairy tale *The Snow Queen* at the Danzig Municipal Theater when I was a child—we went to see a play by Strindberg, *The Father,* with Hermann Speelmans in the lead role. She cried when the curtain fell. I have no memory of the relatives we visited, but I do remember the train ride there and back.

On the way there we soon passed through the bombed-out Ruhr and came to the Westphalian flatlands, which gave the impression that nothing world-shaking had occurred. I watched my mother sitting opposite me in silence.

She didn't care for my questions and was trying to get me to see the landscape as a "sight for sore eyes." "Look at those meadows! All that grass! All those cows!"

But I persisted. "What was it like when the Russians came? What actually happened? Why does Daddau just tell funny stories? Why does Papa beat around the bush? What was it like for Daddau, and for you? Did the Russians ever come and . . . And when the Poles came . . ."

She could find no words. The most she would let on was: "That's all in the past now. Especially for your sister. Don't ask so many questions. It doesn't make things better. In the end we had a little luck . . . We're still alive . . . The past is the past."

Then on the way back she asked me to go easy on my father. He'd been through a lot and lost everything. The shop had meant as much to him as it had to her. Not that he complained. No, and all he cared about was the son. He enjoyed his visits even if they were rare—"No fighting next time, please." The past was over and done with. "Just be nice to him, won't you? Or let's play a quiet game of skat. He's always so glad to see you . . ."

Not once during the few years she had left did my mother ever so much as drop a hint or utter a word that might indicate what had gone on in the empty shop, in the basement, or in the apartment, nothing that might indicate where and how often she had been raped by Russian soldiers. It was not until after she died that I learned—and then only indirectly from my sister— that to protect her daughter she had offered herself to them. There were no words.

Nor could I bear to come out with things long lurking within me: the questions I had failed to ask . . . my petrified faith . . . the Hitler Youth campfires . . . my desire to die a hero's death like Lieutenant Captain Prien of the submarines—and as a volunteer . . . the Labor Serviceman we called Wedontdothat . . . how Fate had saved the Führer . . . the Waffen SS oath of allegiance in the jangling cold: "If Others Prove Untrue, Yet We Shall Steadfast Be" . . . And the Stalin organ and all the deaths it caused, mostly among the young and unprepared like me . . . the song I sang out of terror in the woods until an answer came . . . the Pfc who saved me but lost both legs to a Russian grenade while I was spared . . . my belief in the final victory to the bitter end . . . the lightly wounded soldier's feverish dreams of a girl with black braids . . . the gnawing hunger . . . a game of dice . . . the disbelief at the pictures of Bergen-Belsen, at the piles of corpses—

look at them, go ahead look at them, don't turn away, just because—to put it mildly—it is beyond description . . .

No, I DIDN'T look back, or else took only a short, frightened peek over my shoulder. From the time I received my hourly stonecutter's wage in new currency and shortly thereafter at seven pfennigs more an hour, I lived exclusively in the present, or, as I thought, looked to the future. And there was no shortage of work.

Once the reichsmark fell, Moog started getting even more contracts for non–cemetery-related projects. Façades all over the city were in need of repair. Façades were a lucrative business. Scaffolding sprang up everywhere, and traces of the war disappeared on a piecework basis. The first monstrosities of the soon popular façade art saw the light of day, an especially sought-after material being travertine, the Führer's favorite marble.

We also moonlighted after work, delivering large slabs of dappled marble to a newly opened butcher's shop whose owner wanted bright, colorful walls and counters, or building high tuff walls around the private residences being bought up by the nouveaux riche.

But I was never able to practice art. All the war-wounded sandstone figures had been given back heads, knees, and the folds of their garments; the Lehmbruck torso, which bore my faulty signature, had found a buyer who believed it an original; the Caritas graybeards, who could now buy cigarettes without ration coupons, would no longer model for me beneath the chestnut trees.

No matter how much the new money jangled as I bought surprise presents for my parents, it could not, not even with overtime, assuage my third hunger. It was façades, façades, and more façades. Until I finally heard from the Academy of Art.

WELL before the deadline, I had submitted a portfolio of pencil sketches—the gallery of old men who posed between sneezes— and three small sculptures, the two female torsos, both modeled freely after Lehmbruck, and the expressive head, and appended a certificate attesting to my training and signed by Master Moog. In addition, as he assured his favorite lodger, Father Fulgentius had included a good word for my application in his morning prayers to Saint Anthony, who stood life-size in the Caritas House chapel in all his plaster glory and had charge of all sorts of things.

When I told the good father how fierce the competition had been—only two of the twenty-seven applicants had been accepted—and that although the admissions committee had recognized the potential evident in the portraits it pointed out that my experience in stonecutting was decisive, but that Professor Mataré was unfortunately unwilling to accept new pupils, which meant I would be unable to enter the sculpture program until the winter semester and then not with Professor Mataré but with a Professor Mages, whom I didn't know, the prior of the Düsseldorf-Rath Caritas House proposed another possibility, another way I might serve art.

We had often had conversations during which he would explain, or at least make plausible, the miracle of grace, the deeper meaning of the Trinity and other mysteries, and the joy God takes in the Franciscan vows of poverty.

These chats—sometimes he poured us each a small glass of liqueur—reminded me of the conversations I'd had over dice with my Bavarian friend Joseph when we were POWs together: he too tried to sniff out my childhood belief in the Sacred Heart and the Holy Virgin Mother of God and even then had a dozen or so theological tricks up his sleeve.

And like Joseph in the camp near Bad Aibling, Father Fulgentius, though less of a know-it-all, more peasant-sly and wily, tried to win me over. In the large bay window of the main building, which he called his office, he outlined a vision of the future whose medieval dimensions had a rare, attractive charm and reminded me of my schoolboy fantasies.

Recently, he told me, a sculptor brother, Father Lucas by name, had died at an advanced age in the main monastery of the Franciscan order. His studio, with its skylight and modeling stand and full box of clay, with its access to the open air and the monastery garden, was ready and waiting, waiting for a creative hand to put its full range of tools and stock of stone to use. Thanks to charitable contributions, that stock even included marble from the quarries of Carrara, the great Michelangelo's favorite. I had only to come to it in a spirit of joy. Faith would surely grow, gain strength as I worked on the Madonnas, and was eventually commissioned to do a Saint Francis and a Saint Sebastian. The pious devotion and unremitting diligence required by the work would inevitably lead to enlightenment. The rest, as he knew from his own experience, was grace.

At first he dismissed my doubts as to his view of my future and the outcome he desired, but when I began making reference to my secondary hunger and called it chronically incurable, when I painted my addiction to young girls, mature women, to the female sex as such in all its infernal carnality, outdoing the temptations of Saint Anthony by drawing on congress with animals and fabulous beasts from the Flemish workshop of Hieronymus Bosch, Father Fulgentius gave up his attempts. "Ah yes," he said, "the flesh," and tucked his hands into the sleeves of his habit. That is the first thing monks do when they are tempted by the Devil.

Decades later, however, when success had become a habit, fame boring, and popular resentment repellent and ridiculous, when the struggle with political opponents on the right and on the left had temporarily died down, when as an artist with a dual profession, as husband, father, homeowner and taxpayer, prizewinner and breadwinner for a growing family enmeshed in the business of day-to-day existence, I made excuses day and night, I wondered what my life would have been like had I listened during our games of dice to my Bad Aibling pal Joseph, who had since become a bishop, and swallowed his antidoubt pills like a good boy, revived my childhood faith, and with or without academic training followed the prior's advice, embraced his offer, and—first under probation, as a novice, then as a sworn-in regular—taken refuge in the monastery studio he had so praised . . .

I as monk. What name in Christ would they have given me? What would I have been assigned to sculpt besides the standard saints? Would I, like the Master of Naumburg, have paired important personages from business and politics on the pedestal: Chancellor Adenauer with the much acclaimed pollster Frau Noelle-Neumann? Or his big-bellied successor Ludwig Erhard with the long-legged film star Hildegard Knef? Or made bas-reliefs for cathedral doors: the Descent into Hell or Adam and Eve busy under the Tree of Knowledge, developing a taste for the Original Sin?

I wouldn't have had to worry about the first hunger, and as far as the third goes, I would have become a moderately pious painter, but the second hunger, so keen on flesh of another kind, would have led me astray whenever the opportunity, offered or sought, arose, and therefore dragged me helpless back into the world.

How I Became a Smoker

PEOPLE required by their profession to exploit themselves learn over the years to value fragments. Not much was left. Whatever tangible material enabled me to configure, disfigure, and finally—jumping forward, then back—pass on, has been swallowed up and excreted in cascades of words by the all-consuming monsters called novels. The lyrical gave way to the epic. After all that excrement—all grist to the mill—one hoped to have cleaned the system out, written oneself empty.

And yet there are remnants overlooked by chance: an ID card dating from the winter semester of '48–'49 and bearing the stamp of the State Academy of Art, Düsseldorf. Folded over, fraying at the edges, falling apart, it has a passport-size photo of a young man whose brown eyes and dark hair would lead one to believe he comes from the south, more Balkan than Italian. He has done his best to look presentable by wearing a tie, though he seems to be in the mood which shortly after the war was fashionable under the name of existentialism and visible in the faces and gestures in neorealist films, so god-forsakenly gloomy and self-absorbed is his gaze into the lens.

The physical characteristics entered by hand and the emphasis given to the downstroke in the signature confirm it beyond a doubt: this odd, ominous character is none other than myself in my first semester as an art student. The tie may have come from the charitable Father Fulgentius's used-clothing box. It was knotted for a quick shoot at a shop called Photomaton. The subject is clean-shaven, hair neatly parted, utterly noncommittal, allowing plenty of room for conjecture.

The long-standing affinity that I and my kind felt for existentialism—or what passed for existentialism at the time—was based on a French import adapted to German rubble conditions and could be worn as a mask becoming to us, the survivors of the "dark years," as one of the circumlocutions for the period of Nazi hegemony had it: it fostered tragic poses. You saw yourself at a crossroads or before the abyss, according to your mood. All mankind was supposed to see itself in jeopardy. The poet Benn and the philosopher Heidegger furnished quotes for the apocalyptic mood. The background to it all was the thoroughly researched and soon to be expected death by the atom.

Crucial to this lively going-out-of-business sale was a cigarette dangling from the lower lip. The dangle showed the direction we were headed in, though the cigarette, lit or cold, bobbed up and down in nightlong conversations, during which human existence was summarized as "the thrownness of things being." They dealt with meaning in what is meaningless, the individual and the masses, the lyrical I and the omnipresent nothing. Suicide would recur as a figure of speech, also called "free death." To contemplate it while smoking with friends was considered *bon ton.*

It may have been in the course of just such discussions, discussions so deep they would descend into the absurd, that the young man in the passport photo, celebrating an endless finale in the company of his friends, became first a tea addict and then a smoker, but I have trouble dating his initial, constantly post-poned reach for a cigarette.

And in general, sticking to the chronological course of events constrains me like a corset. If only I could row back to one of the Baltic beaches where I built those sand castles as a child . . . If only I were still sitting beneath the attic window utterly lost in my reading in a way I have not been since . . . or back with my friend Joseph under a tent, rolling the dice, for a future that seemed dew-fresh and unspoiled . . .

In any case, I had reached the age of twenty-one and thought of myself as an adult, yet I was still a card-carrying nonsmoker when, along with a girl from Krefeld whose animal sculptures—does and foals—had made a favorable impression on the admissions committee, I gained entry into Professor Sepp Mages's sculpture class. We were the youngest.

Somebody, presumably Father Fulgentius, had persuaded me to try the invigorating qualities of glucose instead of tobacco. (I assume it was Father Fulgentius, as he was the one who kept me supplied: like the powdered milk, it came from the Canadian fathers.)

But I couldn't help noticing that everyone else in the class, including a war invalid with a glass eye, was a smoker. The nude model, a portly housewife, would also light up during the break following each half hour of *contrapposto* posing, though I always gave her some of my glucose.

One of the students—quite a bit older than the others, who tried to mother me and wore her hair piled high on her head in what during the war had been mockingly called an "all-clear" hairdo—played the grande dame by using a cigarette holder. Her friend, who was the professor's pet and possibly his mistress, rolled her own and puffed away at them nervously until Mages entered the studio, at which point she would stub them out in a lump of clay. Everybody smoked. One of us even smoked a pipe.

I can only suppose that, overzealous beginner that I was, I imitated the way my fellow students picked up or rolled cigarettes just as I imitated the white, knee-length smocks they wore, standing in a semicircle before their modeling stands, looking up at the naked housewife, and going into physical detail with their wooden and wire modeling tools. We were not unlike a bevy of nurses and interns awaiting the visit of the head physician, because Mages, too, dressed in white, down to his beret.

In the overalls and garish wool-end sweater I had fished out of the Caritas clothing box I felt decidedly second-rate, and since the son felt the lack of a proper uniform so acutely, the mother, proud of her "fledgling art student," made a snow-white smock for him out of perfectly decent bed sheets, frayed only around the edges. Pictures taken at the time show me thus attired.

WHAT I can see more distinctly than the belated beginning of my career as a smoker is the first assignment I received, namely, to copy in modeling clay a larger-than-life late-Roman plaster head of a woman that Professor Mages had dug out of the antiquities room of the Academy and more or less foisted upon me.

A scaffolding of iron tubing that rested on a wooden stand and was crisscrossed by wooden sticks—we called them butterflies—provided stability for the clay. The slight twist of the head and copious curls in combination with a tilted profile made the bust difficult to reproduce.

I got some help from compasses and a plumb line, especially as the angle of the shoulder indicated a moderate turn of the body to the right. Another problem was the new material: soft, moist clay, which we covered with damp cloths when we left the studio at night.

Having had figures and heads very different from those of the late-Roman period in mind, I cursed my fate, but the more time I devoted to the plaster cast with a hint of a double chin, the more I learned. I grew curious and found hidden beauty in details, in the curve of the eyelids, for instance, and the set of the dangling earlobes.

The apprentice stonecutter had to chisel away a lot of hard material; the apprentice art student had to mold soft material, to model green-gray clay, and, like God the Father, fashion out of that clay if not an Adam then the head of an Eve.

A FLURRY of activity, because saints' days—Saint Martin's?—were being celebrated somewhere, but then all was quiet and concentration in the Academy's venerable building. Gradually the copy took shape, came to resemble her plaster sister. At the same time, there were drawings of nudes and studies of a complete male skeleton we called Tünnes or Schäl, after two popular Rhineland figures whose heroic deeds were the butt of numerous jokes at the time.

Then there was everything the city had to offer: exhibition after exhibition at the Kunsthalle. The painters of the Rheinische Secession, the "Junges Rheinland" group, Expressionists, the "Mother Ey" collection, Düsseldorf's local celebrities. I saw the works of Goller, Schrieber, Macketanz, the sculptor Jupp Rübsam. A painter by the name of Pudlich was all the rage.

One gallery exhibition featured the watercolors of Paul Klee, who had taught at the Academy until the Nazis kicked him out.

Before Wilhelm Lehmbruck moved to Paris, he was said to have been the star pupil of a Professor Janssen in our very workshop, and August Macke, another legend, was said to have learned what there was to learn here, for a brief spell at least. They were spoken of in hushed tones, perhaps because their brilliant careers had been nipped in the bud.

Sometimes I ventured to visit other studios. In one of them, a holy fool by the name of Joseph Beuys was considered a genius, though he was merely a pupil of Ewald Mataré. Who would have thought he would later occasion a precipitous rise in the price of artificial honey and various fats and felt?

I would look in on Otto Pankok's menagerie, a reserve where talents flourished in rank proliferation and Gypsy families traipsed in and out. No one would be seen dead in a white smock there.

In the class of the man who had given me a short but sweet bit of professional advice on my first day in Düsseldorf, Enseling, I met Norbert Kricke, who, true to nature and his teacher, turned live naked girls into plaster naked girls until he grew tired of them a few years later and switched to decoratively twisted wire figures in the spirit of the times.

There was a genius on every street corner, but none seemed willing to accept the fact that the "Moderne," from Arp to Zadkine, was by now one big museum piece. Disciples posed shamelessly as dazzling innovators.

Did I too take a running jump into the heavenly heights, or was my hunger for art satiated now that I could be sure of a trough that was at least half full?

Perhaps my training as a craftsman working in resistant stone saved me from dreams of grandeur. Mages, who came from a

Palatinate stonecutter's family, also helped to keep my feet on the ground. And then there was that mundane quality that stood at the top of the German catalogue of virtues: hard work drove me on.

Even though I still inhabited the ten-bed Caritas House room deprived of daylight, the spacious studio, with its large windows facing north and the smell of clay, plaster, and wet rags, had become my true home. Having grown accustomed during my stonecutting days to rising early, I was always the first to get to the modeling stand. Yet I was often the last to cover the day's work with those wet cloths. Where else could I grab a few hours alone? Well, not entirely alone: all ten of my fingers were actively involved with a malleable mass, with clay. It was akin to bliss.

Shortly before the Academy closed on Saturday, I would open the lower window facing the street wide enough for me to slip into the studio the next morning after scrambling up the bumpy natural-stone exterior.

This sounds daring, the material for a film sequence: the wild enthusiasm of the façade climber, another Luis Trenker scales the north face of the Eiger. But since both the sculpture studios and the plaster- and bronze-casting rooms were located on the ground floor, my Sunday climb was child's play. Nor was I the only one to do it—I just did it more often than most. No one took umbrage, and the janitor turned a blind eye.

About halfway through my first semester I persuaded one of my Löwenberg dance partners to take part in my Sunday climb and pose for me on our rotating wooden platform in the studio—which, though chilly, was at least minimally warmed by an electric heater. She was devoted enough to climb and pose, though not without complaint.

Unlike the housewife who posed for us during the week and whose mounds of flesh corresponded to the ideal of both the French master Maillol and my teacher, the weekend substitute shivering through her *contrapposto* contortions was slight of build, her collarbone, hipbones, and backbone all clearly visible. There she stood, slightly knock-kneed, while I turned her to catch the light that would show her gawky beauty to the best advantage.

Nervous by nature, she tended to cry when standing in a fixed position became too much for her. I worked quickly and in silence. As soon as she started fidgeting, I would offer her glucose instead of a break. Her mop of curls and her bush of pubic hair were flaming red.

Such was the self-centered determination that gave rise to the first independent piece of sculpture by the art student bearing my name. Our session over and the façade behind us—we never used the studio as a love nest—we would take the tram to Grafenberg, where ragtime was played until past midnight. My weekend model was easy to lead on the dance floor, too: supple and light-footed.

ELSBETH's proportions—was her name Elsbeth?—provided the basis for several clay figures, one of which, *Girl with Apple,* was cast in plaster and later recast in bronze. Also derived from those figures, under the supervision of my usually morose professor with beret, was my first large—just short of a meter high— sculpture, *The Laughing Girl.*

There she stood with hollow back and hanging arms, as far as she could be from Maillol's rotundity. Mages accepted that. The man who had to answer for several Nazi war memorials and two gigantic musclemen for the 1936 Berlin Olympic Stadium took pleasure in my undersized girl. What is more, my statue, with its somewhat foolish smile, and a statue the same size of a girl with markedly broader hips done by my classmate Trude Esser, received belated recognition when they appeared in the Academy's end-of-year report as outstanding class projects in the winter of '49–'50. Photographed head-on, the plaster casting, dyed and therefore looking deceptively like bronze, posed, angular and insolent, in *contrapposto*. The laughing girl had a whole page to herself.

The publication of the Academy brochure did not seem particularly momentous to me at the time, but looking back I can appreciate its importance. It was the only evidence, the only substantiation of my artistic ability—a mere claim until then—that predated my mother's death: she died of cancer at the end of January 1954. Though concerned and even anxious, she had put up with my eccentricities and flights to what she called cloud-cuckoo-land and never swerved in her faith in her son. Now there was something she could show relatives and neighbors with a modicum of pride: "Look at what my boy has done . . ."

Who can tell how this one piece became an icon for my mother. If only I had been able to offer her more to show around. But the sketches I did with a brush or reed pen were abhorrent to her: she found them too dark, too morose. At her request I borrowed some oils from a friend of mine, Franz Witte, and painted a lifelike bouquet of asters, her favorite flowers, onto a board made of pressed shavings. It was to be my only oil painting.

For more than two years my parents had been living near the Fortuna North brown-coal mine in an apartment that came with my father's job there, a two-room place with kitchenette, small but easy to heat, in Oberaussem, a village that was home to many miners. The rent was low, and little by little they added one piece of furniture to the next.

Whenever I turned up there—my visits were mostly unannounced—the Academy report would be lying on the table next to the couch, open to the page with my sculpture, as if Mother had sensed I was coming. She had always hoped her darling son would amount to something, and now that he had she hoped for more.

The tangible proof of accomplishment and the name of the accomplisher in print also seemed to have mitigated the long-standing discord between father and son and softened the tone of our conversations. My sister, who had begun an apprenticeship in business at Saint Mary's Hospital in Düsseldorf, could enjoy the familial peace and quiet occasioned by the Academy brochure when all four of us gathered. The harmony extended even to the times father or son lost ignominiously to mother at our kitchen-table skat games. Skat was a game I had learned by watching my mother play. She was known for making outrageously risky bids—and almost never losing them.

It is probably because she kept such zealous watch over the brochure that the ever laughing, scant-meter-tall girl has retained its significance all these years, although back then it and the rest of my medium-sized plaster figures meant so little to me that I left them all behind in the studio at the end of '52, when I made my next move. A fellow student took the little orphan with him.

A decade later, when I had a name and sufficient funds, he told me he had it, so a bronze casting could be made to ensure her continued existence. The same happened to *Girl with Apple,* the product of my wall-scaling skills: Edith Schaar, who had posed a short time for our class and later became a versatile artist in Spain and Northern Germany, rescued the plaster casting shortly after my sudden departure, thus helping me remember a time that otherwise, for want of tangible mementos, would have become as murky as an underexposed photograph.

TOO LITTLE can be nailed down. Moods at best, rippling through the interstices—some heavy and oppressive, some playfully light, but all unclear; no incident to brand me as player or victim; no memory of what I once recalled in excruciating detail. The onion balks. I can only speculate what happened outside my studio or Caritas House. I even see myself as only one of many sketches, each as far as the last from the original.

The art student in his second and then third semester, though still obsessed by art and fitfully addicted to new, often flash-in-the-pan influences, probably remained love-hungry and dance-mad, but I can't be sure whether I took sides during those years on issues like the break-up of the country, the onset of the Cold War here, and the far-off war in Korea, or if I did, what arguments I used. It was the time of highhanded "Ami go home" slogans.

I had an instinctive feeling of repulsion for the types who found the economic miracle, which happened to take hold first in Düsseldorf, to their nouveau-riche liking. True, I never strayed from that feeling, but now that he was entitled to cast a ballot, did the potential voter exercise his entitlement in the first Bundestag elections? Probably not. I was completely and utterly taken up with my own existence and the attendant existential questions and could not have cared less about day-to-day politics. When rearmament became first an issue and then a reality, the youthful war veteran, the child with burnt fingers, could have been counted among the admittedly large but nonetheless politically passive crowds of the "count me out" movement.

Chancellor Adenauer was like a mask hiding everything I detested: the hypocrisy disguised as Christianity, the mendacious claims of innocence, the effusive philistinism of a band of wolves in sheep's clothing. Amidst so much counterfeiting the only thing that seemed real to me was my lack of money. Machinations behind closed doors and Catholic corruption passed for politics. A detergent produced by the Düsseldorf company Henkel and bearing the name Persil gave rise to the term *Persil certificate*. With its help more than a few brown stains were washed white, and entered public life with clean hands.

And the Socis? The Social Democrat Kurt Schumacher, whom I had heard when I was a coupler boy against the backdrop of Hanover's ruins and whom I count today among the unsung heroes of our time, put me off in the early fifties with his national emotionalism. I found anything with a whiff of the national repugnant. I also turned up my nose at democratic trivialities. Indeed, anything that smacked of politics I rejected out of hand. The Social Democratic views that had been forced down the coupler boy's throat on a potash mine floor 950 meters below ground might as well have fallen into a bottomless pit. Egomaniac that he was, he saw and felt only himself. I would not have wanted to meet him, but had I met him, we would have fought.

During those late-night sessions when so much tea was drunk and tobacco smoked we also imbibed all the clichés existentialism had to offer. Once more the debate was about the whole of life, though this time—or so we thought—on a higher plane. And when we disagreed, it was not over the crimes of the war that lay behind us, let alone the party squabbles of the society that lay before us; we splashed about in the conceptual approximate.

Oh, our nightly word extravaganza may have had a vague antifascist and abstract philo-Semitic tinge to it. Trying to make up for its past, our once failed resistance was now all boastful courage and heroics and did not need to substantiate its claims. I was probably one of those loudmouths, whose pronouncements memory, that indiscriminate glutton, has mercifully forgotten.

Things would begin to change when I came under the influence of a new teacher, Otto Pankok, but at this point I was still the pupil of my respected but not particularly spectacular or charismatic master Sepp Mages. He never spoke about art. His firm, immutable concept of form upheld the plain and simple, and in the early sixties he published a book under the title *Monuments* in which the plain and simple in stone found expression. Under his supervision I learned my craft and remained a hard worker.

But what was my life like outside the studio? I read what I could get my hands on and what Father Stanislaus slipped to me. Rowohlt put out cheap paperbacks of Faulkner's *Light in August* and Greene's *Heart of the Matter*. I produced a continuous stream of poetry that bore traces of Trakl or Ringelnatz or the two combined. I still took my meals at Caritas House and could pick up enough to live on at occasional jobs like window-dressing or working as a stonecutter in construction and by doing portraits of potbellied beer drinkers and their swaying wives, arms linked, at shooting contests on the banks of the

Rhine: two marks apiece. The money I made was sufficient to cover a monthly tram pass, movie and theater tickets, weekend dances, and—yes, by now—tobacco.

Or did I first become a smoker when my father's miners' guild—he was still working for the brown-coal people on the lower Rhine—awarded me a stipend of fifty marks a month?

In any case, I began smoking regularly when the young man bearing my name decided smoking was the thing to do. My favorite tobacco, Schwarzer Krauser, was finely cut and thus suitable for rolling one's own. Factory-rolled cigarette brands like Rothändle and Reval were beyond my means, even in packs of five.

I smoked as if I had come to it early in life. No crisis forced me into it. No affairs of the heart, no doubts. No, it was clearly the heady talk and its superficial profundity, that triggered the desire to belong to the community of smokers and reach periodically for tobacco and cigarette papers. That was what got me hooked—or, to put it more politely, made a regular smoker out of me.

Schwarzer Krauser came in a packet that was blue on the outside and silver on the inside and that I, left-handed as I was, kept readily accessible in my left-hand pocket. I had seen any number of soldiers and miners roll their own, so the coupler boy had no trouble keeping his locomotive driver supplied.

In the mid-seventies, when I switched to a pipe, fearing smoker's leg, I wrote an obituary for my many years with cigarettes under the title "Roll-Your-Own": "When you roll your own, you have to radically renounce all the fluffy pieces that refuse to fit in. Only then, when the tobacco is firmly ensconced along the bottom third of the paper, firm to the touch—only then do you take your tongue and moisten the strip of adhesive along the far edge of the paper, using your index finger behind it as backing." In this obituary, I praise "a type of cigarette paper you can get in Holland, which doesn't have any adhesive but still sticks" and ended by describing a special advantage that comes of rolling your own: "self-rolled stubs are all unique, each is artistically curved, and every day my ashtray lets me know how my crisis is progressing."

Looking back—if I divide my life up to now into three periods: the nonsmoker period, the roll-your-own period, and the pipe period—the war and postwar nonsmoker period was the best. By trading his cigarette coupons and the cigarette ration cards that later replaced them, the nonsmoker could count on all kinds of benefits—there was a time, for instance, when a single active cigarette, which is what factory-made products were called, would bring an egg, whereas the only advantage you could put down to smoking was the brief pleasure derived from each puff. Yet it was a vice I was loath to renounce.

Only after a doctor's admonition did the fifty-year-old, for whom rolling his own had become an obsession, a kind of substitute for religious fervor, give up the daily rolling and inhaling and with the help of broken-in models sent to him by a friend of sorts make the transition to the pipe, which to this day he sets aside and allows to go out only when he is forming clay figures—human or animal—and all ten fingers are satisfied.

In retrospect I might speculate as to whether, had I never left the stonecutting trade in favor of the one- or two-handed writing and typing of manuscripts that took on epic proportions and encouraged the nervous habit of reaching out for tobacco (there was a time when I smoked cigars and cigarillos too), I would now be spared asserting my rights to the self-appointed morals police who (how civilized of them) have narrowed their sights to a ban on the consumption of nicotine and even made provisions for incorrigible offenders in the form of highly restricted smoking zones, though who can tell what solicitous punishment they may eventually—or tomorrow—come up with.

As a virtuous nonsmoker who had given up the obsessive writing habit in time, I would cough less, expectorate no grayspeckled spittle, and walk more nimbly on my pain-free left leg . . . But enough!

WHILE still a nonsmoker—or only shortly after I gave in to nicotine's regular pleasures—and under the sullen eye of Professor Sepp Mages, I was subject to his daily rounds and the laconic instructions he would give about keeping the moist clay surface of the sculpture rough as long as possible, because if it was smooth too soon it tricked the eye: "It only seems finished," he would say.

I later transferred his method to my manuscripts, constantly roughing up the text, keeping it in flux from version to version, and I write at stand-up desks because I am used to working on my feet. Mages would not allow us to sit at the modeling stand.

I remained his pupil until the end of 1950, by which time a number of skinny girls were finished or seemed so. Every day during this period, while I consistently refused to imitate the Maillol-like curves of the generally pudgy-to-portly models, one of my classmates, the veteran with the glass eye, would whistle themes and motifs from all nine Beethoven symphonies, as well as the piano concertos. His technique was amazing. He could whistle whole suites and sonatas, everything classical music had to offer, from Bach to Brahms, so vividly and with such skill that from then on I had no trouble differentiating Beethoven's Third from his Fifth or Schubert from Schumann. He whistled with a reserved passion, that is, not loudly but not to himself. He would take requests, repeating especially engaging melodies, this or that adagio, the Kreutzer Sonata, *Eine kleine Nachtmusik*. He could—if I remember correctly, that is, without my notorious tendency to exaggerate—whistle whole sections of Bach's *Art of the Fugue*.

While the veteran whistled melodies known to the others but new to me, he would use his flat wooden modeling tool to smooth down the surface of a life-size clay figure, a walking woman who had something Egyptian, something mummylike about her, until a jaunty allegro induced him to roughen up the surface with a jagged wire modeling tool. Then a slow movement would return him to his smoothing. The only time the virtuoso interrupted his concert program was when Mages made his rounds.

That is how I acquired my musical education incidentally and, hungry for learning as I was, I would have profited even more from the whistler had I not had a run-in with my teacher.

Not that I provoked him. He also seemed perfectly satisfied with me and my regular attendance and hard work. When a plaster model he had done, large kneeling women in bas-relief, was ready to be transferred to shell-lime, he asked me to take part in the process, at a decent wage. The deadline was fast approaching. His piece was to decorate the portal of a government building on the Mannesmann Embankment, and I worked on the scaffolding next to two men from the Küster firm, chiseling away at the Grenzheim shell-lime, a stone of insidiously varying density.

When, after quite a few standing girls in modeling clay, I added a reclining woman with gaping thighs, Mages took offense at the exposed vagina and the—to his mind—vulgar pose, which ran counter to a "plain, closed form." He strongly urged me to close the thighs. When the pupil refused to honor the professor's sense of decency and form, it came to a showdown. "Nothing like this ever happens under my supervision," the professor said. "And never shall," he added.

Or he may even have taken matters into his own hands and pressed shut what, to his mind, should never have been open: clay is soft and yields.

The memory offers a number of versions, some more flattering to him, others to me. In one of them I restored the position of the thighs immediately after his attempt to correct the offense: because clay yields.

Although the dispute between teacher and pupil was subdued in tone, each stood his ground: they were not made of clay; they were not soft or yielding. Nor did attempts to reconcile them, made by the glass-eyed veteran and gifted whistler, who saw himself as the spokesman for our class, bear fruit.

And so I changed teachers. Mages helped me to gain entrance to Otto Pankok's studio. I was no longer eager to study with Mataré, who had adopted the ascetic Christian, even anthroposophical, trappings of his then dominant pupil, Joseph Beuys. It was time to break free of standards imposed from above and seek a path—or detour—of my own.

Although Pankok was no sculptor—he worked almost exclusively in charcoal and woodcut and was even said to be colorblind—he attracted pupils who were more intense than most and known, as I now was, for having a will of their own. I remained friends with my former classmates Beate Finster, a wallflower, yet constantly in bloom, and, especially, Trude Esser and her handsome Manfred, a curly-haired Viking from Northern Friesland who was later kidnapped—a story in itself—and transported to Paris.

MY NEW teacher must have been in his mid-fifties, though his full, prematurely gray beard made him look older, and imposing, a bit like God the Father. Yet there was nothing of biblical severity about him: he was easy-going, even lax, with his pupils, who thought of him more as a role model than a teacher. And it was not only his height that made him overlook a lot.

The reason the early Christians were dogged by mockers is that they appeared—or, more precisely, revealed themselves as— highly principled in the way Pankok was. He radiated a revolutionary but gentle spirit. His pacifist credo, which found expression in *Christ Breaking the Sword,* a woodcut that reached a wide audience as a poster against German rearmament, served me as a standard for a long time, throughout the protests against Soviet and American medium-range missiles in the eighties or even longer. In the last years of the last century, when setting up a foundation for the Roma and Sinti peoples with prize money I didn't particularly need, I found it only natural to call the prize we planned to award every two years the Otto Pankok Prize.

Pankok was forbidden to paint or exhibit during the Nazi period. He had lived with Gypsies and traveled with them, and he made pictorial poetry out of the lives of this long persecuted and in the end decimated minority in countless woodcuts and charcoal drawings. It was only because he knew them so well that he could transform their trials and tribulations into a series of images depicting Christ's Passion, large sheets full of endless shades of gray between black and white.

Gypsies, young and old, made up his cast of characters, and not only his own studio but also his pupils' studios were visited regularly by the Auschwitz-Birkenau survivors of their greatly reduced line. They belonged to the wild and woolly Pankok clan. They were more than models. It was a time when the old, or so we hoped, shattered principles of order were making a comeback, all nice and polished, before our very eyes, but we were behaving like the wayward children of the Restoration.

Scene change on a stage where the characters appear in my memory, first in one costume, then in another, and help themselves from the props box. And because under the protection of the kind man with the outlandishly curly beard anything and everything in thought and image was possible, a while later when the ink started flowing from my pen, an invented personage found a place in the Pankok menagerie. Not only did he fill chapter after chapter of the time-hungry novel, occupying center stage in each, the be-all and end-all whether passive or active, Oskar Matzerath also got himself a job as a model in the studio.

Coveted by painters and sculptors alike, he was ideal for emotionally charged, symbolic representation. Small and hunchbacked, he embodied the madness of the past era and the era just beginning. And because he was both, he could also be the converse of it all. Meeting him was like standing before a concave mirror: in his presence everyone took on a new shape.

Otto Pankok too became a caricature of himself when he tried to turn Oskar into his vision of a model: he became the coal dust–inhaling Professor Kuchen. And the moment Oskar heard the artist's Siberian charcoal rasp along the paper, he sketched an alternative picture, blackening everything in sight with words.

He did the same with the professor's pupils, whose easels showed their mentor's stylistic influence. He steered clear only of the Gypsies, sensing they could see through his tricks, his games with words and images, and, worse, fearing they would shatter his magic.

I, too, Pankok's most receptive pupil, was excluded not only from the chapters in which Professor Kuchen inhaled coal dust; I disappeared entirely into the endless torrent of words that, pruned into a novel, eventually reached the book market. I was just a writing implement following the trajectory of the plot and allowed to forget nothing, neither the facts poured in concrete nor the deceptions apparent when backlit: Oskar's entrances.

He determined who was to die, who to be granted miraculous survival. It was Oskar who compelled me to haunt the misty corners of my early years. He gave me leave to put everything which laid claim to truth between question marks. He, the twisted metaphor personified, taught me to view everything twisted as beautiful. He, not I, turned Pankok into Kuchen, the gentle pacifist into a volcano whose explosions blackened any sheet of paper with brute expressive power. His mere presence unleashed orgies in black; he saw black and made black; his hump threw pitch-black shadows.

Incidentally, Oskar also worked as a model for Mages, whom he immediately renamed Maruhn. Several of my classmates to whom he displayed his hump in Maruhn's and Kuchen's classes later served as vehicles for his naming mania: my friend Franz Witte, for instance, who shared a studio with me under Pankok's lenient supervision and who plays a ghostly role in the novel; or my friend Geldmacher—more of whom later—who turned into Klepp, the bedridden spaghetti cook who, communist though he was, revered the queen of England and managed to quote "God Save the Queen" in his flute rendition of the "Internationale."

Even if an author eventually becomes dependent upon the characters he creates, he must answer for their deeds and misdeeds. And if on the one hand Oskar was clever enough to use me, on the other he had the generosity to leave me the copyright to everything that occurred in his name. If you write, you renounce your self. Only tax officials refuse to accept the fact that an author's existence is mere say-so, that is, fiction, and therefore nontaxable.

So I must confess I find it difficult to sound out my past for demonstrable facts. No sooner do I get down to business than someone seems to butt in. As a publicly acknowledged protagonist he insists on his birthright and at the same time badgers me for the biblical pottage of lentils whenever an exchange is possible.

Oskar must always be first, Oskar knows all and tells all, Oskar laughs at my porous memory. For him, as is plain for all to read, the onion performs a different function, has a different meaning.

———

To RELIEVE the tension and shake off my immaturity for which I have only myself to blame, I shall now turn without delay to my first important travels. Long summer vacations lasting from July to September made them possible.

Starting in '51 any citizen of West Germany could apply for a passport. Visa requests were approved with relative speed. In anticipation, I had earned enough to travel on by working not only as a stonecutter in construction but also as a float designer for the Cologne carnival. One float showed Adenauer and Ulbricht (in plaster over wire-netting and burlap) swaying arm-in-arm, the picture of pan-German harmony. I can still hear the carnival hit of those years, "Who Will Pay the Piper? Who's Got Money Now?"

But my main source of pecuniary gain came from work on shell-lime and travertine façades: stone window ledges were still in need of repairing. The hourly wage was one mark seventy.

By mid-July I was ready. I promised my parents if not letters, then regular postcards. My rucksack was light: a shirt, spare socks, a box of watercolors, a case of brushes and pencils, a sketching pad, and a few books. I picked up a cheap sleeping bag in a shop selling off U.S. Army supplies. I also bought a pair of marching boots, now billed as hiking boots.

True to the most basic of German instincts and thus following in the footsteps of the Teutons, Hohenstaufen emperors, and Deutschrömer art worshippers, I was drawn to Italy, my ultimate destination being Palermo, where I had felt so at home in my childhood dreams as a squire or falconer for Frederick II and a member of Konradin's retinue when the Staufers went under. Another reason to cross the Alps was a wound that refused to be healed by hasty excretions of verse or increased tobacco consumption: my first great love—apart from schoolboy infatuations—had come to nothing.

SHE, Annerose, had set out like me to be a sculptor. Her eyes were gray—or were they blue?—and she struck me as beautiful, and I knew why: it was the way she swung her skirts and the fact that she came from Stuttgart, where she had studied with the sculptor Baum. It happened in March or early April, in any case at a time when spring was not quite in the air, but inviting changes.

Just before our love bloomed I had finally—and without fanfare—moved out of Caritas House. In a Jülicher Strasse apartment building I had found an empty bathroom with a tub unconnected to the water main and furnished with a dresser and a cot.

Since my sister, who was still an apprentice at St. Mary's Hospital, had managed to negotiate free meals for me there, I not only found myself charitably looked after by Franciscan nuns but also with an opportunity to take one or another nurse out dancing and then for a short visit to the Jülicher Strasse subtenant's cot. The former bathroom also contained a carpet made of coconut fiber, but I refuse to describe it in detail because Oskar will interrupt, move in on me, take over.

My assignations with nurses in the Jülicher Strasse bathroom did not last long. They came to an abrupt end when Annerose entered my field of vision, banishing every other female figure from the throng. She was the only one I could or would see. And as so often happens when one zeroes in on a single subject, everything boiled down to possession: I immediately set about building us a roomy nest, the bathroom with no water having proven too cramped and fraught with past exploits.

And so, with the painter and musician Horst Geldmacher, and assisted by a former Langfuhr neighbor, the master bricklayer Werner Kappner, I undertook to remodel the upper story of a stable in Düsseldorf-Stockum, turning it into a studio with a side room. The goal was to bestow a durable roof upon our homeless love, and upon myself four walls of my own after so many years in rooms packed with bunk-beds. The enthusiasm I brought to building was thus sparked equally by love and self-interest, which in later years always sought outlets: the studio in the ruins of Berlin-Schmargendorf; another, larger one in the Friedenau part of town; yet another in the marshy village of Wewelsfleth; a small one on the Danish island of Møn, in the Baltic Sea; an old Portuguese structure; and finally my Behlendorf stable, thereby assuring me, and only me, the space for new headbirths.

A good part of the material I used—cement, stone, the metal frame for the skylight, and the door leading to an outside iron stairway—came from unguarded building sites or had been rustled up at low cost by our former neighbor, a policeman's son who had become a construction foreman.

We bought the stairway, also at low cost, from a demolition contractor. Geldmacher came up with an iron stove and several meters of stove-pipe to transport the exhaust fumes through the wall and out into the world. From my father, whose job with the brown-coal company was still remunerated partly in kind, I got a delivery of briquettes, which people began collecting in spring for the following winter.

The stable, for which we paid very little, was located behind an apartment building with a ground-floor toilet we were allowed to use. There was a stunted tree, I can't recall what type, growing in the courtyard.

Geldmacher, with his recorders, bagpipe, and doctor's bag full of painting material, occupied the anteroom; Annerose and I had the studio with the skylight, which meant that on clear nights we could count the stars overhead. Our mattress was embedded in a wooden frame designed for stretching canvases. Day or night, when we became one multilimbed flesh, we were accompanied from next door by Geldmacher's recorders alternating blues with children's ditties.

Our short-lived happiness lasted until early summer. Annerose and I could have kept each other warm through the cold season and our coupling instinct would scarcely have abated had my first love not been brought to an abrupt end.

My beloved's mother, a menace from afar and from the beginning, had ordered her in the end obedient daughter in a flood of letters and telegrams to return to Stuttgart immediately: no ifs or buts! The letters included clippings of the terrible things she had read in the local tabloids. One was a long article about the violent murder of a young girl by a stonecutter with his hammer and stippling iron, pictures of which accompanied the story. I was compared in the vigorous calligraphy of a raging mother to the homicidal stonemason. The article moreover described the murderer as from the east and left-handed.

Annerose hesitated for one long night and half a day, but her mother won out. A heartbreaking farewell. I felt terribly lonely in the nearly finished studio with skylight. The bed now too wide. I missed her Swabian intonation. Her short, strong fingers. Deprived of her tenderness, I was left the poor, whining whelp whose yelps I am now trying to put into words, but all attempts at deciphering the thoughts of that abandoned soul are in vain.

Until then he had been the one who had done the abandoning, leaving women and girls, of whom he tired quickly, with no farewell.

My friend Geldmacher, who spent night after night luring German-accented jazz out of his recorders and flutes, was unable, for all his virtuoso blues variations on the folk song "At the Fountain by the Gate," to console me.

Work on the house helped a bit. In exchange for a collection full of rare Free State stamps that my mother had saved from the chaos of expulsion, the janitor at the Academy of Art expropriated a complete outfit of studio equipment—modeling stand, two rotating platforms, several metal compasses, and an easel— from the basement reserves for me. The easel, with Nude Room II inscribed on it, still has its place in my Behlendorf studio, though I can't for the life of me say how it got there.

Not even this exchange—nothing—could have made up for the loss of my beloved. Except perhaps a journey. I quickly applied for a visa. And while I waited I did some more façade work, so that by the time I left I carried a good 300 marks in a leather pouch against my skin. The departure seemed like flight.

I MADE rapid progress hitchhiking southward until a wild impulse led me to break the journey at a Stuttgart rest stop. I hitched a ride into the city. Hasenbergsteige was the address. I made my way up the hill, looking for the villa hidden behind pine trees, in which the love of my life had taken shelter from a murderous stonecutter and where she was now held captive by her wicked mother, whose insinuations had frightened her into believing the story.

Did I want to play the Knight in Shining Armor? Was I motivated by vengeance? Or by a shred of hope?

I rewind and stop the film to see myself standing at the garden gate at dawn—or was it dusk? The gate is rusty and slightly awry but locked. Cast iron with flourishes. I jiggle it, shake it. I wave my arms, demanding they let me in, cursing mother and daughter, whistling on two fingers. Nobody comes. The gate refuses to open. I curse again. Then beg, plead, weep perhaps.

I wish I could see what the film, now running forward again, fails to show: an angry young man tearing the gate from its hinges and flinging it into the garden of the terrified villa with both hands.

I must have been strong enough for that in the years of my youth. The seething maniac must have hurled the cast-iron gate into the garden. So painful was the loss, I didn't know how to deal with this excess of love.

But the film shows something very different. In *Dog Years* a garden gate is torn from the hinges in a fit of rage by someone not me and—as a symbol of thrownness—hurled into the garden of a philosopher with a pointed hat, but that takes place in the Black Forest, on completely other grounds, whereas I stood idle on Stuttgart's Hasenbergsteige, arms hanging by my sides.

There he stood, mute, at the padlocked gate, looking up at a lighted attic window—now I am sure he visited the house at night—and waiting in vain for the silhouette he knew so well, musing on his pain. Nothing moved behind the curtain; no owl hooted, no nightingale trilled. End of film. I made my way down the hill.

———

A SERIES of cars and trucks—at Innsbruck even a motorcycle—
took me and my sorrow, which waned perceptibly from vehicle
to vehicle, over the Brenner Pass to where the lemons bloom.
There I made my way on three-wheeled delivery vans, donkey
carts, and in a Topolino, the much loved two-seater of the time.
Down the boot. And on to the island of Sicily, where at one
point between Syracuse and Palermo—I felt I was in the middle
of nowhere—after hours of waiting for a car, a cart, anything on
wheels, after the shadows had packed up for the night, I spied a
group of armed men emerging from a hollow between two
rocky hills, and the closer they came the clearer it grew that they
were no hunting party, but a band of rural Mafia emissaries. Before long they had formed a circle around the strange straw-
hatted foreigner.

I emptied my rucksack and spread out my belongings for
them to see. No sooner had their leader, who wore a long
gown similar to a monk's habit, inquired after my provenance
and destination than—what else—a Topolino came into view,
puffing its way closer and closer up the hill. He raised his rifle
to stop it. Its terrified driver, a country doctor, took the guest
imposed on him to Caltanissetta, where he let me off in the
marketplace.

And other adventures, which I have told my children too
often and in too many variations to be able to determine which
is true: for example, this one I like to end with a shot warning
me to move on, coming from a rifle of German origin, the .98
carbine I had been trained to handle myself—in other words,
loot from the still-recent occupation. After all, the Mafia in the
person of its leader and New York godfather Lucky Luciano was
said to have helped the American troops take Sicily in '43.

In my encounter with the local members of the island-wide "honorable society," I was taken for a pious pilgrim: the repentant *pellegrino* on the way to Saint Rosalia, who was known to have her seat in Palermo. So they helped me. And from Caltanissetta, a truck driver took me voluntarily to my final destination.

BY THAT time I had traveled through Tuscany and Umbria and visited Rome. In the Uffizi I had finally seen the originals of Titian's *Venus of Urbino* and Botticelli's *Birth of Venus,* and in the Pitti Palace of Sodoma's *Saint Sebastian,* his boyish, arrow-ridden body writhing against a wooded landscape: works that thanks to the colored cigarette cards had made me the art-addicted youth I was. I can easily picture myself standing before the portrait in profile of a man with an aquiline nose and a red hat, by Piero della Francesca.

I slept in youth hostels and monasteries, under olive trees and in vineyards, occasionally even on park benches. Wherever I found a *mensa popolare* open, I would eat cheap pasta, bread soup with globules of fat floating in it, and *trippa alla napolitana,* the latter being my first taste of a poor man's staple the world over, made of the rumen, the first stomach of the cow, which when brushed and given a good wash looks like a terry towel.

I was later to serve this stew many times, with tomatoes, garlic, and white beans, to guests I set particular store by. I made it for the Master of the Naumburg Cathedral and his models—all of whom came from artisan or peasant families that had settled on the banks of the Saale after the military occupation of their land in the early thirteenth century.

They stood the master in good stead when he came to carve limestone likenesses of the cathedral's founders, Countess

Gerburg and Count Konrad, Margrave Hermann and his merry Reglindis, the pensive Count Syzzo and melancholy Thimo von Küstritz, and last but not least the second Ekkehard and his childless wife, the famous Uta von Naumburg.

Though at the time the west choir came by these sculptures—later called Early Gothic—there were no tomatoes or white beans, so I had to leave out the tomatoes and substitute fresh broad beans. Still, it was the same tripe that had filled me up for so little in Rome's soup kitchens.

Even a cooper's wife, the fair Gertrude, who served as a model for the unapproachable Uta von Naumburg, had a taste; the grim carter who became the spitting image of Count Syzzo couldn't get enough of it; and Walburga, the goldsmith's daughter, whose cheery dimples were transferred to Reglindis, the Polish king's daughter, requested a second helping.

Back in the days of East Germany, when the authorities of that so painstakingly insulated state finally allowed me to go on a reading tour of Magdeburg, Erfurt, Jena, and Halle—it was two years before the wall came down—Ute and I visited Naumburg Cathedral. While we admired the august figures on high, Ute looking up at Uta, our guide laid out the real-socialist background of these stone-hewn representations of reality: "The master made a conscious choice to replace canonized saints with working people, who as early as the Middle Ages were imbued with class-consciousness . . ." She went on to state that not even Fascist propaganda, which made a cult of Uta, could diminish the lifelike beauty of these statues. As we left, I could hear Reglindis laughing.

———

I HAD brought three addresses with me to Italy. The first, the Hasenbergsteige in Stuttgart, had already served its purpose. The second came from my sister Waltraut, who had completed her commercial apprenticeship in the spring and was offering her services to a group of nuns just outside Rome who belonged to an order based in Aachen but looked after a number of hospitals abroad as well as at home. The Roman branch included a nursery school, and my sister helped the nuns who ran it.

The nuns were always rushing around or slaving away in the convent's vegetable garden. They seemed to have no time for prayers. Even the abbess did her bit, folding laundry and helping to bring the olive harvest in. It was a convent of open doors and active concern.

On my way to Sicily and on my way back they offered me hospitality in an annex, in a cell with a view of the Alban Hills. Every evening I found a jug of wine waiting for me. The meal was served by a rotund kitchen nun of Westphalian origin who before trundling away liked to leave me with an edifying thought or two.

She would use the as yet empty wineglass, pierced by a diagonal ray of sun, to give the nonbeliever an eternally valid explanation of the miracle of the Immaculate Conception, pointing by way of proof at the glass pierced by light, yet whole.

So did the evening sun acquire an archangelic function, and strength of faith a Westphalian accent.

While enlightening me, though as far from sexuality as heaven is from earth, my kitchen nun would smile a smile so transparent that she, too, might have been made of glass and constantly expecting the miracle. Then, as if there was nothing more to be said, her hands would disappear into the sleeves of her sheltering habit.

No sooner had she left than I drank wine out of the inviolate glass. Lewd thoughts went through my head. Even as a youth I played an archangel who did more than annunciate. And again as a prisoner of war when during our dice sessions my pal Joseph did his best to win his pal over to the One True Faith, I would call the Virgin names and list all the instruments of torture that had been used to torment people of both sexes in the name of the Mother of God.

My sister, though, seemed content among the bustling nuns. Her childhood faith, lost in the face of the violence committed by soldiers at the war's end, had been restored. Which had its consequences.

The third address had been passed on to me shortly before I set off, by the energetic Dina Vierny, Aristide Maillol's last model, who was doing a swift business with his sculptures from her Paris base. She had come to Düsseldorf to sell the city a life-size bronze. The naked girl, a representation of herself in her earlier years, would eventually adorn a pedestal in the Hofgarten.

For us, who looked upon her presence as a natural phenomenon, she would sing German and Russian revolutionary songs. She completely turned my friend Geldmacher's head and stole Trude Esser's beloved Manfred out from under her, spiriting him off to Paris, where he eventually became hard of hearing. But I, immunized against infections of the sort by my recent bout of lovesickness, took away with me the address of her divorced husband, who was doing time on a French government grant at the Villa Medici in Rome. She gave me to understand: "He likes visitors . . ."

And right she was: he took the guest in without batting an eyelid. I must have set myself up quickly in his empty, all-but-unused studio because I have a fuzzy picture of a clay head of my curly-haired, carefree, idle host with which to document the interlude. Expressive but unfinished, it looks like a sketch of a fawn.

He and I and the other guests, whose work on their art was diverted into ever escalating conversations, which I understood only through gestures, would eat elaborate meals at a long antique marble table. We smoked before, between, and after each course. With a hidden camera a director of the wave the French would soon call new, could have captured scenes typical of the times.

Situated above the Spanish Steps, the Villa Medici was like a sanatorium for burnt-out artists: the spacious garden was full of shady stone benches.

By day I walked the streets of Rome, when the heat allowed. Only churches and chapels were cool. Another thing I noticed: every fountain, every pillar stump became a metaphor. Hordes of priests clad in black and with broad-brimmed hats, inspired rapid sketches of motion. I drew with pigeon- and gull-feathers dipped into a bowl of diluted India ink. Everything was amazing, everything became a motif: dozing cab horses, frolicking street children, the washing on long lines. The fat woman on her balcony. The empty, shadowless squares.

I bought a straw hat for myself. Nazionale were the cheapest cigarettes, except for the Gauloises that Dina Vierny's former husband, who lived the life of a banished prince in his Villa Medici residence, provided free of charge. My supply of Schwarzer Krauser roll-your-own tobacco had run out early on.

EVERY day a gift. I went a long way on that first journey alone, and though limited in time that journey has never ended: even now, in old age, every new trip I take—and Ute and I have gone from continent to continent, traveled all over China, India, Mexico—no matter how carefully planned, predictably profitable yet reasonably priced, pales in comparison with the daily enrichments I experienced on that first excursion up and down the boot.

I lived: that is, I took in everything, could never get enough, and hard as I tried, I was unable to narrow down the splendors on view. I stood thunderstruck before gesticulating marble, entranced before hand-size Etruscan bronzes. I looked up Vasari in Florence and Arezzo. At the Palazzo Pitti in Florence and the Palazzo Borghese in Rome I saw more and more of the cigarette cards of my youth turn into pompously framed originals.

I drew whatever landscape, street, or square had to offer, excreting verse as usual, evoking the stagnant heat of the midday calm or a fountain in a shady park.

Happy, sad, I followed the traces of the Deutschrömer painter Fohr, who drowned in the Tiber at an early age, made friendships that did not last, met and parted at crossroads, treated myself here and there to a lemon gelato, raced up the Spanish Steps, let my sister take a snapshot of me in my straw hat as further proof of my identity, restored a damaged plaster Madonna and Child in an Umbrian monastery in exchange for room and board, let myself be carried along Perugia's *corso,* danced in a vine-covered pergola with an English girl who looked like nothing less than a Botticelli angel, got lost in the maze of Naples, wrote a long letter from there to my mother, feeding her longings with minutiae of local color, earned a bit more travel money by painting Butan-Gas advertisements, set off for Palermo—a story I often later dined out on—in the guise of a *pellegrino,* surrounded by the local mafiosi, who gave me tomatoes and goat cheese for the road.

I thought of myself as an outlaw, an adventurer with an insatiable wanderlust who felt chosen, but I was just one of thousands of young men in those postwar years who put their notion of freedom to the test by crossing borders, now finally open, who set off haphazardly yet with a goal, for places like Assisi, Pompeii, and Agrigento *con mezzi di fortuna,* as the Italians call the art of hitchhiking. I met hitchhikers who, seven years previously, in this or that uniform, had survived the battle for Monte Cassino or had met as enemies when the Allies landed on the beach at Anzio-Nettuno, but were now peacefully inspecting the site as equals in mufti. I saw signs to soldiers' cemeteries with neat rows of crosses in battalion strength; I saw rubble quickly overgrown. The sea was lukewarm.

I met girls along the way, alone or in pairs, girls from Sweden, Canada, and Scotland, sending postcards from wherever to Haparanda, Toronto, and Glasgow, but I was unavailable, still under Swabian lock and key. It was not until Palermo, where the putative pilgrim presented himself to Professor Rossone at the Accademia di Belle Arti rather than—as he promised his Mafia patrons—to Saint Rosalia, and there, while attending his sculpture class, I was suddenly taken with his pupil Aurora Varvaro. The bolt slid open; the curtain tore. What can I say? Love at first sight . . .

———

SHE was no more than seventeen, with charms so closely guarded that it was only in the back pews that I could tell her in few words and less grammar all the things I saw in her, what I felt for her, the lovesickness I sought to assuage by her unknowing presence, and why her closely guarded beauty pained me so. Of course I also loved the sound of her name.

When I was granted permission by Rossone to do a portrait of Aurora in clay, we were constantly under the surveillance of her younger, sinister-looking brother or her grandmother, who would nod off now and again. Nothing more than glances were allowed, though fingertips managed to meet, and we could go a little further with English words than with Italian. But what had begun to take the shape of love never took flight; nor did the head, whose elongated form I exaggerated, get beyond a sketch, though one of Rossone's pupils apparently made a plaster cast of it after I left.

I left—she stayed. But even now, after a separation of more than fifty years, broken only once, in the early sixties, which led to something I shall pass over in silence, we keep in touch and have forgotten nothing, not the back-pew secrecy, not the whispered words, not the moments of fleeting closeness.

What would have happened had I stayed in Palermo belongs in a completely different film, a tragicomedy under Sicilian skies that would take me into doddering old age. And whatever was left of Greeks, Saracens, Normans, and Staufers on that insular pile of historic debris would have come together and formed the raw material for a wide-ranging epic novel.

Then what would have become of Danzig? How would I have envisioned the lost city from the perspective of Palermo?

In the truck that gave the hitchhiker a front seat on his way back up the boot in the direction of Cefalù, I opened the package she had presented to me as a farewell offering and found a slice of cake, some dried figs, and a half-dozen hard-boiled eggs. So caring was my Aurora, my unlived but lasting love, preserved in amber.

I arrived back in Düsseldorf in mid-September, just in time for the beginning of classes. The nearly ready remodeled Kirchstrasse studio in the suburb of Stockum no longer looked desolate and lifeless: I immediately set out a paper-thin profile of Saint Francis and Etruscan-looking figurines. There was also Horst Geldmacher with his collection of instruments and his all-pervasive smell.

Pankok gave a positive, if perfunctory acknowledgment to my drawings and watercolors from my travels: many of his pupils had come back from far-flung places with things to show.

Up to now, my memories of the journey to Italy have overshadowed a side plot rich in characters that later took on a life of its own and provided fodder for the practically omnivorous novel, so that only leftovers can be used for this account.

Pictures taken by Trude Esser's brother Hannes show Geldmacher and me smoking what look like cigar butts, together with Franz Witte. We are taking ourselves seriously, each in his role. Oh, my friends! I miss them still. Neither lived long: both were brought low by their talents and by their very selves; I was robust enough to outlive them.

My friendship with Horst Geldmacher, "Flute" to his close friends, and my long-standing love for ragtime and the blues resulted in a jazz band of three, with Günter Scholl on guitar and banjo. Günter, who was studying to be an art teacher, did in fact teach drawing later on and always seemed to be in a good mood.

For percussion I used a household item that had served jazz since its earliest days—in New Orleans!—the washboard, beating out the rhythm on its corrugated steel with eight thimbled fingers.

We played three times a week in the Czikos, a two-story, slit-narrow Old Town restaurant with a pseudo-Hungarian aura. A Gypsy cymbalom player with his son on double-bass filled the rest of the week. Wedged into the space under the stairs leading to the gallery, we played our hearts out for meals and a moderate fee, before a nouveau riche audience and some more or less successful artists and their hangers-on. And because the owners, Otto Schuster and his wife, might as well have stepped out of a novel, they later stepped into the episode in which the washboard takes over from the tin drum.

The author did as he pleased with his cast of characters, granting the Czikos a chapter of its own, "In the Onion Cellar," and therefore great importance, moving the jaded yet life-loving patrons of the exquisite establishment to tears with the aid of knives and chopping boards: the minced onions, a very specific sort of purgative, were well suited to poke a few holes in what later came to be known as postwar society's "inability to mourn." This is how it went. For a fee you could cry your eyes out. Paid-for tears brought relief. Paying guests were reduced to babbling infants who then followed nice Oskar's drumbeat. Which leads me to conclude that of all products of the soil the onion is the best suited to literature. Whether it unwraps the memory skin by skin or moistens dried-up tear ducts and causes tears to flow, it is a valid metaphor, and as far as the Onion Cellar was concerned it was good for business.

Nothing more needs to be said: what is transformed into literature speaks for itself. But even if the Onion Cellar was meant to outlive the Czikos, I can't get Otto Schuster's clip joint—the mood that came of the stuffy air and the dim oil lamps—out of my mind.

WE THREE occasional musicians rarely took a break. Not until long after midnight, when the last customers had left, did we sit down and stuff ourselves with Szegedin goulash. I did not overdo the smoking, but I did drink too much marc and slivovitz, brandies bought for us by screaming lady customers. It was a noisy operation, and its prices had learned to climb from the so-called economic miracle.

I was going to the dogs. The Academy scarcely saw my face. Each night swallowed the following day. Dreary talk. Boozy breath. Customers' grotesque faces, one snuffing out the next. More holes in an already porous memory. And yet there is something I can make out, as if behind a pane of milky glass, something I can halfway believe I remember: the three of us— Geldmacher pushing his flutes to raucous limit, Scholl sometimes picking sometimes thrashing his banjo, and me, now holding back, now giving it my all on the washboard—once had a famous late-night visitor.

After a jam session before a large audience—it had been sold out weeks in advance—the idol of our early years showed up at the Czikos, complete with retinue. From the distance of a few tables back he heard and apparently took pleasure in our kind of jazz, or at least in Geldmacher's ear-splitting eruptions; his sound was unusual.

The prominent guest, as we later learned, had a taxi bring his trumpet from his hotel room, and the next thing we knew, there was his unmistakable presence in our corner under the stairs—I can see him now—lifting the shiny brass to his lips, joining a bunch of poorly paid nobodies who were merely trying to outdo the noise in the restaurant, with a bright clarion call, then taking his cue from the flute's wild stutter, his eyes rolling, launching into a solo, which our soloist, Geldmacher by name, answered with his alto flute and which, while it played on the consonance between brass and wood, was a hundred percent Satchmo, the Satchmo we knew from coveted records, from the radio, from glossy black-and-white photographs. Then he muted his trumpet and pulled back, blending his sound with ours for a brief eternity—letting me and my thimble-fingers switch to a new rhythm, urging on Scholl's banjo, and causing general jubilation—and, once our Moneymaker, Geldmacher, had come down from his piccolo tightrope act, blew one last trumpet blast of gratitude, and giving each of us a friendly, somewhat avuncular nod, was gone.

What a visitation! It was not Scholl and his banjo or me and my thimbles that had lured him, but Flute Geldmacher, who had a knack for turning German folk songs into restless emigrants and transplanting them to Alabama: it was his version of "A Huntsman from the Palatinate"—or was it "O Tannenbaum"?—that had caught Louis Armstrong's ear.

Risky enterprise that it was, the quartet had come together with dreamlike certainty. It had lasted no more than six or seven minutes—when does bliss last longer?—but the scene, which no flashbulb registered, remains fresh in my ear and eye. The honor with which it crowned our attempts at entertainment means more to me than all the prizes I later won, including the most prized of all, which, having been granted me in my biblical old age, gave me an ironically distanced pleasure and has since stuck to me like one more job title.

Yes, even if the writer's occupational hazard were to have tempted me to experience with hindsight what is believable and durable on paper, that is, even if this monumental meeting were not to have taken place in bland reality, it retains a figurative meaning for me: always within reach, trumpet gold, interpretation-free, above suspicion.

NOTHING much went on in Pankok's menagerie other than the miserable failure of Franz Witte's and my daring attempts to soar on canvas or brown paper. There was no miracle to convert us other than Trude Esser's fish soup, which she made for hungry friends out of numerous herrings reminiscent of Peter's miraculous catch.

My sister returned from Rome and her cloistered existence oddly different, as if transfigured. My parents were horrified to learn that she intended to become a nun. Father yammered, while Mother ailed. I drank more than was good for me. Franz Witte began muddling his words, and Geldmacher raged and banged his head against walls that were really and truly hard. Wars had started up in Korea and elsewhere. We had lost faith in ourselves and were living on credit while the nouveau riche crowd flaunted their new riches.

They also left large enough tips at the Czikos to finance my second great journey, in the summer of '52. I saved all winter, wanted to get away, out of Düsseldorf, a town which saw itself as a "little Paris," and whose artistic folk dressed Bohemian style at guild get-togethers.

AT ABOUT this time I inherited two easy-to-lead dance partners from the carnival festivities—one after another and for several weeks both at the same time. They took turns paying visits to my Kirchstrasse studio in Stockum, where, to their horror, I served up dishes hot off the iron stove like hasenpfeffer, sour pig's kidneys, fried horse liver.

One was long legged, the other well proportioned, but my heart or, rather, its chambers, was still uninhabitable even if I was doubly attracted—by desire and opportunity—to them both. After completing dress-making apprenticeships, they had decided, unclear though their talents were, to serve art.

Yet we had a good enough time. There was no question of possession, so our criss-crossing, though not free of tension, was without any tragic finale. We enjoyed one another until further notice.

Both of them had studied with a French mime at the Brücke, a cultural center sponsored by the British occupying forces, and later, when I was long out of the picture, one of them, whose name was Brigitte, followed her teacher to the socialist camp and made a career as a choreographer in East Berlin, but even while we were still together she had started giving her name the French pronunciation, which, lighthearted Rhinelander that she was, she pulled off with aplomb.

The other, though from Pomerania—she was a fascinating, fragile creature who when she strode along in her bilious green-and-purple stockings turned the Königsallee into a catwalk—remained true to Düsseldorf and pantomime for a time. Years later she appeared as a muse by the name of Ulla in a novel often cited since, but this side of literature her name was Jutta and she was called Angel by me and others because of her demeanor. That is what I call her tenderly to this day when we two old-timers greet each other from afar.

I PLANNED my tour of France without Brigitte and Jutta, who were mostly to be found in slow-motion pantomime poses or practicing off-beat walks and neck-stretching before the mirror. Again I hitchhiked, spending most of my time on the way to Paris and between the Mediterranean and Atlantic coasts in trucks, next to dog-tired drivers. I often had to sing to keep them awake. At dawn it was easy to get a ride out of Paris in the direction of Marseilles or Cherbourg or Biarritz by going to Les Halles, the now defunct central market. No matter where I rambled, to the beaches of whichever coast, I made Paris my base, first at the cockroach-infested youth hostel near Porte-de-la-Chapelle, then in a room with a view of Saint-Sulpice, in the flat of a Kleist translator by the name of Katz.

The linguistic pandemonium of Kleist's bloodthirsty plays infected Katz with a kind of antic lunacy: he would summon man-killing amazons from his work in progress and greet everyone with "My swan sings Penthesilea even after death." He held court at the Café Odéon wearing a monocle, which I found embarrassing. He apparently came from Mainz or Frankfurt. And garrulous as he was he would clam up whenever the subject of his origins or how he made it through the war came up.

If the need arose, I could always find a place to sleep among the ex-servicemen back from Algeria or Indochina. They had war written all over them in ways I could recognize, and we understood one another in whatever jumble of languages we used. Anyone who has seen not only individual corpses but corpses in piles looks on every new day as a gift.

For a while I found rent-free accommodations in an attic room with a view over roofs and chimneys in exchange for washing up after a couple belonging to the old nobility—Saint-Georges—who were, both figuratively and literally, at each other's throats. Every morning after breakfast the din of their duel would travel from the living room down the long hallway to the kitchen. I often stood between the two of them, trying with sign language to calm them down, but they, oblivious to the onlooker, would continue throwing the plates I had just washed, or not.

They were always civil, even friendly, to their kitchen help, though they would save up their rage for the periods when I did the dishes. Not only because it was one of the few times they were together; their duelling clearly needed a witness.

Sometimes they threw knives and forks at each other. Once I had to bandage a wound in Monsieur's left hand. My limited knowledge of the language meant I could only guess at what enraged the knife-throwers and eventually brought them to the brink. Maybe an inheritance going far back in history, to the persecutions of the Huguenots, for instance, or even further, to the never-ending Wars of the Roses.

Monsieur and Madame used the formal *vous* with each other. That is how decorous their quarrels were. I could have added a choral commentary and made it a three-hander. My friend Katz would have directed. Besides, our kitchen drama played itself out at one of the most exclusive addresses in Paris: Boulevard Péreire. My address too.

WHO swept up the shards? Probably I did with a dispassionate expression. I was less distressed by the daily plate-smashing sessions than I might have been because the ritual wrangling of the Saint-Georges couple took place at a time when wrangling was rampant. Thesis clashed with thesis. Not that I had read Camus by then, but the verbal jousts between him and Sartre were on everyone's lips, though more as empty phrases than solid information. There was talk of the Absurd and the myth of Sisyphus, the happy stone roller. It was probably Katz who infected me, moving effortlessly from Kleist to Camus, from Kierkegaard to Heidegger, and from both to Sartre. Katz loved extremes.

In the debate among the gods of the existentialist doctrine of salvation, a debate ranging over years and borders, I took sides—first gingerly, then vehemently—with Camus. But I went further: mistrusting all ideologies and rejecting all faiths, I made stone rolling my daily discipline. I liked that Sisyphus. Damned by the gods, as sure of the absurdity of human existence as he was of the sun's coming up and going down, and thus aware that the stone he rolled up the hill would not stay put—he became a saint to me, a saint I could worship. A hero beyond hope or despair. A man made happy by a restless stone. A man who never gives up.

It was in Paris that I began to try on politically committed positions, if only incidentally, staking out my own territory during bistro conversations with and without Katz. I gradually came to see that political power relationships could be measured. I joined the fray—or argued with myself if necessary—and lived on cheap food: pommes frites and boudin, the French counterpart to Blutwurst.

THE paper by-products preserved from my tour of France include a sketchbook plus a pile of medium-size drawings on which gull feathers and a bamboo reed have produced an all but unbroken line forming the heads of men and women who were close enough to sketch for sufficiently long intervals in cafés, on park benches, in the Métro, and in my various sleeping quarters. There are also two dozen watercolors on brown paper showing not only heads with and without hats and half figures but also streets on the outskirts of town. I did several watercolors of the bridge-rich Canal Saint-Martin and of bistro scenes, which from page to page show influences—from Picasso and Dufy to Soutine. They differ from the India-ink impressions of my Italian jaunt of the previous year in their heightened expressiveness. All of them were quickly dashed off, yet they were attempts at finding myself or somebody I wanted to be. But who did I want to be?

My writing during the trip was likewise a groping forward. A series of poems revolving around Odysseus' helmsman is eminently forgettable. Then came an endless poem during which a present-day stylite develops into a hero of the absurd: a young mason who gives up his job, breaks off all ties with his family and society, that is, becomes a total outsider, erects a pillar in the town marketplace and looks down on its daily activities, that is, on the world, the better to inundate it with metaphor-laden curses from his exalted vantage point. Though he does let his mother feed him with a long pole.

The only reason I mention this verse epic, a work fed on a diet of early German expressionism seasoned with Apollinaire and García Lorca and accordingly inordinately rich, a work that flexed its muscles but was never completed, is that this static stylite evolved over the years, and through a lengthy fermentation process became a mobile headbirth cursing the world from the opposite perspective—the view from a tabletop—and in prose.

ON THE way home from France I made a little detour. An address was all it took to lure me to Switzerland, to the canton of Aargau and the spotless little town of Lenzburg.

I went there to see an actress by the name of Rosmarie Loss who had met me in a Düsseldorf cinema that was showing *Les Enfants du paradis*. In the course of our hasty embraces and continuous verbal battles she must have pegged me for a notorious hunger sufferer, because after her return home I kept getting packages full of Swiss treats. Flute Geldmacher and I were thrilled with the Ovaltine, chocolate bars, grated cheese, and cured beef. I showed my gratitude with the only currency I had: poems long and short.

In Lenzburg she and her sister's family lived with her parents. Their private house differed little from the other houses in the town. Her father was a postman, a member of the Gutenberg Book Guild, and a Social Democrat. Her best friend, however, who came to what was intended as an innocent coffee-and-cake farewell party for her, was from solid middle-class stock and only nineteen. She moved like a budding dancer—with pronounced jolts and a head held high at the end of a long neck—and proclaimed, without being asked, that she was making a beeline for Berlin, the reason being that she did not wish to be the teacher her parents expected her to be and had decided to study the expressive barefoot choreography of Mary Wigman, the famous German exponent of modern dance.

A brave decision! And declared in resonant High German. Whereupon something within me jelled, something that had till then been no more than a vague desire. I announced to the assembled company, the Loss family plus the future student of modern dance, that I, too, would be moving to Berlin and soon: the West German climate did not agree with me.

Thus began a chat that had its consequences. She or I speculated that we might perhaps meet in Berlin, though Berlin was a big city, one you could easily get lost in. Still, you never knew . . .

While traveling through France—and especially while waiting for my next ride—I had drawn a lot of chickens, and I compared the jerky movements of the future dancer with the gait of the fowl I had observed, a comparison I immediately, though unsuccessfully, tried to rephrase as a compliment. Then the coffee and cake were served and the conversation returned to Berlin. Rosmarie Loss divined that my heart might have determined my proposed change of residence.

After Anna had gone—she had another farewell engagement to attend—the tone turned Social Democratic: the young lady with the wanderlust came from a cultivated bourgeois family, which through a hardware business had accumulated possessions according to good liberal principles. A good match, to be sure. A good catch, especially for impoverished Germans passing through . . .

Perhaps a bit of hidden jealousy gave our banter an ominous coloration: Rosmarie and I, pugnacious as we were, would have exhausted each other with relish and speed. And here I was, relaxed, unbeholden to anybody, smoking cigarettes called Parisiennes offered to me out of a yellow pack.

In any case, the family gathering around the table was still in full swing—the conversation conducted partly in High German, partly in Swiss German—when a boy about three years of age, the son of my clear-sighted moviegoer friend's sister, entered the smoke-filled room with a toy drum hanging from his neck and struck the round sheet of tin with wooden sticks.

Twice with the right, once with the left. Disregarding the grown-ups, he crossed the room and repeatedly circled the table, drumming his drum. He was not to be deterred by bribes of chocolate or silly distractions and seemed to be looking through everyone and everything. Then all at once he turned on his heel and retraced his steps out of the room.

It was a scene that left its mark, a picture that stayed with me. But it would be a long time before the bolt slid open, the flood of images was released and with the images, words I had been saving since childhood.

As for Anna Schwarz, however brief her appearance, she had left behind more than her name.

AND so my ill-defined desire to leave the economically miraculous Düsseldorf, with its beery Old Town antics and the fuss over its Academy of Art geniuses, received an unexpected impetus. In Berlin I wanted to find a new, more demanding, "absolute teacher," as I put it later in my application, and discipline my straggling talents in a rawer climate.

Earlier in the summer, before I left for France, I had been taken with an exhibition of a sculptor by the name of Karl Hartung, and especially with the monumental quality of his small works. I therefore applied to the Berlin School of Fine Arts, where he taught, with a portfolio of drawings, photographs of several plaster castings, a folder of poems, and a brief autobiography in the form of a letter. The acceptance arrived in late autumn.

I did not waste much time on farewells. "It's so far away," the mother wailed. "Berlin is a 'dangerous place'," the father said, "and not just on account of politics." The sister, about to enter the Aachen convent, wished me "Godspeed."

Both the still unfinished head of St. Francis and the neo-Etruscan figurines in the Stockum studio had dried. I felt drained. Leaving Düsseldorf was easy.

After an all-night New Year's Eve celebration, Flute Geldmacher, Scholl the guitar, and the bassist son of the cymbalist Gypsy saw me off at the station, each smoking a cigarette, as if it were his last. Franz Witte came too. We played our brand of jazz one last time. The washboard and thimbles stayed behind on the platform. That wasn't all.

I departed Düsseldorf on the inter-zone train. It was the first of January nineteen fifty-three, in the middle of the winter semester: with little luggage but rich in words and images that did not know yet where to go.

Berlin Air

Ah, my friends! The train was pulling out and Franz Witte was still horsing around: hopping back and forth on the platform, a dodgy character, you couldn't pin him down, always posing in one way or other. Strutting like a crane or flailing, about to take off, fly away. Yet he stayed behind, turned into a Soonother, as in the book, though now in pictures, in alternating colors, elongated even: another El Greco.

Not so long before, in one of the smaller studios where Otto Pankok's special students were left to their own devices, we had gone our separate ways: he dancing over the colors of the rainbow, I racing crisscross in black and white. I occasionally watched him telling the legends of the saints with a number of brushes at once, spraying the blood of the martyrs as from a fountain.

On his canvases he spoke with absolute clarity: red next to blue, yellow next to green; otherwise his speech was confusing, recalling poetry of an airy beauty that vanishes on paper. He could fashion cloud towers with words and tumble them syllable by syllable. Though fragile by nature, he proclaimed himself an angel in armor whose will no brute force could withstand. He destroyed his pictures with gusto and a carving knife.

It was not long after my departure on New Year's Day—or was it a year later?—that the brick long aimed at him hit him in the head.

There was talk of a brawl in Düsseldorf's Old Town near the Church of Saint Lambert, then of a joker named Franz Witte doing a dance along the Königsallee on the snow-decked roofs of closely parked Opels, Borgwards, Mercedeses, and hunch-backed Volkswagens, though because the dancer was light on his feet no chassis were damaged.

This was later confirmed. But while he leaped from roof to roof making funny faces—he was good at that—a brick or was it a cobblestone? struck the back of his head. That was how the combined rage of the united car owners put an end to his leaps into Nowhere.

Later, when the wound had healed, externally, he was taken to Grafenberg, delivered by the police as a "known criminal." The year after I left I visited him in the sanatorium, took him some sweets. He looked even more unstable than before. He had a slow, odd way of talking and kept pointing a long finger at the leafy trees outside the hall window.

And it is through the hall window that Franz, darling of the gods, is said to have jumped. With a running start, along the hall, and finally through the glass. He wanted to fly again, be a bird or air, wind in the trees.

One of my sons is named after him, my dead friend—after him and the uncle who turned hero against his will in the Pol-ish Post Office. Both Franzes. When I left that day at dawn, I left little Franz—Fränzchen, as we called him—behind on the platform.

NEXT to a Franz Witte so hopelessly unsettled he couldn't sit still stood the rock of Horst Geldmacher, who could do anything—draw with both hands, coax unheard-of tones out of a flute with all his fingers—anything but what his name, Moneymaker, implied: he was hopeless at making money.

And yet I once used the promising name to scare my poor mother. When she asked me nervously how her darling artist son planned to make a living, how I intended to pay for my monthly tram passes—"to say nothing of tobacco and suchlike"—the only answer I could give was a casual reference to our skill, Geldmacher's and mine, with paper and paint. We could easily turn out copies of things that looked just like the genuine article.

No wonder my poor mother connected the name of her son's friend with the worst thing she could imagine: a basement forgery operation, where she pictured this moneymaker and her son—her problem child and his henchman—hard at work. If he got caught counterfeiting, whether passes or banknotes, I'd go down with him. Many years after Mother's death my sister told me that she had long expected every ring at their Oberaussem door to be a member of the local constabulary or, worse, the criminal police.

In fact, Flute Geldmacher was a danger only to himself: he would bang his head against plaster walls or bare masonry to prove how tough it was. This occurred at irregular intervals; otherwise he was a gentle, exceedingly courteous soul, who would greet people several times over with great ceremony and not only painstakingly wipe his shoes on the mat before entering his host's residence but repeat the process on his way out. His comings and goings were further slowed by another self-imposed rule: whether arriving or departing, he never failed to knock.

His flutes, on the other hand, he treated as inconsiderately as he did his head. More than once I saw him snapping them in two and hurling the pieces off the Rhine Bridge, only to mourn their passing.

He played entirely by ear, but the way his music infused these German children's ditties, Christmas carols, and saccharine love songs with the rhythms and harmonies of black cotton pickers, you'd think it came from a freshly minted score. He was also a skillful decorator with a passion for detail: he could turn the most common Old Town beer hall into a Wild West saloon worthy of Hollywood or into the cabins of a luxurious Mississippi steamboat. Düsseldorf had not only the moneyed clientele but also the perfect spirit for "illusionary gastronomy."

He was John Brown and John Brown's mother in one; he was Old Moses and Buffalo Bill; he was Jonah in the whale; he wept with Shenandoah, the Indian chief's daughter, that her river might return to its source. Long before pop art came on the scene, he had invented it in private, outlining his flat saturated colors in black.

In the year *The Tin Drum* appeared and—as a cleaning woman had once predicted from my coffee grounds—I began to be marked with notoriety, I managed to get Dieter Wellershoff, then an editor with Kiepenheuer, to slip Geldmacher's *O Susanna* into their list. This work of art, a combination of jazz images and blues, spiritual, and gospel scores, is now available only in antiquarian bookshops and on the Internet.

Flute hung on longer than Franz. He came to Berlin in the early sixties, when I was beginning to lose myself in the manuscript of *Dog Years,* and visited us on Karlsbader Strasse, bloated from too much beer. In that already terrifying half-ruin, inhabited to the rafters by the horrors of war, he terrified Anna, the boys, and little Laura, born in the Year of the Wall, a serious child who never smiled more than tentatively.

It was because he himself was so terror-stricken and anxiety-ridden that he inspired terror and anxiety in others. He thought he was being persecuted and would leave rooms backward and avoid city streets or, when that was impossible, try to cover his tracks. He would rub his fingerprints off things and begged me to hide him in the small upper-level room of my studio to protect him from the shady characters who were after him. He tried to get me to buy him a special and far from inexpensive camera that would enable him—here he lowered his voice to a whisper—to photograph the streets through his trousers. He laughed and cried at the same time. He banged his forehead against the wall harder than ever, was lost without his flutes and disappeared one day, never came back.

Shortly before that, however, he had a lucid interval; that was when the two of us made a record in honor of Willy Brandt, then the mayor of West Berlin—he playing on a number of flutes, high and low, I reading ten or twelve poems from my third book, *Gleisdreieck,* which contains my credo, "Asceticism." Another tape, made in the late fifties, of the sugar-sweet glaze and shrill forced tones he composed for *The Goose and the Five Cooks,* a ballet libretto I wrote for Anna, was unfortunately lost. It débuted in Aix-les-Bains, although—again unfortunately— without Anna.

It's all gone. Nothing left but a few LPs, collector's items I covet. Nothing but them and two friends I left behind, sitting in my memory, a crowded prison from which no one is released.

HAD we agreed to meet or did Chance, once again, play director? The man sitting opposite me was someone to be approached with caution. In the sparsely occupied inter-zone train to Berlin either he or I could easily have ended up in another compartment.

Ludwig Gabriel Schrieber—Lud for short—was two decades older than me. He was a painter and sculptor who belonged to a generation of artists too unformed to be banned in '33; by the time he was no longer able to exhibit in the Galerie Stuckert or at Mother Ey's, the war had begun, and he spent the entire war in the army.

Recently he had been named professor and begun training future art teachers in an undamaged Grunewaldstrasse building, but I had met him as a heavy drinker at the Czikos, where he usually sat by himself, moistening his forehead with brandy between each gulp, as if he felt in need of constant rebaptizing.

Once, during a break, I laid my washboard and thimbles aside and gathered up the courage to go and speak to him. When he heard I wished to go to Berlin to study with Hartung, he was surprisingly helpful. It was he who advised me to include a handwritten letter along with the required portfolio: it would make a good impression, he said, make it more personal.

Now I was sitting face to face with him. He was smoking Rothändle, I rolling anemic cigarettes from my supply of Schwarzer Krauser. We avoided each other's eyes.

Lud sighed now and again, was silent. I wanted to say something, but didn't dare.

In Düsseldorf, where he was known and feared as a loner easy to rile and fast to strike, he had been visiting his mistress, who was married only on paper. Lud, too, lived apart from his wife. He commuted between Berlin and Düsseldorf, studio and mistress.

As the train pulled out, I could probably have seen her stranded on the platform like the friends who had come to see me off with banjo, flute, and bass. I knew her narrow face from brief encounters and, in profile, from his small wooden sculptures. Itta, which is what he called her, would surely have accompanied him to the station, if not all the way to the platform.

It wasn't until we got to the Ruhr that a pallid light broke through the January morning. Lud had been friends with the painters Goller, Macketanz, and Grote since before the war. The Nazi years and then the war had held them back. They made a belated attempt to distance themselves from their influences. In Lud's paintings, fine gradations in color had to hold their own against austere structures.

I own two Schrieber watercolors that date from his time as a prisoner of war in England. They are park landscapes done in bright hues economically applied. Later, after we had become friends and after three or four glasses of Doppelkorn, he spoke about the lost years and grew so enraged that he toppled several innocent bystanders in the pub with karate chops by way of compensation.

During the first part of the trip we didn't talk much. Could we have been sleeping? Not likely. Did the inter-zone train have a Mitropa dining car? No.

Once in snowy Lower Saxony, he hinted at something to do with physical changes. I thought he intended to apply some more plaster to one of his sculptures to increase its girth. But then I realized he was trying to say that his mistress was pregnant. All of a sudden he was humming; then he sang something Catholic about celebrating the arrival of an Emanuel. But when his and Itta's son was born, they baptized him Simon.

Lud's wife, like Itta, had a narrow face and a stern profile. Her eyes were close together and slightly bulging. I had seen her at an opening, lost and speechless in the bustle of lively conversations.

We got through the East German border check at Marienborn without incident, though Lud frowned as he grudgingly pulled his passport out of his pocket. Neither of us had much in the way of luggage.

Scattered in with the shirts and socks I had stuffed into my little black bag were a few tools, including a stippling iron, a roll of drawings, my folder of poems, and a slice of roast lamb between two pieces of bread with caraway seeds, compliments of the Czikos. The suit I was wearing came from my Caritas days.

I wish I knew what was going through my head at the time besides the desire for a change of scene, the desire to put the stultifying atmosphere of Düsseldorf behind me, but no matter how I try, not even the echo of a thought comes back to me.

I am only externally present: in the black bag on the luggage rack and the herringbone of the suit. Though it is also true that during the trip from west to east the constant pressure of words nearly blasted my skull apart: the fragments of thoughts, the din of isolation, the frightened souls I saw running next to the train—headbirths that would not let me be.

Tangible, and therefore certain, was the man sitting opposite me, Ludwig Gabriel Schrieber, whom only after we became first tentative, then fast, friends did I call Lud.

Though shortened to Lud and lengthened to Ludkowski, Ludström, Prelate Ludewik, and drinking buddy Ludrichkait, to Ladewik the Hangman or Ludwig Skriever the woodcarver, and changed from century to century, he is woven into the story I was telling and at the same time became a participant in my novel *The Flounder*, which I worked on during the mid-seventies. One of its short chapters bears the title "Lud" because my friend died out from under me as I was writing away.

Lud is gone. Lud lives in my memory, so I can't give him up. The way I described him is the way I experienced him during my early Berlin years, when we got together often and got too close at times: "Like a man buffeting a strong wind. Bent grimly forward when entering closed rooms like the studio full of pupils. Prominent forehead and cheekbones, but all finely modeled. Light hair and soft. Eyes red because there was always a strong headwind. Delicate mouth and nostrils. As chaste as his pencil sketches."

All contour with few details sketched in—that was more or less how he looked as he sat facing me in the inter-zone train to Berlin, though he was twenty years younger than when I wrote that obituary. Billows of smoke in a compartment empty except for us.

Was it underheated, overheated?

Did he rail at nonrepresentational artists as if they were the original iconoclasts or did he hold off until our bar-room discussions?

Did we share the lamb sandwich?

Outside, the landscape lay flat under sparse snow, inhabited by fictions because people were nowhere to be seen. After Magdeburg, whose remains we could only imagine, Lud spoke: about the son—he was sure it was a son—he had begotten and would name, with great fanfare, Emanuel; about the art of the Hittites and the great form we lost; about Mycenae and the joyous grace of Minoan miniatures; he spoke in half sentences about Etruscan bronzes, then moved on to the Romanesque sculptures of southern France and to his time as a soldier there and later in Norway and at the Arctic front—where "you could hardly make out the Ivans camouflaged in their white anoraks"—to end up, after a meaningful reference to the Naumburg Cathedral and its Early Gothic figures, in Greece, though glossing over the military operations on this or that island to praise archaic austerity, form coming to rest, and the inner sensation of joy it still arouses in us. "We are too late," he said, "followers, Ptolemaists . . ."

And between the stops of this grand tour of Europe, which, though a tour of duty seemed to have been focused solely on art, he would quote, without glasses brimfull, the toast of the old baas in his favorite book, Charles De Coster's *Uilenspiegel,* in the Flemish: *"Tis tydt van te beven de klinkaert . . ."* He, the experienced drinker, could talk himself drunk without schnapps.

Then came Potsdam and sobered us up. A platform full of Vopos, the People's Police. Announcements in Saxon dialect translated by loudspeakers into military German. After pulling out our passports again for the border guards, we were on our way through West Berlin: pine woods, allotments, the first ruins.

Lud kept interrupting himself and sighing habitually, then suddenly and for no apparent reason took to grinding his teeth, thus becoming the character known as the Grinder in the future novelist's *Dog Years,* and when the train pulled into the Zoologischer Garten station he casually offered to put me up for the night in his Grunewaldstrasse studio.

How did he know I had nowhere to sleep? Was he afraid to be left alone among his unfinished sculptures?

There we drank tumblers of Doppelkorn with an especially high alcohol content and without the *Uilenspiegel* quotation, and ate the supplies he had brought with him: smoked mackerel with eggs that he salted, peppered, and stirred in a small pan on the hot plate in the kitchenette. Then I lay down on one of the two plank beds at the far end of the studio and fell asleep, but not before watching him standing there amidst a number of veiled clay figures, sanding down a plaster bust that looked like his distant beloved in profile.

THE next day I found a room on Schlüterstrasse that a widow with wavy white hair sublet to me for twenty marks a month. "No women allowed, of course," she said.

Amid the useless items of furniture crowding the subtenant's room there was, at least, an old-fashioned bed. The clock did not work and presumably remained on the wall to confirm the impression that time had stopped. "Only my husband was allowed to wind it," I was told, "nobody else, myself included."

She would, however, heat up the tile stove on weekends, she promised—for a fee, of course.

My miner's guild stipend had recently been raised from fifty to sixty marks a month. In addition, Otto Schuster's widow—the owner of the Czikos had lost his life in an unexplained accident—had handed over a tidy sum for a portrait in relief I had done of her husband. I paid the rent and heating fee in advance.

The ornate plaster design decorating the exterior of the apartment house that had just provided me with a steady address had been only lightly damaged by bomb splinters, but the buildings on either side of it had been completely destroyed at the end of the war, and it stood there like a lone molar. Later, when spring came, I saw from my window a surviving chestnut tree in the courtyard with plump, shiny blossoms.

Facing the apartment house were the remains of a façade with nothing to the left or right of it: the rubble had been cleared, leaving empty spaces through which the wind whirled, first powdery snow and later dust, which spread so evenly over the city that wherever I went—the school nearby or the registration office—I would soon be grinding chips of brick between my teeth.

Masonry dust blanketed all of Berlin, the eastern and the three western occupation zones. But when snow fell the air was again true Berlin air, dust-free, as celebrated in the hit song blaring from my landlady's kitchen radio: "Das ist die Berliner Luft, Luft, Luft . . ." Not until a decade later did I write a long poem entitled "The Great Rubble Lady Speaks" as an amen to the situation. The final stanza reads: "Berlin lies there scattered./Dust flies up,/And then a calm sets in./The great lady of the rubble is canonized."

Everything stretched farther in Berlin: the city had a shabby, gap-toothed, closer-to-the-war look about it. Large, empty spaces between extensive firewalls. Few new buildings, lots of shacks and makeshift stalls. The Kurfürstendamm was having a hard time rebuilding its image as an elegant promenade, though on Hardenbergstrasse near Steinplatz, between the Zoologischer Garten station and the Am Knie—later Ernst-Reuter-Platz—station, I did see the scaffolding behind which the many-storied monstrosity that became the Berliner Bank was taking shape.

At Aschinger's you could get pea soup and all the bread rolls you could eat for pfennigs. Everything was cheaper, even Max Krause-brand writing paper: WRITE LETTERS QUITE EXTRAORDINARY, USE MAX KRAUSE STATIONERY rode on double-decker buses with me from neighborhood to neighborhood.

I ARRIVED. And the moment I arrived, I shook the dust of Düsseldorf off my feet. Or did I always have an easy time casting off ballast, never looking back, arriving and being there and only there?

In any case, the School of Fine Arts building took my arrival so for granted that it might have survived the bombing especially for me. My new teacher, Karl Hartung, also made little fuss, introducing me to his pupils and the nude model, who happened to be taking a break and was knitting something socklike.

I was given a hook in the wardrobe for my work pants and a modeling stand. Lothar Messner, who came from the Saarland and rolled his own, like me, offered me some tobacco. I was accepted into a men's club to which Hartung's only female pupil, Vroni, could also belong, thanks to her robust constitution.

Behind the school's main building and a courtyard full of trees were the studios for both students of sculpture and professors—Scheibe, Sintenis, Uhlmann, Gonda, Dierkes, Heiliger, and Hartung. We had a view of the Technical University on the far side of an empty plot of land to our left and a corner of the School of Music to our right. In the distance we could also see uncleared rubble, half hidden by bushes.

The clay sculptures produced by Hartung's pupils during the live model sessions had a certain independence to them, though they still bore traces of their master's sense of form. The only female pupil endowed her reclining nude with the ample proportions of her own body. She struck me as the most gifted.

The atmosphere in our studio was quite sober. No bohemian pretenses, nobody playing the genius. The youngest of us, Gerson Fehrenbach, came from a Black Forest family of wood carvers. Two or three students came from East Berlin and received meals at the Technical University canteen. Fehrenbach showed me a nearby shop, Butter-Hoffmann, where I could buy inexpensive bread, eggs, margarine, and cheese spread.

In my very first week I gave the traditional newcomer party, at which I served green herrings rolled in flour and fried on a hot plate. I bought the herring fresh at the weekly market for thirty-five pfennigs a half-kilo, and it became a staple of my diet.

No sooner had I settled in than I began to work on a chicken, an independent project apart from the standing nude model. The red potter's clay was later pressed into a plaster mold and fired to become my first terra-cotta. The chicken sketches from my French journey had proved their worth, and I would continue to be stimulated by roosters and chickens, verbally as well as visually, right down to my poem "The Merits of Windfowl."

One day, after making his rounds, Hartung, who usually kept his distance, told us the story of his visit to the Paris studio of the Romanian sculptor Brancusi. "As a member of the occupying forces," he added, to be totally aboveboard. Brancusi's formal language, the "condensation of the basic form," had made a deep impression on him. Then, pointing to my chicken in progress, he said: "Natural, yet aware."

He used words in the same sober way the northern light

shone through the large studio window. His goatee was always neatly shaped and clipped. He was able to apply the then fashionable concept of "abstract" to every object or body that could be abstracted. That I remained representational was in accordance with his understanding of abstraction. He did, however, take offense at the smell of fried herring wafting through the door connecting his studio to ours, but then understood our need and occasionally treated us to *Buletten* with potato salad from Butter-Hoffmann. He was friends with Schrieber and tolerated his growing influence on his pupils.

AT SOME point in January I had to take an oral exam because I had entered mid-semester. The school's director, Karl Hofer, who said not a word, and three or four professors carried on an exploratory conversation with me in the course of which the poems I had included in my dossier piqued the curiosity of Professor Gonda. He praised passages from the stylite cycle and quoted several genital metaphors, calling them "bold, even audacious," which I found embarrassing: I felt I'd gone beyond that kind of imagery.

From the other professors' ironic comments I gathered that Gonda had written and even published a novel years before. He also turned out to be a Rilke enthusiast. This enabled me to bring up *The Notebooks of Malte Laurids Brigge,* a work which Father Stanislaus had used to draw his book-hungry charge into conversation. We then moved on to Rilke's place as Rodin's secretary and biographer. Gonda and I pelted each other with quotes, which I no longer remember, though they most likely included the line from the Paris merry-go-round poem "And then and when an elephant all white . . ."

Throughout this exchange the rest of the examining committee remained mute. Then Hofer broke the silence and declared, "Enough, one could talk endlessly about Rilke, the candidate has passed."

I am still surprised by this exam that was no exam, and the uncritical approval of poems that were, all of them, suffering from an advanced case of metaphoritis. Perhaps the new arrival got extra points for what they considered his potential as a poet, what he might yet become.

I was even more surprised by the patience with which Karl Hofer, who seemed completely isolated from the other committee members, tolerated my at first timid and then self-assured performance. I would have been stricter with myself.

I remember Hofer's face, a face marked by loss. Present yet distracted, he sat there looking as if his paintings destroyed in the bombings were passing before his mind's eye, as if he had to repaint them, one after the next, in his head.

I seldom saw him after that, and when I did it was only as he walked slowly through the school. Soon he would be hard hit by a dispute with a pope of the art world. He never got over it, and it has not been settled to this day.

ON MY very first day I noticed the telephone booth to the left of the main entrance. I was relieved when I saw it occupied, comforted when there were three or four people waiting for it. Another tactic was to avoid looking in its direction. Because as soon as it was empty and ready for use I would be tempted and tell myself: *Now, now, now* . . .

Many times I screwed up my courage and dialed the number, which I knew by heart, but hung up after the first ring.

Once or twice the office answered, but got no response from me. A waste of coins.

But I couldn't avoid the telephone booth forever. There it was, waiting patiently, waiting for the procrastinator. A trap. After a while I started picturing it on my way to school or from the studio to class.

It came up to me, ran after me. It turned me into a hermit tantalized by the dial, the number. It appeared, open and inviting, in the Schlüterstrasse subtenant's dreams. In the dreams I was often defeated by the busy signal, though only in the dreams did I ever get an answer and a long, pleasurable conversation. To call me a coward would be only half correct: I would recite the number over and over, like a litany. That helped, but only briefly.

Once, while waiting in line for the phone, I thought an intense flirtation with a girl called Christine from Sintenis's class might prove beneficial. There was something foal-like about her. In any case, she had a ponytail, and all I had to do was stroke it, nothing more. But I didn't, and when she stepped into the booth before me someone who looked just like me and had the same ingrained fear of commitment fled.

So timorous was my love in its raw state, buried lifeless under tender words meant to suffice, that I positively enjoyed my procrastination and feared, and therefore avoided, anything leading beyond it, since every time I made for the booth I knew that if you contribute two groschen to the slot and dial one number after another, you will hear one beep after another followed by a voice announcing that you have reached the office of the Mary Wigman Studio, and you, courteous or gruff as the spirit moves you, give the first and last name of a person to whom it is your urgent desire to speak, and you wait until she dances up to the phone and says "Ja, bitte," in the most beautiful High German, and you're done for, there's no going back, you're tied, hooked. Something is happening, coming close, becoming flesh and blood, whose name has until now been written in the clouds.

And when I finally did exchange a few sentences over the telephone with a dance student by the name of Anna Schwarz, they resulted in our first date. All it took was one call.

HARD as it is for me to remember the birthdays of our younger children and grandchildren, I still remember that date: we met on January 18, 1953. For me—I have always perceived historical events such as battles and peace treaties as occurring in the present—the date Bismarck willed the Second Reich into existence is still helpful, a fact that comes to mind whenever I remember that ice-cold day, was it Saturday or Sunday?—and its less clear course of events.

We had agreed to meet at one o'clock at the U-Bahn exit of the Zoologischer Garten station. Since the time I had been wounded and lost my Kienzle wristwatch between Senftenberg and Spremberg, I had no means of telling the time. I arrived at the station clock early, paced back and forth, withstood temptation for a while, then had two glasses of schnapps at a nearby stall, which meant that my breath smelled when Anna turned up on time, looking younger than twenty.

There was something angular and boyish about the way she moved. Her nose was red from the cold. What was I to do with this young thing all afternoon? Dragging her back to the sub-tenant's room, where women were not allowed, did not enter my mind except as something to be strenuously avoided. We could have gone to the cinema on nearby Kantstrasse, but the Western showing there didn't seem right. So I did what I'd never done before, I gallantly invited Fräulein Schwarz to join me for coffee and cake at Schilling's on Tauentzienstrasse, or was it Kranzler's on the Kudamm?

I'm at a loss for words as to how and where we spent that long afternoon. We must have talked: What's it like to dance barefoot? Did you have ballet lessons as a child? And what's the famous Mary Wigman like? As strict and demanding as you'd hoped?

Or did we talk about the uncrowned kings of poetry, of Brecht over there in the eastern part of the city and Benn here in the west? Did we get political?

Or did I let on, before the first piece of cake, banking on the effect, that I was myself a poet?

I am like a gold miner shaking his sieve, I shake and shake, but no sparkling nugget, no speck of wit, no echo of a daring metaphor turns up. Nor is how much cake or pie we polished off, and in how many places, listed on any of the onion's skins. We got through the afternoon in one way or another.

Things didn't take off until evening, when we got sucked in by the then famous dance hall known as the Eierschale. It's not enough to say we danced: we found each other in dance. Looking back over the sixteen years of our marriage, I must admit that no matter how lovingly we tried, the only times we were truly close, one and the same, a couple, was when we danced. Too often we avoided each other's eyes or strayed, looking for something that didn't exist or existed only in phantom form. And when we became parents, duty-bound, and felt lost to each other, the children were the only thing that kept us close. Bruno, our last, didn't know what to make of it.

The band in the Eierschale went from Dixieland to ragtime to swing. We danced every dance, giving our all. It was if we had practiced together our entire lives. A dance couple made in heaven. We took up a lot of space. We barely noticed others were watching. We could have gone on for a small eternity, at arm's length, cheek to cheek, eyes making brief contact, fingers pressing lightly, swinging apart the better to merge, swirling as one on feet made to swirl, playfully earnest, out and then back, up she goes weightless, faster than thought, dragging more slowly than time.

After the last blues—it was around midnight—I saw Anna to the tram. She had a room in Schmargendorf. The story goes that between dances I said, "I'm going to marry you," and she said she had a friend she was serious about, which prompted me to say, "That's all right. We can wait it out."

Easy beginnings make up for the hard times to come.

AH ANNA, the time we shared. The gaps that couldn't be filled, the things best left forgotten. Things we never asked for that came between us and then had to be treated as desirable. How we made each other happy. What we thought beautiful, what deceitful. Why we became strangers, hurt each other. Why for so many years, and not only because I like diminutives, I called you Annchen.

A picture-book couple, people said of us. We seemed inseparable, made for each other, and we were equals. You willfully proud, I self-taught to be self-assured. In a rapid sequence of images designed to celebrate the young couple I see us as united:

In theaters east and west, where we saw *The Caucasian Chalk Circle* and *Waiting for Godot*, or in the Steinplatz cinema, where we saw the French classics *Hôtel du Nord, Casque d'or*, and *La Bête humaine*. I wanted to go up to your room, not yet, you said. We would match Lud Schrieber glass for glass at Leydicke's long bar until you had to drag me home, blind drunk. You would come and see me at our studio, where Hartung called you the Helvetian muse, and I watched your barefoot dance at Mary Wigman's highly disciplined establishment. You couldn't cook, so I showed you how tasty and cheap mutton could be with lentils, and how simple it is to remove the flesh from the bones of a fried herring. And when I missed the last tram and asked to stay over, we hoped your landlady, that battle-axe, wouldn't notice.

Our mutual friends: Ulli and Herta Härter, with whom we put God and the world to right. Rolf Szymanski, whom we called Titus and with whom, dead drunk, I pissed at the gate of the Berliner Bank because we thought it was one big urinal, for which we paid the hefty fine of five marks each. And later Hans and Maria Rama, who took the first pictures of you dancing: you brightly lit in tutu and à pointe. Even then you wanted to switch from modern dance to classical ballet, though your arches were too low and your legs too short. More often than I would have liked we went to the Hebbel-Theater for ballet: all those endless pirouettes and flashy grands jetés. Ulli and I would whistle the moment the curtain fell.

We wanted to see ourselves intertwined on paper as well. I drafted the libretto for a short ballet in which a frightened, trembling young man in a baker's cap, with two policemen at his heels, seeks and finds refuge under the skirts of a ballerina dressed as a peasant woman, which could have been you, until the danger has passed and he can come out and dance a pas de deux with her: a funny, vulgar piece, as far from classical discipline as could be. It remained a draft and never saw the boards, though it later turned into narrative prose, its slow-motion leaps and pantomimed sprints injecting some jerky, silent film–like motion into the first chapter of *The Tin Drum*.

We loved each other and we loved art. And when we stood at the edge of the usually deserted Potsdamer Platz in the middle of June and watched the workers hurling stones at Soviet tanks, we didn't leave the American sector, we remained at the eastern edge but experienced power and lack of power at such close range that the symbolic stones and their ricochet made an indelible impression on us. That is why twelve years later I wrote my German tragedy, *The Plebeians Rehearse the Uprising*, in which the rebellious workers, lacking a plan, run around in circles, while the intellectuals, who are good at using plans to find the right words, are brought low by their arrogance.

At the time we merely looked on. We didn't dare do more. Since you had been protected by the safe haven that was Switzerland, your horror was new; mine was revived by a long-dormant fear. I knew the panzers: they were T-34s.

We had seen enough, it was time to go. Violence scared us. Throwing rocks at panzers could succeed only in the imagination. We had ourselves and art. That was nearly enough.

And so we bought a tent for two. Reddish orange. And with that tent rolled up in a rucksack we set off for a summer in the south. Ah, Anna . . .

While Cancer, Soundless

This time over the Gotthard Pass. But before we set out on our first hitchhiking venture together, Anna and I visited my parents, and then my sister, who was in Aachen doing her novitiate at a Franciscan convent. That journey before the journey is still painful.

Gray skin, shadows under her eyes, Mother was ill; Father was worried. Both suffered from having lost their daughter, but they had turned their grief inward. They did their best to welcome us, though they were a bit surprised: this was the first time I had introduced them to one of my "conquests," as my mother put it. Anna had never experienced such cramped quarters. My sister had bought some new furniture with money she had saved up.

When I try to recall our visit, I feel unsure of myself because I have trouble picturing the place where the kitchen cabinet stood, the color of the curtains. Was the floor made of wood—pine boards—or covered with artificial material of a nondescript color? Did the tablecloth have a crocheted trim? Why did we eat in the tiny kitchen and not in the main room? Or was it the other way round?

I can picture Anna standing next to the stove, which used brown-coal briquettes from the Fortuna Nord mine for fuel, and try to see her at the kitchen table, which was covered with oil-cloth for the occasion. Father had probably cooked one of his favorite dishes for our visit: *Königsberger Klopse* in pickled-caper sauce with boiled potatoes.

Now Anna lifts a "nice little teaspoonful" of the sauce to give it a taste. Mother is darting here and there, not knowing what to say. Now Anna sits at the table and answers questions in the beautiful High German she learned in school, questions about the war-free wonderland known as Switzerland. Now she gazes out of the window in the direction of the mine and sees smoking chimneys.

At one point, shortly before we leave, mother takes son to one side: "You can't treat Fräulein Anna like your other girls. She's from a good family, you can tell."

We hardly speak about my sister and then only in guarded tones: the cloudy waters of grief have settled somewhat, and there is no point in roiling them again. I probably say something lighthearted like "If she's happy there . . ."

I look around as if for the last time. I see the asters I painted, I see the newly acquired furniture, piece by piece. I see the dresser in their bedroom. It has a framed picture of my sister on it. She is smiling—showing her dimple—and wearing a flowery dress.

Now I hear Father saying, "She's passed the postulant stage, as they call it; she's a novice, our little girl. Her name is Sister Raffaela . . ."

There is also a picture of her as a nun. Framed in black and white, her face looks childlike. It also looks proud, though a bit worried that her new outfit doesn't become her. Her body is gone, as if it had never existed. Her parents stand on either side of her, both in hats. They look uncomfortable, out of place.

Nuns peopled my prose and poetry from the late fifties well into the sixties: *Magical Exercise with the Brides of Christ* is the title of a verse cycle I wrote then and accompanied with my own illustrations. "They are made for the wind./They always sail, even without sounding the depth."

I did drawings of nuns as large-scale études in the play of black on white, using a brush soaked in India ink on large-format paper: nuns kneeling, flying, and hopping, crossing the horizon against the wind; abbesses domineering, assembled at Eucharistic congresses; nuns on their own and nuns in pairs, habitless except for wingèd coifs—all these I have my sister's misfortune to thank for—and then to see her, all devout and pious, taken in by organized cant, and anxiously, in the negative sense, awaiting the vow when Anna and I visited her at the Aachen convent.

Draped in heavy cloth, she stood weeping in the inner courtyard. Old brick walls on all sides, ivy running up to the rain gutters. Flat, neatly trimmed boxwood hedges lining carefully measured paths and surrounding long, narrow beds of decorative plants. Everything in perfect order. No weeds. Gravel raked. Roses smelling of curd soap.

There we stood, waiting for her to stop crying. Stumbling, as if every word required courage, she told her woe. Life at the convent wasn't at all the way she'd thought it would be . . . The way it was when she'd done social work two years before in Italy . . . that was the true Franciscan spirit, full of joy . . . Here she had to pray all the time, do what she was told, self-flagellation even . . . There were punishments for the slightest infraction of the rules, and everything was a sin . . . She liked to whistle, to take three stairs at a time—even that was forbidden . . . You had to eat everything put in front of you, even bread smeared with lard . . . and not a word about aiding the poor and sick; just repentance, introspection, that kind of thing . . . She wanted out, as soon as possible, that very day . . .

Then she paused and said, the tears still running down her cheeks, "The supervisor of novices is so strict . . . you have no idea how strict she is . . ."

And so I requested or, rather, demanded, a meeting with this much-feared disciplinary officer. She immediately crossed the inner courtyard and came up to us, introducing herself as Alfons Maria and thus giving the impression of bisexual legal authority, a kind of archangel sent from on high to run a reformatory here below.

My demand that she release my sister from the convent bounced off her as if it had not been made. She spoke instead of well-known temptations and enticements and how a heart imbued with faith could learn to withstand them, "couldn't it, Sister Raffaela?"

The enclosed courtyard awaited her word; it heard only sparrows twitter: the novice held her tongue. The bespectacled archangel spake with the authority vested in him/her, enunciating each word precisely: "We shall embark upon a novena and, thus fortified, find our peace . . ."

Anna and I were appalled to see my sister respond to the order from that narrow mouth with a devoted nod of the head. Alfons Maria's spectacles registered triumph.

And we departed. When the nine-day period was up, we received a letter in a childlike hand informing us that prayer and humble introspection had granted her the strength to use her faith to defy temptation in general and, by the grace of God, the wiles of Satan in particular, and to continue renouncing the world. Though not in so many words, the role of the Devil was imputed to me, her brother.

Any answer we might send would presumably pass through the supervisor's hands. I made it menacingly clear that my period would be fewer than nine days: If my sister were not released from her convent prison forthwith, I would pay it another visit. Daddau later maintained it was a telegram rather than a letter whose intimidating contents had the desired effect.

Be that as it may, my threat succeeded in opening a chink in the red brick–walled bastion. The moment she emerged, my sister, whose sense of earthly essentials had clearly remained alive through her period of convent captivity, sought out a hairdresser, who for a pittance—the nuns were not particularly charitable to her in their severance pay—and with great skill managed to turn the hair left by the regulation shear into the semblance of a hairdo. "Okay, girl. Now you can venture out into the world again," he is said to have told her.

The atmosphere of my ailing mother and depressed father's two-room flat brightened up a bit, though not for long: even after returning home my once lively sister never laughed.

AT WHITSUN of the year now ending my sister and I visited Gdańsk to bring back Danzig and our childhood. I also invited the older grandchildren, that is, Laura's daughter Luisa and her twin boys Lucas and Leon, Bruno's daughter, Ronja, and Raoul's eldest daughter Rosanna, plus Frieder, a friend of the twins, and took them on grandfatherly walks through the town and nearby Wrzeszcz, the former Langfuhr, and to get-togethers with our Kashubian relatives. The two of us chatted while the children searched the foam of the listless Baltic waves for slivers of amber, and eventually came to the convent interlude of more than fifty years ago. I had the feeling Sister Alfons Maria, the harsh supervisor of novices, was still breathing down my sister's neck. And what was even more surprising: Daddau had retained her Catholic faith, though with the leftist bias of the former midwife and trade union official. She turned a skeptical eye on the newly elected Pope Benedict: "As German as he may be, I can't say I'm thrilled." And after a short pause: "Now if they'd chosen a Brazilian cardinal or an African one . . ."

While the two of us old-timers—she in her compact rotundity, I with my round back and faltering step—made our way through the sand between Glettkau and Zoppot, and the children, energetic Leon out in front, dreamy Lucas bringing up the rear, Rosanna, energetic as ever on her stork legs, Luisa, hesitant at first, and Ronja, self-assured, were gathering nuggets of amber, the two of us condemned the public death of the previous, the Polish pope as shameless histrionics, I calling it "repellent," she "impertinent," though I could have come up with worse adjectives, and she swallowed a few that might well have trumped mine.

And after once more going through various incidents of our childhood, keeping them alive by juxtaposing our personal versions of them, I told her the story of how as a seventeen-year-old POW I had sought refuge from the rain under a tent with a boy my age and how we chewed caraway seeds to stave off our hunger. My sister doesn't believe my stories on principle, and she tilted her head distrustfully when I said his name was Joseph, he had a marked Bavarian accent, and was a dyed-in-the-wool Catholic.

"So what," she said. "There's a lot of them about."

But, I protested, nobody could be so downright fanatical and at the same time tender and loving when referring to the Only True Church as my pal Joseph. "He came, if I'm not mistaken, from somewhere near Altötting."

That made her even more suspicious. "Are you sure? Sounds a bit far-fetched to me. Just like one of your stories."

"Well, if my camp experiences under Bavarian skies are of no interest to you . . ." I said.

To which she replied, "Oh, go ahead."

I conceded a certain lack of confidence to make myself more believable—"We were just two among thousands"—but refused to rule out the possibility that my pal Joseph, who was as lice-ridden as I was, whom continuous hunger had driven to chewing caraway seeds from a bag, and whose faith was as securely bunkered as the Atlantic Wall once was, might well have had the surname Ratzinger and so be the man who today as pope claims infallibility, if only in that familiar shy way of his, speaking softly, the better to enhance its effect.

Whereupon my sister laughed as only off-duty midwives can: "It's just another one of those yarns you told to pull the wool over Mama's eyes."

"Who knows," I conceded once more. "I can't swear that the spindly kid I sat with in early June '45 in the Bad Aibling camp, looking out over the Bavarian Alps when the sun was out and huddled in a tent when it rained, actually had the name of Ratzinger, but that he wanted to become a priest, was not interested in girls, and was planning to study all that damned dogmatic claptrap the moment he was released from captivity—of that I'm sure. And that this Ratzinger, who had previously served as prefect of the Congregation for the Doctrine of the

Faith and now held sway as pontiff, was one of the ten thousand interned in the Bad Aibling camp—of that I'm sure as well. Apparently," I added, again to make myself more credible, "That's what the tabloids say."

And then—while the children, innocent of my early encounter with Catholic fundamentalist theology, poked about in the seaweed, and Luisa, Rosanna, and Frieder proudly showed us their meager finds—I told my sister about the cigar box full of Siegfried Line souvenir pins and the three ivory dice and leather dice-holder I had lifted when the occasion presented itself in Marienbad, shortly before or after the war ended. "And since we had nothing better to do, Joseph and I, we rolled dice to tell the future, our future. Even then I wanted to be an artist and famous, and he a bishop and more, the devil only knows what. We also fantasized about exchanging roles."

I may have gone a bit overboard with my constantly suspicious if loving sister when I asserted that gazing up at the less than communicative sky, behind which Joseph saw the heavenly abode while I saw a gaping void, we both responded by writing ostentatious verse, which, however, proved insufficient. That is why we let the dice make the final decision as to who would become what. To needle my pal, I claimed that, as church history demonstrated, even an atheist could become pope.

"Anyway," I said to bring my account of those early years to a close, "Joseph threw three points more. Call it bad luck or good. So I became a mere writer, whereas he . . . But if I had thrown two sixes and a five, then today I and not he would be . . ."

My sister's response was curt: "You're lying through your teeth!" Then she was silent, but I could tell she was working on one of her irrefutable objections and had something up her sleeve.

Just before Zoppot, as we got to the promenade and the children were showing one another rice-kernels of amber, she peered over the top of her glasses at me and pointed out that this nice family outing, the whole Whitsun trip with all the sweet grandchildren, would have been impossible had her brother and not that Joseph character been pope. "Or are you saying that even as pope you'd have brought a brood like this into the world?"

Then we went back to digging around in the attic of our young years, and as usual came up with opposing memories. But when I called Sister Alfons Maria, the supervisor of novices', a sanctimonious bitch we broke out in harmonious laughter.

WHAT came before, what after? The onion cares little for sequence. Sometimes house numbers are written on it, sometimes snatches of idiotic pop songs and film titles such as *The Sinner Woman*—the names of legendary soccer players, but seldom an accurate date. I have to admit that I have a problem with time: many things that began or ended precisely didn't register with me until long after the fact.

The older I get, the less stable is that crutch, chronology. Even when I open yellowing art catalogues or pore over several issues of the journal *Der Monat* from the mid-fifties on the Internet, one event that had a great impact on my life remains mired in the approximate. Only the following is certain: before Anna and I set off for the south with our reddish-orange tent, Berlin had become the scene of an art controversy that lasted well into the next year, no, longer, beyond Karl Hofer's death, and even today it must rankle with the former avant-gardists, so fiercely was the claim to "the modern" disputed. I took sides, if only from a distance.

Offended and hence angry, Hofer defended representational art, art determined by the human form, against the absolute priority of non-representational art at the time, whose approach was termed *l'art informel* and praised in art catalogues as the most modern stage of Modernism. His opponent in the controversy was an art critic named Will Grohmann who accepted only what Hofer felt would result in "a slide into the misty distance of nothingness." Hofer lambasted the reigning intolerance in a number of articles, even warning of a rapprochement with the "Nazi Gauleiter state."

He waged his war not as an official, as director of our school, but as an individual. He regarded art as endangered by "surface decorators" like Kandinsky, and defended Paul Klee, whom he called a "painting poet," against the Russian's "death-tinted kitsch."

He was subsequently condemned from many corners as "senile and behind the times," "blind with rage against the modern," and, in a word, "reactionary." It was a period when words, concepts, the latest -isms were vying with one another. The controversy reached the Artists' Union. Members started resigning.

When Hofer went so far as to accuse America of being the source of the fashionable dogma—in America anything that was new was ipso facto good and good for society—he was decried as a crypto-Communist. There was another suspicion at the time, one that was, as was then customary, nipped in the bud but which returned a few decades later among scholars doing archival research, namely, that the CIA had promoted the non-representational school called *l'art informel* in Germany because of its harmless, decorative quality and because the concept of the modern was and promised to remain the property of the West.

Looking back on the controversy from today's perspective, I can see what a strong influence the quarrel between Hofer and Grohmann, the adamant figure painter and the art pope of the period, had on the direction of my work as a visual artist. Just as in the quarrel between Camus and Sartre that determined my later political position, I sided with Camus, so here I chose Hofer.

His cry "O holy Klee, if only you knew what was being done in your name!" became a byword. And what he told us art students in the early fifties—"The central problem of the visual arts is and remains man and the human, the eternal drama"—has retained its ring, lofty as it may sound, into my old age. Perhaps that is why I remember more or less exactly what the controversy meant for me and how it split teachers and pupils at the school into factions until after Hofer's death and the choice of his successor—and not only because I took part in the student protest against the choice of an artistic nobody to replace Hofer.

When Karl Hartung decided it was time for me to submit some of my chalk drawings—including *Haystacks Over the City* and *K the Beetle,* pictures based on poems—to the Artists' Union so they could be exhibited in the forthcoming annual show, he was forced to report in a few weeks that while the jury had recognized their quality it had rejected them as "too representational." From then on I kept my distance from all dogmatic constrictions, maligned all popes, for instance, the media-savvy one who later took it upon himself to judge the literary firmament exclusively according to his standards, and made my peace with the risk of having to resist the Zeitgeist as an outsider. Which had its consequences: the only way my work as an artist could gain exposure was in one-man shows, steering clear of changing fashion. It has remained on the fringe to this day.

EVEN that first year in Berlin I went my own way. It was not so much the work we did with models—the standard *contrapposto* nude girl, which was supposed to teach us everything there was to learn—as the massive chicken, then the body of a bird stretched out on a stick and the flatfish with a piece missing in the middle, that made me the artist I am. The fish was based on early drawings later relevant to the themes of *The Flounder;* and in poems like "Hurdy-Gurdy Shortly Before Easter" and "The Flood," the latter a text that led to my first piece of theater, I found the tone I had been seeking, if only playfully. The Berlin air laced with brick chips helped.

Love drove me on: I wrote and drew for Anna, who was wrapped up in dance. Her teacher, Mary Wigman, was commissioned to choreograph the Venusberg scene for the Bayreuth Festival the following year, and Tannhäuser, making his way among a wild mass of barefoot and virtually naked girls, was going to experience unbridled lust.

Ulli Härter and I went to see his Herta and my Anna just before the dress rehearsal. They were both suffering from all the stomping required but were eager to perform.

In a park Ulli and I saw a group of oddly dressed figures standing in a row. They had velvet berets on their heads and were draped in black cloaks: latter-day Wagner disciples conducting invisible orchestras, as if they had a large audience behind them. Some had scores open on stands they had brought with them; others were conducting from memory.

Otherwise, all I took home from Bayreuth and the repulsive

posturing of the nouveau riche rabble around the monstrous cult barn was hysterical disgust. The men in bloated dress shirts, the women laden with jewels, the moneyed nobility, everything was on display. But the memory of a ramble through the neighboring woodlands that began innocently enough rates an onion skin all its own.

We had been roaming through a forest dark as a fairy tale when we came upon a clearing from which noise and an oom-pah band announced a shooting contest. People dressed in folk costumes and hats with tufts of chamois hair were sitting at long beer tables. Booths invited you to topple pyramids of tin cans or shoot at targets to win artificial flowers and other prizes.

Although I had been taught how to shoot humans at a tender age, I had never fired a shot. Here the targets could not be harmed: the guns were air guns and the ammunition of the lowest caliber. I hesitated at first—should I pick up the butt, touch the barrel?—but in the end stepped up to the stand hoping to win a rose for Anna.

I carefully aligned the sights and squeezed the trigger, but fate directed my shot to a target that won me a stork with a tiny basket containing twins hanging from its beak. This was before the pill and the age of contraception.

Who was frightened more? Not even the rose, which I won immediately thereafter, could comfort Anna. The prophetic reference to the birth of our sons Franz and Raoul three years later could not be washed away with steins of beer or joked away with a reference to the poet Jean Paul's archetypical adolescents Walt and Vult. Nor did a reference to Wunsiedel, the poet's nearby birthplace, serve to dissolve the fatal shot in irony. Never again did Anna allow me to shoot for a rose.

———

THE year before, Bayreuth had been nothing more than a vague promise on the horizon. Summer vacation began shortly after the workers' uprising in East Berlin and shortly before West Berlin's mayor, Ernst Reuter, died. Anna went to Switzerland, and a little later I too hitched south with our tent in my rucksack.

In Lenzburg Anna prepared her parents for my visit—quite what she told them I don't know. Much as they tried to bridge the distance with hospitality, the have-not from Germany who showed up at their door in corduroys and with a rucksack couldn't have struck them as more alien. To soften my appearance, I had shaved off the luxuriant beard I grew more as a whim than as an existential gesture. Now I felt naked the moment anyone looked at me. Luckily, Anna's sisters—one of whom was somewhat older, the other much younger—helped ease me into the unwonted surroundings.

During an introductory visit to Anna's widowed paternal grandmother, a Calvinist from the south of France who had married into this Zwinglian family, we sat on the terrace of the upper-middle-class house speaking a French that flew over my head as if I were air. Scarcely a word settled on the new arrival, who felt miscast in a comedy of manners, drinking weak tea, nibbling away at pastries, and glancing furtively toward an out-of-reach brandy bottle or the garden and its gate, concealed by rhododendron bushes, that gave onto the road for Wildegg and Brugg.

I had just hitchhiked from there. The gate was tempting. Why not flee? There and then. I was agile enough. All it would have taken was a vault over the terrace wall into the garden.

That's it! A standing jump and I'm on my way. A few short steps across the lawn, through the gate, and into the street, where the first or maybe second car, or a truck from the nearby Hero jam factory, picks me up and I'm released from the embarrassment of being on display, I'm unattached, free again.

What was I doing there, anyway? What show of mercy would have redeemed a hard-boiled doubter like me? What business did a pagan Catholic have among Zwinglianists and Calvinists? A lone Papist from the Huguenot wars. And not a shot of brandy within reach. No, he had to get out of here!

I had surreptitiously patted the breast pocket of my jacket to make sure I had my passport; in my head I was ready for the leap, only my legs were trembling. I took a deep breath, doing my best not to look at Anna, who may have felt for me and sensed there was something wrong, when her grandmother turned a face framed in silver curls to mine, fixed me with an amused and curious gaze, and—her mouth in a smile, her curls trembling slightly—said in a High German purged of all but the trace of an accent, "My son Boris tells me you are studying art in the former capital of the Reich. During my youth I was acquainted with a man who went up in balloons. He too was from Berlin . . ."

Suddenly my carefully planned—and mentally executed— flight had gone up in smoke. There was no backing out now. The moment Grandmother addressed me, I had been accepted into a rock-solid family founded on property, a family that, as was the way with their countrymen, lived modestly on the interest from their savings, and was as tolerant, true to tradition, of my origins as if the Edict of Nantes had never been repealed on a whim by the Sun King.

So I acquiesced, though still mindful of a possible vault into safe territory. Besides, the Berlin balloonist's heir always had accommodation in the form of the reddish-orange tent Anna and I would be taking with us to Italy.

The day of departure was set, the rucksacks packed. Their contents included some old-fashioned guidebooks plus Burckhardt's *Culture of the Renaissance in Italy* to heighten our sense of the beautiful. But before we could set off, Anna had to allay her mother's fears about what might happen in the tent at night. She did so with an explanation as innocent as could be, namely, that the two poles keeping the tent up would also keep us apart. To Greti Schwarz's credit, she believed her.

From Capo Circeo we continued south to Naples, and no matter where we pitched our tent—on the beach, under the pines, in the ruins of abandoned houses—we grew closer and closer, unimpeded by the imaginary line of demarcation between the two poles. But since our love was and remains ours, Anna's and mine, and resists all attempts at putting it into words, the only thing I will say about the tent is that the canvas bore a number of blood-red splotches that no rain could remove: unmindful of the consequences, we had pitched it under a mulberry tree full of overripe fruit.

One day we were cooking on the beach—fish was cheap—and a band of young Fascists brought us some driftwood for the fire. They gave us quite a scare. These kids in their black shirts—their greeting still smacking of Mussolini, of their Duce—were as incorrigible as I had been in my brown *Jungvolk* shirt. Weeds do not die; they keep coming back, keep spreading. And not only Italy offers a conducive climate.

ALTHOUGH we covered a lot of ground, we didn't see that much: Anna and I were still discovering each other, experiencing each other with amazement. She was sensation enough for me, I for her, and there was little that could distract us from each other. Even sketching or painting, we would sit close together.

Apart from the usual hitchhiking incidents—frightened by two Neapolitan men, Anna surreptitiously passed me her Swiss Army knife—and an encounter with a bearded Capuchin monk who took us down into his catacomb and, laughing a great resonant laugh, proudly showed us the pile of skulls he had collected—the only thing I remember about our trip down and back was the visit we paid to Giorgio Morandi, a painter we greatly respected. We were young and brash enough to seek out his house in Bologna and present ourselves unannounced.

We were received by the maestro's sisters. After we had made it clear in response to their inquiry that we were not *americani* and Anna, who was fluent in Italian, pulled the name of the Swiss collector Floersheim, an acquaintance of one of her aunts and a known Morandi collector, out of her sleeve, the two rather scatterbrained ladies ushered us into the maestro's studio. Although all he had to show us were blank canvases on stretchers, he assured us, tittering like an elf, that the as yet unpainted pictures—there were a dozen or more—had been sold. To *americani,* of course.

The tables and shelves on the veranda, which he used as studio space, were covered with groupings of vases, jugs, and bottles on low pedestals standing in front of taut cloths and positioned seemingly at random. At one time models for typical Morandi still lifes, they had taken on a layer of dust over time, and the collected vessels had turned a uniform gray-brown, thus giving a hint of the spare charm of the maestro's pictures.

He wore round-rimmed glasses and smiled when we gazed in wonder at the models for the art we so admired. Cobwebs, some even inhabited, had formed between vases and bottles. Nowadays, dust-laden and randomly positioned as they were, they would have appealed to an undemanding art world as Concept Art and would certainly have found a buyer.

After we drank green liqueur, sweeter than sweet, from tiny glasses, the maestro's sisters, dressed all in black, bade us farewell. I should have asked whether he had any proofs from his etchings. Had the old man been in a generous mood, Anna and I might have come away with a signed Morandi. But it was empty-handed that we left Bologna, Bologna *la rossa, la dotta, la grassa,* the red, the well-read, the well-fed.

NEAR the harbor in Naples we saw a band of tearful German scouts whose rucksacks had been stolen and who could think of one thing only: how to get home. Colorful washing hung out across the street to dry. Hordes of noisy children. Adrift in the narrow streets, we saw processions whose heathen Catholic pomp we knew from neorealist films. The stink of fish and rotten fruit.

Otherwise nothing left its mark except for the poste restante letter from my mother. She, whom I'd promised fairy-tale journeys to the south, the land where the lemons bloom, to Naples, she, who dressed her promising little darling in the name of a theatrical hero, a man whose life's onion, after skin upon skin had been peeled off, proved devoid of any meaningful core; she, who despite all my boastful promises had ended up as empty-handed as Peer Gynt's mother, she who had a sense of beauty and hungered after beauty all her life, was overjoyed that her "dear boy" was yet again "lucky enough to see all that beauty," and with "such a nice young woman from a good family."

Not until the very end of the letter, which urged me "to be considerate with Fräulein Anna," was there a reference to her illness—"It keeps refusing to get better"—which could hardly be missed, but which I failed to take seriously: everything that happened afterward happened without her knowing, beyond her suffering.

No SOONER had we returned to Lenzburg than Anna's father called me in for a man-to-man talk. While we were away, his daughter's Berlin landlady had sent him a letter filled with dubious insinuations. He was not one for lending credence to idle gossip, but one thing was unambiguous: I had repeatedly spent the night in his daughter's room. In his wife's view, a view to which he too subscribed, my relationship with his daughter, which, he assumed, was based on genuine affection, now needed to be accorded legal status. He spared us both further words.

We were standing beside shelves full of books whose titles I tried to decipher from their spines. Anna's father found the conversation embarrassing. I didn't, especially as I responded pointblank Yes and Amen. All that remained was to set a date for the wedding.

The father of three daughters, Boris Schwarz would have liked to see us married if not immediately then as soon as possible, preferably before the end of the year. But I didn't want to be married in corduroys to say nothing of my threadbare Caritas jacket; I wanted to earn enough money during the winter semester to fit myself out in brand new clothes, that is, to be able to stand before the Lenzburg justice of the peace in a suit fresh off the rack. Anna was also in favor of a spring wedding. She wanted to have perfected a solo dance to a Bartók piano piece for an important exam.

We were as nonchalant about this marriage as if it had been a pill for mumps or measles. It doesn't hurt. The quicker it's over the better.

We settled on a day in April. I was against the twentieth, Hitler's birthday, but my future father-in-law said that as tainted as the day might be in Germany it had no political overtones in Switzerland; besides, hadn't he heard from his daughters that as a young soldier I had survived an attack on the twentieth of April 1945, wounded, but only lightly.

The highly principled ironmonger and reserve officer of the ever ready Swiss Army was at heart a mild-mannered man. He was obviously under a great deal of pressure. But looking into his eyes while reexamining my blithe Yes, the loner precipitantly turned bridegroom did not feel pressured. I was willing to make good on the promise I had made. I could already see myself decked out in finery, buttonhole carnation and all, gazing into the future.

WHAT followed sped by so fast that I would be hard put to reduce it to a chronology, especially as it proceeded so differently for my far-off, suffering mother.

I am uncertain as to whether it was during those weeks in Lenzburg or on our visit there the following year that my in-laws' richly stocked bookcase became more important than the marriage discussion that took place next to it. In any case, I read and read. I devoured Klabund's *Brief History of Literature,* then the sumptuous soft-leather, two-volume edition of *Ulysses* published by Rhein-Verlag in Zurich and translated by Georg Goyert. I still treasure it. Anna's mother, who read widely and into a ripe old age—she was 104 when she died—found Joyce too difficult, too "ungainly," and made me a present of it, little suspecting what the miracle of its language would set in motion, especially when combined with another piquant work lent to me shortly thereafter by Anna's Uncle Paul, an eccentric who lived with his equally eccentric sister in a large villa and who kept a monkey on a chain in the garden: Alfred Döblin's *Berlin Alexanderplatz,* the masterpiece of an author whose every book I later used as a writing manual and in whose honor I created a prize.

Then there was the edition of Charles de Coster's *Uilenspiegel* illustrated by Frans Masereel, a tale teeming with picaresque incidents that would eventually fuel my as yet pent up mania for writing. And that was only the beginning of it. It was as if I had to build up a reserve before the wedding to last me on the long road ahead: *Manhattan Transfer* by Dos Passos, *The Captive Mind* by Czesław Miłosz, Churchill's memoirs, which brought me the war from the victors' point of view, and Gottfried Keller's *Green Henry* for the second time. I had come across the latter in my mother's bookcase when I was a boy, and now she was undergoing radiation for the cancer in her abdomen.

Or was it in Berlin that I did all that reading while she suffered? Could it have been Ludwig Gabriel Schrieber who pressed his all-time favorite on me: the adventures of Uilenspiegel and his pal Lamme Goedzak? Because Lud, who grew more Catholic with every drink, cursing the Inquisition as the

Devil's handiwork—to hear him, it was still going on—would, whenever he was drunk at Leydicke's long counter, shout, *"Tis tydt van te beven de klinkaert,"* which meant more or less "Let us clink glasses" and thus prompted, he smashed the glass he had just emptied. But no matter who set me on the endless narrative trail, it began with a teacher by the name of Littschwager, who gave his pupils injections of Grimmelshausen's *Simplicissimus*— my in-laws' bookcase was Anna's dowry: marrying her enriched me in this way as well.

THE Bäumliacker, or Tree Field, as the house and garden in Lenzburg were called, had another asset: Anna's two sisters. The elder, Helen Maria, could have made me waver and did so in secret, while the younger, Katharina, was a strapping girl still in school. And just as the bookcase set me off on a life of telling stories, with varying degrees of truth, and retying the string when it snapped, so the three-sister pattern has remained with me, one might say inexorably, over the years: Veronika Schröter, the mother of my daughter Helene, is the middle of three Saxon sisters; Ingrid Krüger, to whom I owe my daughter Nele, grew up the youngest in a Thuringian three-sister family; as for Ute, who has stuck with me through thick and thin and who brought her sons Malte and Hans into our extended family, she is the eldest of a doctor's three daughters from an island off the coast of Pomerania.

No, I can't come up with any more threesomes, except perhaps the pit foreman's three daughters, the eldest of whom the coupler boy had taken a shine to. I might put all these three-star constellations in my life down to some quirk of fate, but wasn't it the Devil—or my onetime caraway-chewing friend Joseph, the current pontiff?—who said "All is chance!" on the long-ago day when, having asked the dice about my future with women, I rolled three threes four or five times in a row?

Like so many Graces the sisters waved good-bye as I left Lenzburg for Berlin via Brugg with the mulberry-speckled, reddish-orange tent in my pack. Shouldn't I have made a detour and paid a visit to my parents in Oberaussem? Mother was still suffering at home, though she took the bus into Cologne for her radiation, more and more radiation.

Throughout the autumn and winter I did a number of plaster death masks for a Berlin undertaker. It brought in enough money to finance a black jacket that fit me, from the department store Kaufhaus des Westens, and pin-striped trousers, a silver-gray tie, and black brogues, which I never wore again. I had nothing in my pockets, but I wanted to cut a fine figure as a bridegroom.

WHAT went on before and after the wedding, while other things began, began and ended, was only briefly interrupted by a hurried change of living quarters and reports of my mother's suffering—now she was in a hospital in Cologne-Nippes—things that later nearly tore me to pieces, made me a cripple, set me free, then ended up on paper or in clay, bringing in a bit of money and my first taste of success—the sale of a bronze crab the size of a hand—it all proceeded according to a certain order, one thing hiding another, all striving to be present, vying for priority.

It was around the time that Anna and I first saw the black-and-white flickering of a television screen in the window of a radio shop near Roseneck, and while the art controversy between Karl Hofer and Will Grohmann was shaking the School of Fine Arts down to its plastering room, that my mother was moved to the hospital for treatment and we moved to the Schmargendorf district, where our landlady, a German Russian, had her cleaning woman, who came from the Eastern part of the city to earn West German marks, read the coffee grounds once a week. Far from a death in the family, she predicted nothing but fame and glory: "Good fortune is your constant companion . . ."

We had a large room and were allowed to use the kitchen. While I was writing my four-liners or drawing my animals, while Anna was dancing barefoot to her Bartók, while we were out watching French films of the thirties, far away my mother was slowly dying.

We were there when debates were held before a politically divided public, sometimes in East, sometimes in West Berlin, the Cold War providing ample tinder and the winter proving neither particularly severe nor particularly mild. While the disputes between East and West covered the same ground over and over, we watched Bert Brecht smiling up there on the podium as if he had no opinion about the Korean War or the nuclear threat. But as poor B.B. chomped mutely on his cigar and the intellectual representatives of the world powers—Melvin Lasky for the West, Wolfgang Harich for the East—enumerated each other's crimes and threatened each other with preemptive nuclear strikes, cancer was eating away at my mother.

We bought a used refrigerator, our first purchase as a couple— my mother's insides burned under the radiation.

We danced at every opportunity, and thought being young was all there was—her abdomen became a wound that would not heal.

I would like to report on other things that happened before our wedding, one after another or all together; however, her slow dying, of which I know nothing, took place outside our time and with nothing much happening at our end.

The discussions between East and West—the comparison was always between the victims of Stalinism and the estimated number of deaths caused by the bombs dropped on Hiroshima and Nagasaki, never a word about Auschwitz—may have moved the world, as had Stalin's death the year before; my mother's death proceeded in silence.

My teacher, Karl Hartung, who belonged to a men's drinking club that assembled weekly in Bayerischer Platz around the poet Gottfried Benn, showed a few of my poems to the otherwise inaccessible master; my mother, who was in completely different company, had no part in the transmission of rhymed and unrhymed verse.

And when my sister—or was it my father?—wrote to say I should come, come immediately, the end was near, I left—it was just after I'd heard from Hartung that Benn had called my poems "highly promising" but added "Your pupil will eventually write prose"—without Anna on the inter-zone train for Cologne, where my mother lay dying in Saint Vincent's Hospital.

Gradually she came to recognize me. She kept asking to be kissed by her son. And I kissed her lips twisted in pain, her forehead, her restless hands. Her bed had been rolled out of the ward into a storeroom that served as the death chamber, a windowless hole lacking even the obligatory cross on the wall. The only light came from what I judged to be a forty-watt bulb up near the ceiling.

She could no longer speak, but her dry lips kept moving. I talked to her, what about I don't know. My father and sister were there too. We would take turns keeping her mouth moist. As soon as I was alone with her, I would lean down and speak softly into her ear, make the usual promises, the same old story: "When you're better, we'll both of us go . . . down to the sunny south . . . yes, where the lemons bloom. . . . It's so beautiful, beautiful everywhere. . . . All the way to Rome and on to Naples. . . . Take my word for it, Mama . . ."

Every now and again nurses and nuns came by. Shielded by their wimples, they would take away bandages, bedpans, a wheelchair. They were always in a hurry. Later I was inspired by the wimples to do frontal and profile drawings of the Vincentians.

One of the nuns who came and went made an unsolicited promise as she rushed past: "The Dear Lord will release the poor soul before long."

Had I brought flowers? The asters she so loved? The onion isn't saying.

While I sat there sleeping—how long I don't know—she died, Father said. "Lenchen, my Lenchen . . ." he kept stammering.

SHE, out of whom I crawled screaming one Sunday—"Sunday's child, that's what you are," she liked to tell me; she, whose lap I still sat in at the age of fourteen, a mama's boy who clung to his complex; she, for whom I promised, evoked, and painted riches, fame, and the south, her Promised Land; she, who taught me to collect her customers' debts in small increments—"Knock on a Friday, when there's still something left of their pay"; she, my good conscience appeased, my bad conscience repressed; she, upon whom I heaped cares and woes that multiplied by the dozen like rodents; she, for whom I bought the electric iron— or was it a crystal bowl?—on Mother's Day with the money I'd earned from debt-collecting; she, who refused to come to the station when I, silly boy, volunteered for the army—"They're sending you to your death"; she, who said not a word when I asked her in the train from Cologne to Hamburg what had happened to her when the Russians arrived with such force—"Bad things should be forgotten"; she, who taught me skat and who counted out banknotes and ration coupons with a moistened thumb; she whose fingers played languorous piano pieces and who put books she didn't read on the shelf for me; she, who had nothing left of three brothers but what could fit easily into a medium-sized suitcase and who saw her brothers living on in me—"You get it all from Arthur and Paul, and some from Alfons too . . ."; she, who stirred sugar into egg yolk for me; she, who laughed when I bit into the soap; she, who smoked Egyptian cigarettes and sometimes blew smoke rings; she, who believed in me, her Sunday's child, and so always opened the Academy's end-of-year report to the same page; she, who gave me, her darling boy, everything and received little; she, who is my vale of joy and my vale of tears and who, when I wrote before and write now, looks over my shoulder even after death and says "Cross that out; it's ugly," but I rarely listened to her and when I did it was too late; she, who was born in pain and died in pain, set me free to write and write; she, whom I would so like to kiss awake on paper still-white, so she could travel with me, only me, and see beauty, only beauty, and finally say, "That I should live to see such beauty . . ."; she, my mother, died on January 24, 1954. Though I did not weep until later. Much later.

The Wedding Gifts I Received

At the funeral in the Oberaussem village cemetery I stood next to my sister, who stood next to my father. The only job she could find after leaving the convent was as a lowly filing clerk in a Cologne hospital. She was languishing there and didn't know what to do. Who could lessen her grief now that, for her, God was no longer within range?

Mother disappeared along with the coffin on which clods of earth reverberated. The brother thought only of himself and the good fortune he had been rashly assured of; he was detached as always, in his own world. The father, who, like the sister, remained behind, disconsolate, seemed smaller somehow, even shrunken.

He looked as if he would be unable to withstand so much solitude. Soon after his wife's death he took up with a widow who like him eventually drew a pension, and lived in what was known as an "uncle marriage." He was content in his own way. The two of them would indulge themselves on occasion, taking pensioners' bus trips to Bacharach on the upper Rhine for wine tastings, or to Spa in Belgium for the thrill of risking their minuscule savings in the casino.

Years later, when I had, as he put it, "made a name" for myself, the father claimed to be proud of his son, in whom, as he assured me, his blue eyes unblinking, he had "always believed." And I replied, "Yes, Papa, where would I be without you," and from then on our meetings were always peaceable: whenever he and his new wife Klärchen came to call on us and the children, she, Frau Gutberlett, would sit on the sofa leafing through magazines and he would play skat with Anna, who was on her best behavior, and me.

At the Oberaussem cemetery, however, we had practically nothing to say to each other. Perhaps it was the sight of all those graves that robbed us of speech. But the smoking chimneys of Fortuna Nord gave a very clear message: Life goes on, life goes on . . .

The mourners were surrounded by tombstones of diabase, Silesian marble, limestone, and Belgian granite, set between rows of boxwood hedges. The stones could all have come from Göbel's workshop, and while senior journeyman Korneff and I had transported single or double stones to several neighboring villages in the firm's small van we had never gone to Oberaussem.

We stood at the grave with Father's neighbors and fellow-workers. I can't be certain if it was raining or snowing or if there was already a layer of snow on the ground. I don't know exactly who came and who didn't. I can recall nothing about the service except that the priest had only one acolyte. I was empty, or I felt empty. I tried to cry, but in vain. Though what does that matter.

And when the weeping sister asked—we had left the cemetery by then—"What will become of me? What should I do?" the brother had no answer, so preoccupied was he with himself, only himself.

FATHER died at the age of eighty in the summer of '79. The coffin was still open when I arrived. He looked good, well-groomed as always and peaceful. He is buried in Opladen with the Widow Gutberlett, who preceded him there. Whenever we saw each other, he felt the need to encourage me: "Keep it up, boy. Keep it up."

His wallet contained positive reviews of my books, none of which he had read. When my son Raoul was an apprentice radio technician at Westdeutscher Rundfunk in Cologne—and with long curly hair was trying his best to look like his idol Frank Zappa—he and his friends would drop in on his grandfather for an occasional game of skat, his innocent passion.

During the mid-sixties when the extreme right party, the NPD, or National Democrats, came out with yesterday's slogans, I asked him who he had voted for in the Bundestag elections. "The Socis, of course," he said. "As usual." Then after a pause he added, "If I didn't vote Social Democratic, you'd stop sending me money." We understood each other well.

Several years before his death, by which time he was in a nursing home, Ute and I brought him to our house for a visit. He enjoyed the long car ride and refused to take a nap, taking in the rich meadowland and the cows, cows everywhere. But in our Wewelsfleth kitchen nook he sat dozing for hours on end. And at noon, before Bruno, Malte, and Hans came home hungry from school and their various noises took over, he would sit near the stove and listen to the potatoes cooking. "I always liked to hear them boiling in the pot," he said, "when I cooked for Lenchen and then Klärchen . . ." He wasn't much for talking anymore and was at his happiest when Ute gave him a good-night kiss: "A real one. On the mouth."

AND my sister? The question she asked me at the Oberaussem cemetery or after the service was one I would hear many more times: "What will become of me? What should I do?"

Toward the end of April, right after the wedding, for which she had come to Lenzburg, she drove with Anna and me to my in-laws' summer cottage in Ticino, where she tried to assuage her sorrows with mounds of Swiss chocolate, milk and bittersweet, and didn't know what to do, except weep in the most beautiful weather. Yet her never-ending complaints had a social element to them, a desire to help others, help them in practical ways, here and now.

And when she came to visit us in Berlin in the autumn of '54, shortly after our trip through Franco's grimly locked-up Spain, which gave me the material for my first story, "My Green Meadow"—by then we were living in the Dianasee basement flat—and asked the same question with the same urgency—we were coming home from a film and waiting at Budapester Strasse for the light to change—I finally gave her a piece of advice that came out less than brotherly, more like a command.

In a flash of inspiration I snapped, "Cut the whining, dammit! Be a midwife! There'll always be kids to deliver."

And a midwife she became, after completing her training at the Women's Clinic in Hanover. She worked in Rheydt, Bonn's University Clinic, and in Lüdenscheid, outside Düsseldorf, and presided over roughly four thousand births. Her agile hands and no-nonsense words stood her in good stead over the years, and she eventually not only supervised and instructed midwives at her own institution but also headed committees for improved working conditions and higher salaries at a number of hospitals. She still does a lot of traveling as the representative of her trade union's Senior Citizens Committee. She is loved—and a bit feared—by our children and grandchildren as someone who knows her own mind and can hold her drink at festive gatherings, and as a

Catholic Social Democrat and friend of a nun by the name of Sister Scholastika, also known as Scholli, she takes a firm stand. Even at her advanced age she finds occasion to inject her rough-and-ready humor into conversations, but she can also lose her temper and give the representatives of officially sanctioned wrong-doing here a piece of her mind. "I mean, really. It's outrageous!" is one of her refrains. She is also working on the declining birthrate with my youngest daughter Nele, who is herself a mid-wife. They console each other: "Luckily there are enough for-eigners to keep the world going . . ."

So a word spoken on a street corner while waiting to cross can mark the direction of an entire life. Which reminds me of Professor Enseling, who in the ice-cold winter of '47, when the Düsseldorf Academy of Art had temporarily closed for lack of coal, pointed me in the only right direction.

THERE is a picture from our wedding—Anna in a wine red suit, me in the pinstriped trousers—showing us smiling at each other as if we'd just pulled off a hilarious prank. She is twenty-one, I'm nearly twenty-six. It means a lot to us that we don't yet need to be quite grown-up. We are wearing our rings on our left hands; they are gold and therefore valuable. But, given that I already thought of Anna as property acquired, the most valuable yield of the hasty wedding was the wedding gift of an Olivetti portable typewriter, the Lettera model, which, if not immedi-ately, then little by little, made me a writer.

To all intents and purposes I have remained faithful to her: I've been neither willing nor able to give her up. I have always treated my Lettera with deference. She has me in her thrall to this day. She has always known more about me than I wished to know about myself. Her home is one of my stand-up desks, where her keyboard is always waiting for me.

Granted, I did try other models along the way—short-lived affairs, so to speak—but the Olivetti never wavered in her devotion, nor I in mine, not even after it could only be found in flea markets. Every so often someone would make me a present of one he no longer had use for, with the caveat that it had seen better days. Which was wrong.

My everlasting Lettera. She has stood the test of time because she is so easy to repair. She looks so discreetly elegant in that blue-gray, rust-free metal cover. Her light touch, so attuned to my two-finger system, is music to my ears. Sometimes one or another letter jams and teaches me patience, just as she is patient with me when I keep typing wrong letters.

Oh, she has her quirks. The ribbon tends to get stuck. Yet while she may be aging, I am confident she will never grow old. The clatter passing through the open window tells the world we're alive, both of us. Listen! Our dialogue is far from over: To her I am Catholic enough to confess.

At present three Letteras occupy my stand-up desks in Portugal, Denmark, and the Behlendorf studio. As a trinity, they take care that my flow of stories does not dry up. The mere sight of one or the other or the third is enough to give me an idea, and soon they are babbling away, sisterly, cheerfully, filling the silences.

All three are mechanical muses; I have no others. I devoted a quatrain to them in *Lost and Found Items for Non-Readers,* a volume of verse from the end of the last century listing my belongings in the genre I call aquaverse. The Portuguese Olivetti is never jealous of the Danish one or the Behlendorf Olivetti of the two foreign ones. And just as they love me with their three voices, so I am devoted to them and them alone.

No matter how many new and newfangled goods have come on the market, nothing has lured me away. Neither the electric model nor the computer has proved seductive enough to replace even one of my Olivettis, just as no one has succeeded in dumping me on the scrap heap as "old iron."

In the mid-seventies, when my marriage was on the rocks and I was no longer assured of a roof over my head—which is why the manuscript of *The Flounder* didn't know what happened to it—I fled Berlin for London with one of my Olivettis, and once I had found refuge with a kind-hearted colleague by the name of Eva Figes, it took to clattering in the new setting until, thanks to Ute, I settled down again.

I've coddled her, believe me: I've never hurled curses meant for others at her. Nor do I blame her if I'm too lazy to change the ribbon and the print gets dimmer and dimmer. I've never lent her to anybody.

By the same token she has never let me down, no matter what demands I make on her. A change of climate after a long flight, for instance. In Calcutta, where we took up residence for quite some time, she had to endure great heat and humidity and was plagued by insects using her innards as breeding grounds. Though the earlier years were even worse.

In the early eighties, when humankind seemed to me on the way out for good, I developed a writer's block that went on for four years, during which time the only thing I used my fingers for was modeling clay into sculptures and all three Letteras felt forsaken. They sat there collecting dust until stories began coming to me, apocalyptic farewell stories, which I first scribbled out with my brush on sheets of white-burning clay, then by hand on the blank pages of a thick printer's dummy in cramped lines under the title *The Rat,* and which then needed to be brought together and typed up in definitive form.

Day after day. Sheet after sheet . . . For five decades. Two or three typescripts after the handwritten version. The Olivetti can take anything: novellas and novels, an occasional poem by way of relief, so to speak, as well as dry Social Democratic election speeches and—after reunification in '89—speeches about the bargain buy-up of the East by the West.

If I vented my anger on her, I never meant it personally. And I held on to her when my evaluation of the privatization swindle quite isolated me, when *The Call of the Toad* had died down, and while *Too Far Afield* grew and grew into something substantial enough to encompass the sorted detritus from two centuries of German history, as well as of my hero Theodor Wuttke—also known as Fonty. As ribbons for my Olivetti portable were no longer on the market by then, my writing would definitely have come up against a material, if not existential, crisis had it not been for the help of friends.

During a visit to Madrid with Ute—I was being given the *hidalgo,* an award in the form of a walking stick fashioned from a reed, by the elder of a group of *gitanos* who had their camp near a dump outside the city, an object that would soon come in handy as I was having more and more trouble walking— some young people who had read a newspaper article that waxed ironic over my out-of-date writing habits presented me with a box of typewriter ribbons fresh from the factory, enough to keep me going for some time . . .

But my first Olivetti—a wedding present from my father-in-law's sister Margot and her husband Urs and currently in the possession of my youngest son Bruno, who is preserving it as if it were an integral part of me—was of special consequence: it was the one I used to type up the poems that would soon become my first book, *The Merits of Windfowl*.

THEY must have come to me without effort because there are no drops of sweat or other traces of exertion on any onion skin. There can be no doubt that the germ for the poems came from a damp cellar room with a window overlooking a garden, a room Anna and I took in a house whose upper story, complete with turret and bay window, had been gutted in the war and was inhabited since by changing weather and pigeons. We had discovered this half ruin between the Königsallee and the reedy waters of the Dianasee and had no trouble renting the cellar room, which had once been part of the janitor's living quarters, for a modest sum. The only people living above us were a professor and his wife, whom we would greet and who would greet us.

The quarters were cramped, but we could always go out into the overgrown garden, happy or at least living a fairy tale that promised a happy ending. Anna felt more at home there than I did, because after a sheltered childhood in safe Swiss surroundings our idyll in the ruins gave her the illusion of freedom. She allowed her thoughts to wander much less than I did. In summer the window, which faced the garden, was left open all evening to let in the sunset.

I would cook lentil dishes on the two-ring gas stove and fry green herrings and whatever else was cheap—sausage, kidneys, spare ribs—in a cast-iron pan. On Sundays, when we had guests, I stewed beef hearts stuffed with prunes, and in autumn I put lamb chops with beans and pears on the table. "Beans and Pears" was the name of one of the poems I typed on the Olivetti. Another one, "The Midge Plague," had its origins in the nearby Dianasee, the mosquitoes' breeding ground.

We would have friends over. Hans and Maria Rama, who decided our love needed to be made permanent in black-and-white photographs. I also made friends with another flautist, this one curly-headed, with Mozart pigtails, a master of the silver flute and surrounded by swarms of young girls. Aurèle Nicolet was his name, and he was Anna's other love, a love always waiting in the wings but never lived. The Härters would come to visit and with them we enjoyed making fun of people. Then there was Fridtjof Schliephacke, an architecture student who later designed furniture and a floor lamp, now bearing his name, for the student community of Eichkamp, and the sculptor Schrieber, sober by day, with his pupil Karl Oppermann, who before long took up advertising on the side and went to work for a large dairy, Bolle. Some time later Oppermann commissioned me to put together a pamphlet celebrating the dairy's seventy-fifth anniversary and the opening of its first self-service store.

And so on my Olivetti wedding present I wrote a squib of six or seven pages with the title "Convert the Heathen or Sell Milk?", which was then dispatched in a mass mailing of supposedly 350,000 copies to West Berlin households. They were my first large audience.

Only a byproduct, of which I don't possess a copy to quote from, but it celebrated Carl Bolle, the first and legendary purveyor of fresh milk to a large city ("Bolle on the Milk Cart"), in amusing terms and earned me 300 marks then and a good deal more some thirty years later, when the still thriving firm reprinted my milk fairy tale, thereby fulfilling Gottfried Benn's prescient judgment of my poetry: "He will one day write prose . . ."

Yet the Olivetti kept spitting out poem after poem. I had found my tone, or a stray tone without a master had found me. I kept the poems together in a folder, and one day Anna and my sister—who had come for a visit—selected a half dozen and sent them off to Süddeutscher Rundfunk, South German Radio, because the station had announced a poetry contest in the newspapers and together they persuaded me to give it a go. Their choice included the all too metaphor-laden "Lilies from Sleep." And it was not the beautiful hymn to smoking, "Credo," or the lyrical inventory, "Open Wardrobe," or even "Beans and Pears," but those anemic flowers, lilies born of my perfectly healthy sleep, that won me third prize and—as my debt-collector mind recalls—350 marks. I also received the airfare to attend the award ceremony in Stuttgart. It was my first flight.

Thus blessed, I bought myself a winter coat off the rack at Peek & Cloppenburg. The rest of the prize money went for the asphalt-gray mohair skirt that Anna and I bought at Horn, the most elegant shop on the Kurfürstendamm, so matter-of-factly, as if we knew we would never again want for funds. I can still feel the texture of the material, picture its fine cut: so gracefully did Anna move in the proceeds of my poems.

This could be the beginning of a tale that I did not write and that does not belong to those collected by the Brothers Grimm. Perhaps only Hans Christian Andersen could have come up with something of the sort: Once upon a time there was a wardrobe in which memory hung on hangers . . .

That wardrobe is still open, reciting stanza after stanza—what is kept on the bottom, what on top, what is almost new and what is threadbare—and whispering to itself.

Our wardrobe was a narrow affair we had picked up at a junk shop, in which only Anna's mohair skirt hung. When open, it told a tale of white balls sleeping in pockets and dreaming of moths, of asters and other flammable flowers, and of an autumn that turns garment . . .

And so the tale with no attested author became reality: Once upon a time there was a sculptor to whom verse came occasionally and in passing, and who had written a poem called "Open Wardrobe." When he received a modest prize for another poem, he immediately bought a skirt for his beloved and a coat for himself. From then on he thought of himself as a poet.

And so the tale continued: The poet—also a sculptor, who made chickens, birds, fish, and suchlike creatures—responded with poems in his pocket to an invitation delivered to the cellar flat of his villa in the ruins during the spring of '55. The lilacs were in bloom in the villa's overgrown garden; the evening wind blew mosquitoes from the nearby lake to the open window.

The telegram was signed by a man named Hans Werner Richter. It requested the young poet in a reticent telegraphic style to present himself at Rupenhorn House, on another, larger lake, the Wannsee, where the literary coterie Group 47 met at his invitation. It ended with a terse command: "Bring poems."

To make the tale more credible, let me add: One of the jurors of the poetry contest had called me gifted and recommended me to the man named Richter as a participant, but the latter had hesitated until then to invite me.

Anyway, the poet kissed his young wife, who was a dancer,

tucked seven or nine poems into his pocket to keep the tale going, boarded the bus, descended at Rupenhorn House, and entered the sumptuous villa—once inhabited by some Nazi bigwig—in the early afternoon, when the members of the group, founded in 1947, were taking a coffee break and were talking cleverly with and past each other. This too was worthy of Hans Christian Andersen.

The vague impressions that I, the sculptor who thought of himself as a poet, had of the group's existence and what held it together came from newspaper reports. Of the year '47 itself, however, I had very clear impressions based on my own experience: it was then—the year of that hardest of winters, a winter that refused to give in, and of more paneless windows than panes available on the market—that I began my training as a stonemason, using pointed and toothed chisels to turn Silesian marble into children's tombstones, and wrote poems on the side, mere ditties, really, of which not a line has remained.

As I entered the Wannsee villa I saw men and women sitting at neatly laid tables. They were drinking coffee, eating cake, and talking clever. Knowing none of the assembled poets yet wishing to move the tale forward, I took a seat at an unoccupied table and possibly thought about the year '47, when the winter was so severe that the Düsseldorf Academy of Art was closed because of a coal shortage.

A waitress wearing an apron and cap came up to the table where I was sitting so lost and forlorn and asked the new arrival if he was a poet. It was a question that hurt.

When the fairy-tale prince responded with a casual yes, the waitress took him at his word, curtseyed, and brought him a cup of coffee and a piece of cake that tasted like the cake the master stonemason Göbel's wife used to bake. She who kept a goat named Genoveva that I had to take out on a rope to forage in the spring of '47, and that made me a sorry sight.

The story of the goat came back to me in the form of a fairy tale, comparable to the one that had just begun, though I was no longer a sorry sight; no, I was a confident young man with nothing to lose and everything imaginable to gain, like the soldier home from the wars who makes his fortune in Andersen's tale "The Tinderbox."

What I saw and experienced seemed oddly unreal or of an exaggerated reality. Nevertheless, I knew some of those gathered there by name. I had read something or another of Heinrich Böll's. I liked a few of Günter Eich's poems: I had read more of Wolfgang Koeppen and Arno Schmidt, but they didn't belong to the Group. Böll and Eich were interwar years and war years older than the sculptor who saw himself as a poet.

Suddenly a portly man with full eyebrows appeared at my table to help the tale along. He gave me a stern look. He wanted to know what I was doing there with all the coffee-drinking, clever-talking writers, who I was, where I came from. Later he said the new arrival had looked suspicious to him. He'd seen me as a shady character up to no good, possibly even an agent provocateur intent on disrupting the gathering.

Only after I had produced and smoothed out the telegram did the stern look disappear. "I see. So that's who you are. Right. We were expecting another poet this afternoon."

Then the man named Richter, who plays the King Thrushbeard role in the tale and who had invited me as a stopgap but couldn't see that he would soon become the young poet's mentor, said, "Right after the coffee break so-and-so is going to read, then Bachmann, and then someone else. And then—what's your name again?—it's your turn."

Who "so-and-so" and "someone else" were I didn't know. The only name that had something vaguely familiar about it— she was well enough known for him to have used her surname only—was Bachmann.

"There will be criticism afterwards," he announced. "That's the way the Group does things."

It is certain that the man named Richter turned back after moving away and told the young poet, "Make sure your voice is loud and clear."

I've kept that in mind all my life when I give public readings. My friend Joseph, who by 1947 had become a student of philosophy and theology at the seminary in Freising, read his pious rubbish to me from a little black book as we huddled there under the tent at the Bad Aibling camp in a voice so soft and breathless that in a tale sewn of a completely different cloth I thought, He won't amount to much.

Everything proceeded as my "fairy-tale uncle" Richter had predicted. When a man I didn't know read a prose passage before Bachmann and another man I didn't know read a prose passage after her, both readers were criticized by the Group members almost before they could close their manuscripts: roundly, brutally, some accurate, some wide of the mark.

That was the way the Group did things. When the group first met, which was the year before they had taken a name, there were readings immediately followed by criticism. Father Stanislaus, the man in charge of the library at Caritas House, had read poems by Georg Trakl to the young poet when he was still a stonecutter. They were very sad, very beautiful, and easy to imitate.

One of the critics who appeared in the never-ending tale had the last name of Kaiser—though an emperor he was not—and the first name of Joachim. He looked about my age but spoke so like a book—though with an East Prussian tinge—that, ashamed of my inner stammer, I said nothing, much as I would have liked to contradict him.

And when Bachmann, who struck me as diffident, began to read or, rather, weep her extraordinarily beautiful poems—the weepy quality coming from the quivery plaintive tone of her delivery—I said to myself, If that ever so eloquent Kaiser comes down on the terribly frail Bachmann the way he did on the unknown man who preceded her, you will ask for the floor and stand up for the weeping or near-weeping poet, stammer or no stammer. Didn't one of the poems she read, "Tell me, my love," have a line in it tantamount to a cry for help: "One stone can soften another"?

But that Kaiser, who in the year the Group was founded was just as much a twenty-year-old as the former junior stonemason but was studying how to talk like a book with Adorno in Frankfurt-am-Main and learning to analyze everything, including the dialectics of Grimms' fairy tales, played the part of "the stone to be softened" and lauded everything Bachmann read: she was "clearly on her way to consummate form."

The well-read Franciscan Father Stanislaus had said much the same thing when he solemnly entrusted the small Trakl volume to me. So the young poet held his tongue and did not open his mouth until he was sitting on a chair beside the man named

Richter and began to read his poems, seven or nine in number, including "Open Wardrobe," "Polish Flag," and "Three Lord's Prayers," to the members of Group 47 in a "loud and clear" voice, as he had been advised.

And so the tale moved on: Once upon a time there was a young sculptor who made his first appearance as a poet. He did not suffer from stage fright because he was confident in his poems, having inhaled them from the Berlin air. And since he followed the instructions and read each line loud and clear, everyone in the audience could understand every word.

Afterward what he had read received praise from all sides. Someone spoke of a "predatory spirit" and hazarded an evaluation that other critics took up and, searching for other comparisons, varied. Though it may be that someone, possibly the Kaiser whose first name was Joachim, warned against exaggerated praise. But since even the man, with the bushy eyebrows, called Richter, who sat next to the reader's chair—the "electric chair," as it was called—appeared satisfied or at least said he had heard "a refreshingly new voice," he asked to be told again the name of the young sculptor who had just performed as a poet, because he had forgotten it and now felt it should be written down in full, and that is how the man to whom I later, much later, dedicated my story *The Meeting in Telgte* got to hear my name.

Even when the young sculptor who had just proved himself a poet got up from his chair, the tale did not want to end. He immediately found himself surrounded by half a dozen editors, who introduced themselves as representing the publishers Hanser, Piper, Suhrkamp, and S. Fischer. They grabbed the seven or nine poems the poet had typed up at home in his damp cellar room on his Olivetti portable in two copies, thanks to a sheet of blue carbon paper. They refused to give them back and kept talking about themselves in the plural—"You'll be hearing from us," "You can expect to hear from us soon," "We'll be in touch"—so he was tempted to think that before long he would experience if not a golden, then a silver, age.

AFTER that the tale loses its momentum: I heard not a word from the editors who had promised so much. Only a man with a physique that looked somehow askew who had introduced himself as Walter Höllerer, the publisher of a literary journal called *Akzente*, kept his promise and published several of my poems.

Then, once the recently praised poet had got his sculptor hands full of clay and plaster, the tale started up again. An editor from Luchterhand who claimed to have been elbowed out of the crowd by the other editors after the young unknown poet's reading asked me politely whether—if I had not long since signed up with Suhrkamp or Hanser—I was still free. If so, he, Peter Frank, would like to publish a selection of my verse.

What a beautiful beginning, a beginning that put an end to both the poet's anonymous existence and his hidden innocence: "How good it is that nobody knows my name is Rumpelstiltskin . . ."

Because Peter Frank, a gentle soul with an Austrian lilt and a tendency to stray from the beaten path, paid a visit to our idyllic ruin, and no sooner did I show him some of my sketches with lyrical motifs than he agreed to include, as I had suggested, a dozen of my pen-and-ink drawings in the poetry volume and to pay, as I had demanded, extra for them. He even agreed—in the name of the publisher, Eduard Reifferscheid—to my request for a royalty of 12.5 percent of the retail price for each copy sold. If I was so straightforward, it was because I saw the rate as the basis for my material existence.

The Luchterhand house, so I had heard, had made a success of publishing chiefly legal literature, including a loose-leaf compendium, but at the publisher's express request now wished to expand into postwar German literature and had charged the well-known writer Alfred Andersch to run their literary journal *Texte und Zeichen.* Some of the poems could appear there first and—"it goes without saying"—I would receive separate payment for them. How good it was that my poor mother taught me so early on to collect debts.

But, to bring the tale to a close, when signing the contract, which provided me with yet another payment, this time for the cover image, I was blinded by fairy-tale thoughts of a young poet's first book and overlooked the option clause, that paragraph of small print stating I was obligated to offer my next book to Luchterhand first.

WAS there any reason to believe in a next book? Was there anything besides *The Flood,* a play in two acts, the one-act *Ten Minutes to Buffalo,* and some sketches for a play in four acts that was to be called *Uncle, Uncle* and was meant as my tribute to the absurd? Was there even an inkling in the direction of a book? Or to put it another way: did I see my debut as an event that could be repeated in the foreseeable future?

Not likely. I had been writing poems for as long as I could remember. Writing them and throwing them away. I would never have just foisted such things on the reading public just because I felt compelled to write. I was as certain of the inadequacy of everything my pen had created until then, as I had been confident in earlier years about my future possibilities.

The poems that came to me in the Berlin air were the first that were entirely my own, the first that demanded to be spoken, read, printed. At the same time, the pen-and-ink drawings for the small paperbound volume *The Merits of Windfowl* that was to become my first book were no mere illustrations; they were a graphic anticipation and continuation of the verse. They were done with a very fine point and arose out of a series of sketches in which filigree fowl are scattered by the wind, spiders sink into glasses, locusts occupy a city and at the same time are food for prophets. A doll squints and thereby escapes being hit by arrows; twittering scissors fly; piles of ears lie on the beach; and human-sized midges become visual metaphors. Word and image flow from the same ink in a highly personal and concrete take on the world.

Whenever I call to mind where my sorcery on paper took place, the basement of a world-war ruin near Berlin's Dianasee, I get the feeling that without seeking it I had found something on a double track that suited my egocentricity and sense of humor and made the author think it perfectly natural to have the poems and drawings published together. The first printing proceeded according to contract—a contract reflecting my fairy-tale wishes—though only 735 copies were sold in the course of three years.

NOT until later did it become clear, in isolated lines and half-lines, to what extent the poems foreshadowed my second book. From "School for Tenors," in which glass-shattering songs are tested, to the final poem, "Music for Brass Band," in which there is a child with a helmet folded from an old newspaper on his head, motifs come to the fore that point to things still concealed in the white-red and red-white play of the "Polish Flag."

One could have taken all of it as finger exercises sufficient unto themselves. When I read "My Green Meadow"—my first prose piece, the result of the previous year's trip to Spain—at a meeting of Group 47 six months later, there was no way of knowing that, "naked and sensitive," the snail made monumental in the course of the narrative would pave the way to future prose: that its slimy trail would later measure out political battlegrounds and that it would talk progress out of the dream of a great leap forward.

At first, however, there were only hints, gropings, and unconscious anticipation for which there was no explanation. We might surmise that a vast mass of material lay trapped and was showing signs, but lacking form it was not yet ready for the light of day.

Writing or drawing, I practiced the art of evasion with all the skill I'd picked up along the way; I delicately circumvented obvious abysses, had no qualms about making excuses, and chose material that celebrated stasis: fiction nurtured on Kafka and suffering from anorexia, drama reveling in hide-and-seek language, wordplay that led merrily to more wordplay.

I could easily have engaged in productive time-wasting and made myself look interesting at Group 47 meetings with new artistic devices if the massive weight of the German past and hence my own could have somehow been ignored. But it stood in the way. It tripped me up. There was no getting around it. As if prescribed for me, it remained impenetrable: here was a lava flow that had barely cooled down, there a stretch of solid basalt, itself sitting on even older deposits. And layer upon layer had to be carried away, sorted, named. Words were needed. And a first sentence was still missing.

THE time has come to close the drawers, turn the pictures to the wall, erase the tapes, and bury the snapshots, in which one after the other I look older and older. The junk room full of archived manuscripts and accumulated prizes must be sealed. Everything left over after word making, the unused grist, the dust-laden glory, the obsolescent disputes must be removed from view, so as to focus, with memory now unburdened, on the young man who around the year 1955, wearing a beret, then a cap, is trying to form a first sentence out of as few words as possible.

Without actually intending to, he had not so much abandoned the world of earthy clay and plaster dust as expanded into the field of literature. This is known as the split in gymnastics. Was it so strenuous that it tore me apart?

Until then I had propped up the bar drinking beer and schnapps among painters and sculptors; now I found myself in the company of writers drinking red wine into the dawn. Only yesterday I had listened while Lud Schrieber went on about his doings, the sufferings of superfluous Ptolemaists, the splendors of antiquity; now I had the ring of my literary contemporaries in my ear: Hans Magnus Enzensberger's verbal acrobatics took my breath away, Martin Walser's torrent of words swept me into unknown regions.

My teacher Karl Hartung had with few words turned me into a master pupil, but I was still spending a good part of my time in the ruin near the Dianasee, where the clattering, stuttering Olivetti ate up sheet after sheet of typing paper and never seemed sated.

The dancer at two weddings. I could go on listing reasons for my unrest, but no clearly delineated picture would come of it: I am unable to piece myself together, there are only fragments. In one photograph I'm sitting next to a standing bronze figure that resembles a bird in its upward stretch and appears in a prose poem of purely literary provenance: "Five birds. Their childhood was: being a post, casting a shadow, being nice to every dog, being counted . . ."

Anna, however, was still keen on leaps and turns, even after she exchanged Mary Wigman's temple for Tatjana Gsovsky, trading the constant foot pain of modern dance for the torture of classical ballet. In "The Ballerina," my first essay for Höllerer's *Akzente*—written in the following year, after we had left Berlin—a declaration of love now plain-spoken, now concealed, I compared the agony and ecstasy of both forms of dance and came in the end to an appreciation of Kleist's marionettes, Kokoschka's life-size dummies, and Schlemmer's triadic figurines.

Then, after a cold, wet winter, Anna began to have health problems. The idyllic basement flat, where summer was not long enough for our togetherness, proved hard on her kidneys and bladder. The outside wall had dry rot. Everything smelled musty. The window wouldn't quite close. And the stove smoked even though its flue went through the outside wall and into the open air.

I was insisting on a move. Anna wanted to stay. And when at last in early '56 or late '55 we loaded the rented van with our cheap furniture, the wardrobe, the double mattress, she couldn't tear herself away from the view of the garden's undergrowth, the neighboring villa in ruins, and the sunsets; so permanently had she nested. As the sunlight filtered obliquely through the window from the west, she kept sweeping the flagstones so people would say that when we moved from the Königsallee to Uhlandstrasse we had left our rented basement in mint condition.

AND then, and then? Then this happened, then that. But before that, in November of '55, before we moved to the center of West Berlin and became urban dwellers, my first exhibition opened and made the newspapers . . .

But to go on like this would be to get bogged down in lists and force things that resist categorization into categories. Besides, others have written about my before, my then, and my after, assigned them precise dates and places, put them in order. As follows: "From October 19 to November 8 the Lutz & Meyer Gallery, Neckarstrasse 36, Stuttgart, exhibited the drawings and sculptures of the young and gifted . . ."

Yes indeed. And so it went. Everything is listed and dated, printed in neat lines, given marks as in school. My beginnings were promising, my plays short on plot, the poems eccentric and playful, the prose scathing or otherwise and, later, its political message too strident. The animals were gathered and called by name: the merits of the early fowl, the walk of the late crabs, the extensive pedigree of the dog, the unscathed flounder and its bones, the cat with its eye on the mouse, the rat I dreamed of, the toad I became, and the snail as well, catching up to us, passing us, and silently hastening on its way . . .

Which is just what our Schmargendorf landlady's cleaning woman, who came from East Berlin and read the coffee grounds, predicted: I began to make a name for myself. My years of apprenticeship—my *Lehrjahre,* were over, according to time-honored guild rules, but there seemed to be no end to my travels, my *Wanderjahre.*

IN THE late summer of '56 Anna and I left Berlin. My wedding present, the Olivetti portable, came along. With little money but an inner world rich in characters I now sought a first sentence in Paris, a sentence terse enough to blow up the dam and let the words flow. And Anna was resolved to go on enduring the tortures of classical ballet exercises. It was at Madame Nora's Place Pigalle studio that she would learn to turn perfect pirouettes and stand steadily on her toes.

In Paris we lived first on the Rue Alibert, near the Canal Saint-Martin, where one of our favorite films, *Hôtel du Nord,* with Arletty and Louis Jouvet had been shot. We had sold our Berlin wardrobe and mattress and were looking for an apartment.

Having arrived in August, we found Paris empty. Along the Canal Saint-Martin, among its locks and variously curved bridges, I came upon the bench where Gustave Flaubert had seated his protagonists at the beginning of *Bouvard et Pécuchet,* in the first sentence, so to speak.

Then we moved to a different part of Paris, where we looked after the studio of a Swiss sculptor on the rue de Châtillon while he was away. Back in Berlin a dancer friend had helped Anna to apply for a job with the Blue Bell Girls, but her legs were a little too short, or not long enough, for their chorus line, which was all the rage in Paris at the time.

I was restless at first, because we were looking for a flat and I was looking for the words to make a sentence that would open doors. Or was I already typing my hymn to "The Ballerina" on the Olivetti, breaking off occasionally to search for an apartment and for words?

There was a war going on then in all the newspapers and in the Paris suburbs, but the previous war was still foremost in my mind, the war that had begun in Danzig, when my childhood came to an end with the defense of the Polish Post Office. Even so I could not find the first sentence.

Then Anna's father bought us a courtyard building on the avenue d'Italie, with two small upstairs rooms connected by a narrow hallway, next to the tiny kitchen and sitz bath. A worker lived downstairs with his wife and child. All the windows looked out on the courtyard, which was enclosed by run-down workshops.

I immediately turned the boiler room in the basement into a studio by furnishing it with a stand-up desk and a potter's wheel, and started working on manuscripts I had begun in Berlin: the five-act *Wicked Cooks* and a few prose sketches that didn't know where they were going despite the move. Chantal was the name of the girl who was so regularly beaten by the wife of the worker in the flat below that I wrote a poem entitled "Right on Time."

When my daughter Helene—who cuts a fine figure as an actress—and I recently performed our program of *Des Knaben Wunderhorn,* set to music by Stephan Meier, for 900 scholars of German literature in Paris, I made time for a brief visit to avenue d'Italie 111. The courtyard looks pretty now that the workshops are gone, especially as flowers have been planted. But the former boiler room still houses the stand-up desk at which—I don't know how many times—I thought I'd found that first sentence.

In Paris Anna and I heard from afar that Gottfried Benn and Bert Brecht had died in close succession, thereby orphaning their many followers. I wrote a poem as an obituary to both.

While the war in Algeria was echoing through Paris with plastic bombs and we sat in cinemas watching Soviet tanks—which reminded us of the tanks we had seen in Berlin's Potsdamer Platz not so many years before—on the streets of Budapest, I finally found the first sentence. Standing at the damp, dripping wall of my studio, I wrote: "Granted: I am an inmate at a mental institution . . ."

In Paris we forgot Berlin.

In Paris Paul Celan and I became friends.

In Paris I wrote chapter after chapter once the first sentence had been found.

In Paris my sculptures dried out and crumbled on the armature.

In Paris we were always short of money.

I had to hitchhike from Paris to Germany and sell my poems for cash to Cologne, Frankfurt, Stuttgart, and Saarbrücken radio stations for their late-night programs so as to keep us for three more months in fresh sardines, mutton, lentils, the daily baguette, and typing paper.

How did I become an inveterate word-maker in Paris?

In the year 1973 I made an attempt to plead my own case in "*The Tin Drum* in Retrospect, or The Author as Dubious Witness," which describes our stay in Paris and poses the question of the motivation for the lengthy job of writing a novel. I answered it as follows: "The most reliable driving force was probably my petty-bourgeois background, the desire—a musty megalomania aggravated by the fact that I didn't finish school, that I had three years to go—to produce something stupendous."

But there was another, equally important motivation: after I found the first sentence at that dripping wall, the words never stopped coming. I had no trouble writing from dawn till dusk. Page after page. Words and images pushed and shoved one another, trod on one another's heels: there was so much that wanted to be smelled, tasted, seen, named. And while I scribbled chapter after chapter in the boiler room and the cafés of the thirteenth arrondissement and then typed them on the Olivetti, and at the same time kept up my friendship with Paul Celan, who could speak of himself and the unutterable only in his verse and of his grief only in solemn pared-down passages, as if placed between candles, our twin boys, Franz and Raoul, turned us into parents, something we had not yet learned to be in Berlin or Paris.

The twins screamed alone or together, which drove the now thirty-year-old father to grow a mustache, which, as the years passed, gave rise to many self-portraits, pencil-drawn, copper-etched, and printed as lithographs from Solnhof quarry limestone: me with a walrus mustache and a snail-shell in my eye, me opposite the flounder, me with coffin nails and dead bird; me while the rat dreams of me, me with cap and toad, me and my walrus mustache hiding behind a cactus, and finally me with knife and half an onion.

In Paris walrus mustaches were common. In Paris we bought a used baby carriage with enough room for the two very different twin brothers to lie next to each other. Our few Parisian friends were amazed to see Anna and me appear as parents so suddenly and in an unrehearsed play. And Paul Celan, whose anguish could only be assuaged for a few hours at a time, gave me courage when work on the manuscript began to falter because of the two screaming children and in spite of the dripping wall.

Shortly after the birth of the twins, Konrad Adenauer won an absolute majority in the West German elections, which from Paris made Germany look very bleak, lapsing into old ways.

During writing breaks I would draw nuns, preferably Vincentians, whose winglike wimples had been on my mind since the death of my poor mother in Saint Vincent's Hospital in Cologne and whom I now sketched in the Paris Métro or the Jardin du Luxembourg. And it was there, not far from Rilke's carousel, that I sometimes managed to lure Paul Celan out of the cycles in which he saw himself as persecuted and from which he believed there was no escape.

As soon as Franz and Raoul started walking, we bought a wooden playpen, and in August we took our nearly one-year-old twins to Switzerland, where, gazing up at a backdrop of Ticino mountains shimmering in the heat, I fed my Olivetti chapters in which snow fell upon snow and the Baltic lay under a sheet of ice.

Back in Paris again Anna danced under the stern tutelage of Madame Nora while I wrote, though listening out for the twins. Every so often friend Höllerer came through, scribbling postcards with purple ink and dispatching them all over the world. He once bought a dress for Anna which we called the Höllerer dress.

It was from Paris that I traveled to Gdańsk via Warsaw in the spring of '58 looking for traces of my lost city. I would sit in the undamaged Municipal Library and observe myself as a fourteen-year-old sitting in the Municipal Library. I kept finding and finding, and when I found my Kashubian great-aunt Anna I had to show her my passport, so grown-up did I look to her and such a stranger. Her house smelled of sour milk and dried mushrooms. I got more ideas from her than I would have from a book.

I returned to Paris with a large supply of material: fizz powder, the sound of Good Friday and carpet-beating, the escape route of the money-order postman who survived the battle for the Polish Post Office, paths to and from school, the newspapers kept by the Municipal Library, the films being shown in the autumn of '39. Along with whispers in confessionals, inscriptions on tombstones, the smell of the Baltic, and bits of amber from the waves between Brösen and Glettkau.

And it all became words and stayed fresh, as if preserved under a cheese dome in Paris. And I wore myself out, but was not yet empty, and though still writing by hand, I was then a mere tool and beholden to my characters, especially the one who—why I can't tell—was called Oskar. I have little to say about how things came and come about; if I tried I would have to lie . . .

And when in October of that year I traveled from Paris by way of Munich to a Bavarian or Swabian backwater called Grossholzleute to read the chapters "The Wide Skirt" and "Fortuna Nord" to a Group 47 gathering, the author of a nearly finished novel was awarded the Group's prize: 4,500 marks, contributed spontaneously by publishers. My first windfall. It helped me to retype the whole thing on the Olivetti in peace. To make a clean copy.

The prize money also paid for an elegantly designed Braun record-player known as "Snow White's coffin" that I bought in Munich after my first reading on the radio and brought back to Paris, where we listened to Stravinsky's *Rite of Spring* and Bartók's *Bluebeard* over and over. We were no longer poor and could afford calf's liver and records.

In Paris Anna and I danced often and close. In Paris we were happy and knew not for how long. In Paris de Gaulle came to power and I learned to fear police truncheons. In Paris I grew visibly more political. In Paris a number of tuberculomas got a foothold in my lungs while I stood at the dripping wall, and were not ousted until we got back to Berlin. In Paris the twins would run along the avenue d'Italie in different directions and I didn't know which to chase first. In Paris Paul Celan was beyond help. In Paris before long there was no reason to stay.

And when the first edition of the novel *The Tin Drum* came out in the autumn of '59, Anna and I went from Paris to the Frankfurt Book Fair and danced till morning.

And when we left Paris for good a year later and took up residence, now as a family, in Berlin in another half ruin, this one on Karlsbader Strasse, I immediately began to draw and write in the one of our five rooms allotted me, because back in Paris with my Olivetti, the wedding gift, I had made a start . . .

And from then on I lived from page to page and between book and book, my inner world still rich in characters. But to tell of all that, I have neither the onions nor the desire.